BAD SEEDS

THE TRUE STORY OF TORONTO'S
GALLOWAY BOYS STREET GANG

BETSY POWELL

Toronto Star Crime Reporter

John Wiley & Sons Canada, Ltd.

Library and Archives Canada Cataloguing in Publication Data

Powell, Betsy
    Bad seeds : the true story of Toronto's Galloway Boys Street Gang / Betsy Powell.

Includes index.
ISBN 978-0-470-84060-3

1. Galloway Boys Street Gang. 2. Organized crime—Ontario—Toronto. 3. Juvenile delinquency—Ontario—Toronto. 4. Murder—Ontario—Toronto. 5. Murder—Investigation—Ontario—Toronto. 6. Trials (Murder)—Ontario—Toronto. I. Title.

HV6439.C32T67 2010   364.106'6083509713541   C2010-900212-1

Production Credits
Cover Design: Adrian So
Map, p. xxii: Mapping Specialists, Ltd., Madison, Wisconsin
Interior Design: Michael Chan
Typesetter: Thomson Digital
Printer: Friesens Printing Ltd.

Editorial Credits
Editor: Don Loney
Production Editor: Pamela Vokey

John Wiley & Sons Canada, Ltd.
6045 Freemont Blvd.
Mississauga, Ontario
L5R 4J3

Printed in Canada

1 2 3 4 5 FP 14 13 12 11 10

ENVIRONMENTAL BENEFITS STATEMENT

John Wiley & Sons - Canada saved the following resources by printing the pages of this book on chlorine free paper made with 100% post-consumer waste.

TREES	WATER	SOLID WASTE	GREENHOUSE GASES
57	26,159	1,588	5,431
FULLY GROWN	GALLONS	POUNDS	POUNDS

Calculations based on research by Environmental Defense and the Paper Task Force. Manufactured at Friesens Corporation

DEDICATION

For Clay and Julie

CONTENTS

FOREWORD

When my friend Betsy Powell told me she was writing a book about black street gangs in Toronto, I thought: It's about time. For too long, people in this city, in this country, have lived in blissful ignorance. Gangs were an American phenomenon. Black ghettos were an American problem. Not here. No way.

Sure, Canadians know there are gangs: Mafia, bikers, Asian, aboriginal, black. But it's not as if there are drive-by shootings in Rosedale or Forest Hill, Westmount or Shaughnessy. Sure, Canadians know there are racial tensions in their cities. But it's not as if there are altercations on Bay Street, or St. Catherine Street, or Robson Street. As long as the gangsters are killing each other in their own neighbourhoods, who cares? It's only when they bring their guns downtown that anybody—the politicians and media that fuel outbreaks of hysteria—notices.

In Toronto, starting in the early 1990s, there were episodic eruptions: the race riot that the white power structure insisted was not a race riot; the shotgun blast fired by a black robber, killing a young white woman sitting in a trendy café; the 15-year-old white girl gunned down by black kids in a shootout on a busy downtown street. These were the stories that created the boldest headlines—each time young blacks broke the peace in Toronto the Good.

But this book takes a look at Toronto the Bad, the separate society that exists across an unmarked border, where poverty, drugs and guns create an explosive mix, where people live in fear in their neighbour-hoods, where a generation of Canadians has been lost to the lure of crime, where clueless cops sometimes crash the party, and oblivious politicians show up only during an election campaign.

This is the backdrop for *Bad Seeds*. But this is not some thumb-sucking dissertation on the roots of poverty or black alienation, though that's a part of it. It is a true-crime story of how one senseless shooting eventually blew the lid off a shocking spike in gang warfare in Toronto in the early years of the 21st century. It is a sometimes touching, often frightening, tale with real heroes and real villains.

You'll meet Brenton Charlton, a young man with a future, murdered in a case of mistaken identity, and his friend Leonard Bell, who still lives with bullets in his body. You'll meet Tyshan Riley (pictured on cover), the scariest kid on the block, who rises to the top of his unlawful and immoral world, gaining power with the gun to feed his insatiable appetite for money and sex. You'll meet the man who brought him down, Roland Ellis. He sold drugs with Riley and subscribed to much of his criminal code, but resisted the seemingly random violence that Riley unleashed in their community.

You'll meet the cops who turned Ellis into a witness, finally crack-ing the case of the shooting of Charlton and Bell, while employing an extensive network of wiretaps to nail most of the Galloway Boys gang. On these taped conversations, you'll hear the nearly incomprehensible lingo of the streets, where gang members are known only by a strange assortment of nicknames—one after a bear in a Disney movie—and give pet names to their guns.

To make sense of all this, Betsy sifted through hundreds of hours of evidence, from wiretaps to police interviews with suspects and wit-nesses. As a reporter for the *Toronto Star*, she covered the marathon preliminary hearing that ultimately resulted in murder charges against Riley and two cohorts—and the murder trial that followed. She got to know the families of the victims and the accused, especially Charlton's mother, Valda Williams, who lost her only son.

Betsy also often went into their community—the once-sleepy suburb of Scarborough, known as Scarberia and later called Scarlem—to talk to people who knew Riley and Ellis and the rest of the

Galloway Boys when they were growing up. In many cases, these citizens were afraid to speak if their names would be attached to their words.

When Betsy first approached me about working with her on this project, I thought I might bring a certain perspective. As an American who arrived in Toronto in 1975, I had seen some of the signs of the times earlier than my Canadian friends and colleagues. Growing up in New York in the 1950s and early '60s, I had watched the city slide into the chaos of random violence and racial hatred. As a reporter in New York in the late '60s and early '70s, I had covered riots and slaughter in the streets. When I came to Canada—first Vancouver, then Montreal and finally Toronto—as a correspondent for United Press International, I found an oasis of peace and civility. But I brought my American wariness with me.

I recall standing on a subway platform at Union Station one night with a fellow journalist who had lived in Toronto most of his adult life. A small group of young black men huddled nearby. It was the spring of 1981, when race riots were sweeping Britain.

"It's going to happen here," I told my friend.

He laughed. "You're nuts," he said.

"You watch," I said.

I was wrong. But I was also right. Over the ensuing decades, crime rates rose, guns arrived by the truckload, and the Canadian security blanket became a bit tattered.

Many of the characters in this book are as creepy as any you'll find in the most gang-infested neighbourhoods of Los Angeles, Chicago, Mexico City or Rio de Janeiro.

That prompted me to ask Betsy whether she feared any of the gangsters she was writing about. She told me a story about December 26, 2005:

> It was a relatively quiet day in the *Star*'s downtown newsroom. So, as the crime reporter, I worked on a feature about evidence police were using to prosecute members of a northwest Toronto gang. It was a DVD called *Rapsheet* and featured young black men, their faces covered with bandanas, rapping and waving

guns in the air. Some of these young men were now facing charges, the police said.

Around 4:30, quitting time, I left the *Star* and headed up Yonge Street. It was still light, not all that cold, and I thought I might see if there was anything left from the Boxing Day sales that I probably didn't need.

When I got to Shuter Street, between Queen and Dundas, I had a weird feeling. I'm not someone normally given to premonitions, but there was a sense of menace in the air. Was it coming from the clusters of young black men I saw, with their hoods raised? Or did I focus on them because I'd spent the day watching a DVD of young black men waving guns around? What prompted me to cross the street? Or to consider calling the *Star*? To say what? That I had a feeling there was going to be trouble on Yonge Street?

At around 5 p.m. I went into the Guess store at Dundas to try on jeans. Music was thumping when I went into a change room at the back. I didn't buy anything and left the store about twenty minutes later. There were cops everywhere. People were crowded behind yellow crime-scene tape. Some were talking on cell phones, or using them to take pictures.

Jane Creba had already been taken away. Some of the other victims remained. I was back in the newsroom that night—with others who had jumped in—filing a story for the front page.

But Betsy wasn't interested in writing a book about the 15-year-old white girl killed downtown on Boxing Day, the bystander in a shootout between young black kids. It was the exception, the cliché that got the media's juices flowing. She was more interested in the shooting of Charlton and Bell a year earlier, the black innocents among many black casualties. And she wanted to know more about the gangs that populated her city, the neighbourhoods where she grew up.

As a fourth-generation Canadian and lifelong Torontonian, Betsy Powell was raised in Scarborough, the daughter of Clay Powell, a celebrated Crown prosecutor who successfully prosecuted such high-profile cases as the one that sent Maple Leafs owner Harold Ballard to prison, before switching sides and defending the likes of Rolling Stone Keith Richards on drug charges.

As Betsy's editor at The Canadian Press in the late 1980s and early 1990s, I knew the criminal justice system was in her DNA—which is most obvious as she takes the reader through the investigation of the Charlton/Bell shootings, the police tactics in solving the crime and the often outrageous antics of the lawyers involved in the case.

This is not a bedtime story. But it should be a wake-up call to all Canadians.

Ken Becker
Mississauga, Ontario

ACKNOWLEDGMENTS

Crime journalist Lee Lamothe planted the seed for this book when he made the flattering suggestion that I write a book about street gangs. Thank you, Lee. I am also indebted to Wiley editor Don Loney for his unwavering enthusiasm despite the glacial pace of the trial process. Thank you also to Nicole Langlois for her careful and invisible copyediting and Pamela Vokey for shepherding *Bad Seeds* through the editorial and production process.

Many people went out of their way to help me, especially Bill Blair, Fred Mathews, John Muise, Pat Monaghan, Richard Schofield, Lew Golding, David Boulet, Luis Carrillos, Frank Skubic, Geary Tomlinson, Kathryn Martin and Andy McKay. Special thanks to Daniel Brown, David Berg, Maureen Pecknold, Emma Rhodes and Rosemary Warren. David Midanik wanted no part of this book. I thank him nonetheless for sharing his insights into the criminal justice system. Also, thank you to Wayne Banks and Dean Burks for their unqualified support and for always returning my calls with alacrity.

I was privileged to spend time with Leonard Bell, Valda Williams and Uleth Harvey. Through them, I came to know "Junior" and why he was so loved and mourned. I am also grateful to Alice Thomas, who trusted me when others wouldn't.

Many thanks to my colleagues and friends for their support and encouragement, including John Ferri, Peter Small, Peter Edwards,

Wendy McCann, the courthouse cabal and the indomitable Michelle Shephard, who was writing about gangs long before most of us were paying any attention. Ron Pietroniro, thank you, for not only taking a terrific photo but generously sharing it for the front cover of the book.

There are a number of people to whom I am indebted but cannot properly acknowledge. I hope you know who you are. I owe inexpressible gratitude to Ken Becker, one of the best who, in a perfect world, would be a media mogul. XO.

Finally, I am especially grateful to my parents, who graciously proofread *Bad Seeds*. And, most of all, I am indebted to Jeff, for his love, support and patience through a long process.

Galloway Boys (G-Way) Gang Members and Associates

Norris Allen: G-Way gang leader shot to death on his driveway in 2002. Street name: Bolu

Philip Atkins: High-ranking member of G-Way, a lieutenant to Tyshan Riley. Street name: Brub

Omar Demetrius: G-Way leader who was inseparable with Norris Allen. When he was deported to Jamaica, Allen took over. Street name: O

Roland Ellis: A leader of G-Way "southside" gang called Mad Soldiers before turning into the Crown's key witness. Street name: Sledge

Heather Kerr: G-Way associate.

Maxeen McPherson: Her Scarborough apartment is main G-Way hangout. Street name: Smokey

Frances Newby: G-Way associate. Street name: Frano

Gary Reid: Moves to Kingston/Galloway area in late teens, becomes mentor to Tyshan Riley, later an enemy.

Marie Riley: Mother of Tyshan Riley, and Carl and Courtney Francis, also members of G-Way, and two younger sons.

Tyshan Riley: Leader of Scarborough street gangs Bad Seeds, Throwbacks and ultimately Galloway Boys or G-Way. Street name: Greeze or Nitti

Damian Walton: Tyshan Riley's "secretary," or runaround guy. Street name: Burns or Smithers

Dana Lee Williams: Mother of Norris Allen's two daughters. After his death in 2002, she becomes girlfriend of his successor, Tyshan Riley.

Marlon Wilson: "Like a cousin" to Philip Atkins before he becomes a key Crown witness. Street name: Mardawg

Jason Wisdom: Member of G-Way and younger brother to Dwight Wisdom. Street name: C.D.

Malvern Crew

David Francis: Malvern Crew leader caught on wiretaps talking about Tyshan Riley shooting up Malvern.

Alton Reid: Malvern Crew leader and intended target of the March 3, 2004, drive-by shooting. Murdered in November 2009. Street name: Ross P

Dwayne Williams: Malvern Crew leader shot in 2000 in a Scarborough high school. The spark is believed to have ignited the Malvern/ Galloway gang feud. Street name: Biggs

Victims and Family

Leonard Bell: Home renovator shot nine times in 2004 drive-by shooting. No gang connections.

Brenton Charlton: Thirty-one-year-old restaurant manager shot to death in drive-by shooting. No gang connections.

Omar Hortley: Twenty-one-year-old shot to death in 2004 steps from his home in Malvern. No gang connections. Riley and Atkins charged with his first-degree murder. No trial date set.

Chris Hyatt/Kofi Patrong: Two teens shot in Malvern in 2004. No gang connections. Atkins and Riley charged with attempted murder. Trial scheduled for April 2011.

Mark Jones: Teenager hit by numerous bullets in 2004 as he washed a car in the driveway of his mother's home in Malvern.

Eric Mutiisa: Malvern gang associate shot to death in 2002. Tyshan Riley charged with first-degree murder. No trial date set.

Police

Wayne Banks/Al Comeau: Homicide detectives assigned to investigate 2004 murder of Brenton Charlton.

Dean Burks: Detective Sergeant put in charge of overseeing Project Pathfinder, a homicide investigation turned gang project.

Julian Fantino/ William (Bill) Blair: Toronto police chiefs during first and second half of the '00 decade.

Darryl Linquist/Roger Caracciolo: Detectives involved in various stages of the Project Pathfinder investigation.

Kathryn Martin: Investigator for Eric Mutiisa homicide before being appointed first woman in charge of Toronto police homicide squad.

Lawyers

Suhail Akhtar: Lead prosecutor at both 2005-2006 preliminary hearing and Charlton/Bell murder trial.

David Berg: Defence lawyer representing Philip Atkins.

Patrick Clement: Crown attorney at Charlton/Bell murder trial.

David Midanik: Defence lawyer representing Tyshan Riley.

Maurice Mirosolin: Defence lawyer representing Jason Wisdom.

Maureen Pecknold/Lesley Pasquino/Scott Childs: Crown attorneys at both 2005-2006 preliminary hearing and Charlton/Bell murder trial.

Judges

Ontario Court of Justice David Cole: Co-author (with community legal worker Margaret Gittens) of 1996 report into systemic racism in the justice system.

Ontario Superior Court Justice Michael Dambrot: Presided over Charlton/Bell trial.

Ontario Court of Justice Paul Robertson: Presided over preliminary hearing for seventeen co-accused in Project Pathfinder.

GLOSSARY

Beast/Boydem/Poo Poo/Feds/Jakes/Five O: Police
Cheese(d): Mad or money
Chopping: Selling drugs
Clap 'em up: Shoot someone
Dump: To kill someone
Grains/teeth/shells: Bullets
G-Lock: Glock firearm of any calibre
Lick you down: To shoot someone
Maggie: .357 Magnum revolver
Neen: 9 mm handgun
OG: Original Gangster or Original Galloway
Passa passa: Bullshit, gossip
Ray ray: etc., etc.
Stizzy man/Burner/Toast/Piece/Strap: Gun
Talking on the low: Keeping things quiet
Trees: Marijuana

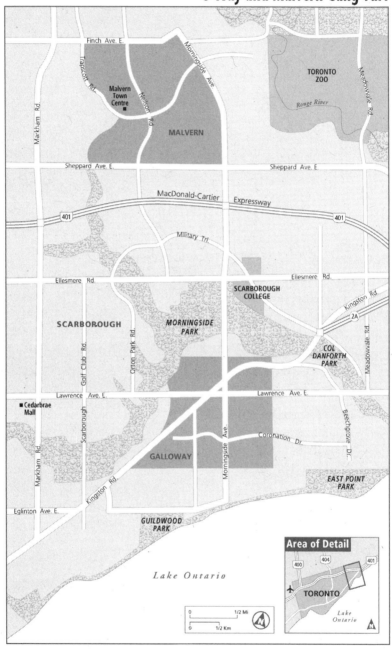

CHAPTER 1

Wrong time, wrong place

On March 3, 2004, the last day of his life, Brenton Charlton drove his mother to her job as a personal support worker looking after residents of a Toronto nursing home. At 31, Charlton still lived at home and was considered a bit of a mama's boy. Before driving away, he told his mom he loved her and waved goodbye.

When he returned home, Leonard Bell was there, repairing the weather stripping on the front door of the modest, two-storey house in the Scarborough section of Toronto.

Bell, then 43, had met Charlton's mother, Valda Williams, after he emigrated from Jamaica to Canada in the mid-'90s. Both came seeking a better life and, in part, to escape the crime and violence in their homeland, a country with one of the world's highest murder rates.

They both came to Toronto. It was considered one of North America's safest cities, though statistically the chances of becoming a homicide victim jumped substantially for those who were young, male, black, disadvantaged and involved in what the police referred to as the "criminal lifestyle."

The Day Everything Changed

On this Wednesday in March, Charlton was on a day off from his job as the manager in one of the concession stands at the SkyDome. Bell, a skilled tradesman who did home renovations, finished the work on the door and agreed to keep his friend company as Charlton ran some errands.

Charlton stood six feet tall and had an athletic build after years of playing football, basketball and cricket. He wore his hair closely cropped and, on that day, dressed casually, a pair of corduroys and a fleece jacket over a T-shirt. Bell wore jeans and a light jacket over a grey sweatshirt. He also kept his hair short and had a trim beard. Neither man was wearing a hat.

They drove in Charlton's 2002 blue Chrysler Neon to a nearby bank, where Charlton applied for a line of credit. He wanted the money to take his girlfriend to Florida.

It was after 5 o'clock, nearing sunset, the streets clogged with evening rush-hour traffic as the two men headed for Bell's apartment. They chatted about a variety of things. Charlton said he was thrilled that his mother, who had never married, had recently started seeing a man with whom she was happy and appeared to have a future. "He was very supportive and looking forward to having him around," Bell recalled.

On Neilson Road, as the men approached Finch Avenue, the light turned amber and Charlton, driving in the centre lane, hit the brakes. Bell gently teased him about not trying to beat the red light when he suddenly felt a jolt in his back and pitched forward. "At first, I felt we were being rear-ended, but I kept hearing the continued explosions and realized it was gunshots," Bell recalled later. Charlton pushed open the driver-side door and stumbled a few metres before collapsing on the hard, cold median. As the Neon began to roll forward, Bell reached for the handbrake. But his left hand was useless. He reached across and used his right hand to bring the car to a stop in the middle of the intersection.

Toronto pastor Juliete Wallace heard four distinct popping noises as she climbed onto a bus with her fare in hand. She and other passengers stepped off the bus. They saw Charlton, covered in blood, lying face-down on the median.

Wallace spotted a passenger in the front seat of the Neon with blood running down his neck. She rushed to him and reached inside the shattered window. Bell was conscious and told her: "I'm getting numb. My back. I got shot." He told her he was dying.

"I said to him, 'Hold on, hold on, you won't die. Keep praying for Jesus to help you.'" Bell asked her to call his family. They prayed together until paramedics and police arrived.

The Toronto Police Service operated on a computerized dispatch system, assigning an event number to every incident. All calls to 911 are recorded. On March 3, 2004, at about 5:20 p.m., there were several calls about a shooting at the intersection of Neilson and Finch, in front of the Free Presbyterian Church.

The callers included a Toronto Transit Commission driver who reported that one victim was lying on the road in the intersection and a second was inside a Neon with the licence plate AMWX 820. A woman reported seeing a man lying in the road and a black SUV speeding through the intersection. She didn't get the licence plate number or supply a description of the occupants.

Surveillance cameras north of the intersection recorded images of what appeared to be Charlton's Neon being tailed by a black SUV and a silver Chevrolet Impala. Police said later they believed the SUV to be an older model Nissan Pathfinder. But the footage failed to focus on the licence plate or any people in the vehicles.

By the time police arrived, Charlton was dead. An autopsy would find three slugs had hit him. The kill-shot had perforated his right lung and aorta.

Bell was rushed to Sunnybrook Hospital, which handles some of the most serious trauma cases in the country. He had four gunshot wounds to his back, two to his left shoulder and what appeared to be two bullet grazes to his neck and head.

Forensic firearm tests determined that at least two, and up to six, guns were used in the assault on the Neon. But police couldn't be sure how many shots were fired. Detective Gerry Storbeck collected slugs from the car at the scene, placing wooden dowels into the holes to show the direction of the shots, suggesting they came from behind the Neon. But no shell casings were found. This was not entirely surprising. In some cases, criminals put a sock over a gun so the shells land inside. Alternatively, if a gun were fired from inside a vehicle, the casings would land inside that vehicle.

Excruciating Pain

Bell had company that night in Sunnybrook's busy trauma centre where doctors were treating three other gunshot victims. His fiancée, daughter, and ex-wife arrived to a chaotic scene of other frantic relatives trying to find out about their loved ones. Bell was having trouble breathing— fluid was building up in his lungs—so the doctors inserted a chest tube down his throat without using anesthetic. "I was in excruciating pain,"

Police walk by Charlton's bullet-riddled Neon on March 3, 2004.

he said. After undergoing tests and X-rays, he was moved into a room with a police guard posted outside the door.

He would later recall "the look of fear on my younger ... daughter's face when she had to come see her father riddled with bullets, lying in a hospital bed and told 'Your father is in a critical state'; having to see the pain and constant tears in the eyes of my then-fiancée, now my wife, the months of work hours she lost to be by my side all the time without complaint. She suffered many sleepless nights and what seemed like endless crying as she watched me in pain and agony."

Bell remained in Sunnybrook for four-and-a-half weeks, during which time his lung collapsed—another chest-tube was inserted—and he developed pneumonia. He didn't have any surgery until three months later, when doctors extracted two of the bullets. Four bullet fragments remained in his left lung. He would later go to Scarborough General Hospital for a consultation to have them removed. A doctor "looked at me and said, 'You people are always killing each other.' I got up, said thank you, and walked out. Never had that surgery."

Still, Bell would hang on to his faith in God and country. He credited his survival to prayer. "I'm not mad," he said years after the shooting. "I trust in God and I'm going to rely on the justice system to make things right."

A Gangland Connection

Bell told police he had no idea why anyone would try to kill him or Charlton. He said he did not see the vehicle that pulled alongside the Neon, or who was in the SUV.

In the hours after the shooting, police conducted criminal record and background checks on the victims. They were quickly convinced a couple of innocent men had been gunned down.

"There was absolutely nothing on either of them that showed up or gave us any reason for why they would have been targeted," homicide detective Wayne Banks recalled years later. He and partner Al Comeau were assigned to the case. The story was on the front page of the *Toronto Sun* and *Toronto Star*. The *Star* ran it under the headline: "We aren't safe—It's so frightening," quoting a woman who lived nearby with her three children. Both newspapers mentioned other recent shootings in Malvern, an area in the northeastern part of Scarborough plagued by gun violence. The cops had no idea who was responsible for the brazen attack.

"We had no suspect description," said Banks, and noted that the vehicle description was almost non-existent: all they knew was that it was a black SUV.

He was instantly struck by the brutality of shooting two people going about their lives, for no apparent reason. The timing—during a Wednesday night rush hour and not under the cover of darkness—also bewildered police. But Banks was certain there was a gangland connection. "It had gang written all over it from the get-go." Comeau agreed it was a "targeted" ambush, with all the hallmarks of an American drive-by gang shooting. But how could you explain the fact the victims were not in any way connected to gangs?

Most gang beefs play out over drug turf, or perceived disrespect. Yet the loss of innocent lives, while rare, is not unheard of, as gangs protect

A distraught Valda Williams leaving the funeral for her son, Brenton Charlton.

their territory and criminal enterprises from rivals with intimidation, threats, assaults and murder.

Both seasoned investigators in their mid-40s, Banks and Comeau knew that any killing related to gang activity would be tough to solve in an environment where "no snitching" was the code of the streets.

The day after the shooting, police put out a news release that concluded: "Brenton Charlton, Homicide #10 of 2004, and Bell, appeared to have no involvement in any criminal activity or gang-related activities. It is believed that both are hard-working family men and well respected by their friends." The news release also contained some emotional language, beyond the by-the-book recitation of the facts generally employed by the Toronto Police Service's public relations department. It said the shootings had "struck this city in the heart."

Ten days later, at the Malvern Christian Assembly, friends and family gathered for the funeral. "Oh God, I have nothing left," cried Valda Williams as she followed her son's casket out of the church. She was so overwhelmed by grief, she needed family and friends to hold her up.

"Black people, stand by your youths," the 600 mourners were told. "If they're doing wrong, tell them they're doing wrong." Charlton never had to be told to do the right thing.

CHAPTER 2

Junior and Leo

In 1989, Brenton Almondo Charlton Junior came to Toronto from Jamaica to live with his mother, Valda Williams, and his mom's sister Uleth Harvey, who was only three years older than her nephew. Also in the townhouse on Cass Avenue in Scarborough was another aunt and her boyfriend. Williams immediately laid down the law, telling her 17-year-old son: "So many things are happening, you could fall into the wrong crowd. If you're brought home in a police car, tell them your mother is dead." A curfew would be followed, house rules obeyed.

It was not the first time the boy, whom everyone called Junior, had been in Canada. At age five, dressed up in a royal blue suit and standing alongside the flight attendant assigned to mind him, he waved goodbye to his mother and the many relatives gathered at the airport in Kingston, Jamaica. Uleth Harvey remembers that day. "It was a big thing to see him off. Everyone was crying, it was horrendous." He was going to visit his father, Brenton Charlton Senior, in Hamilton, where he had settled with a new family and worked in construction. He and

Williams had had a brief relationship. She was just 17 when she gave birth to their son.

Brenton "Junior" Charlton, 31

At the time he first went north, in 1977, Jamaicans were leaving in droves. The Caribbean island was increasingly beset with political strife and violence associated with the drug trade. Many headed to Canada, where the federal Liberal government had laid out the welcome mat. For decades, Canada had traditionally accepted immigrants from countries such as England, Germany, Italy and the United States, with preference given to residents of Commonwealth countries. Once Liberal prime minister Pierre Trudeau opened the doors further, immigrants started coming from the Caribbean, Africa and Asia, changing the complexion of this country.

Canada, and Toronto in particular, was a popular destination for Jamaicans for a number of reasons, including the relatively short flying time—less than four hours. In the 1950s, the federal government introduced legislation that allowed eligible Jamaican immigrants—mainly women—to work as "domestic servants." By the '70s, many of the Jamaicans entering Canada were the children and husbands of the Jamaican women already here. Between 1973 and 1978 some 42,500 obtained permanent resident status—more than doubling the number of arrivals from the previous five years.

But little Junior was miserable in Canada. "He hated it," his aunt Uleth Harvey recalled. He found the winter as harsh as the separation from his mother. He cried every day and longed to go home, which he did after about five months. His father, who adored his son, promised to visit regularly and try never to miss the boy's birthday on November 13. It became a must-attend event on the family calendar, and his parents relished the planning and preparation.

Back in Clarendon, in southern Jamaica, Charlton and his mother went to live with his grandmother, Elsada Harvey, who still had six of her ten children at home. The family was poor but the house was filled with love.

Still, in 1982, Valda Williams moved to Canada on her own, leaving her only son behind, settling in east-end Toronto, where she poured all her energy into making a new life: babysitting and cleaning houses, while taking courses at night school. She lived frugally, collected furniture from garage sales in some of the city's tonier neighbourhoods and reupholstered the castoffs herself. "I never got a cent from the government," she would boast. Williams sent whatever money she could back home to support her son on the island.

She missed him desperately. "I was counting the days until I could hug my son again," Williams remembered. Her dream of a reunion was realized when he boarded a plane in Jamaica with his aunt, Uleth Harvey, and once again headed to Toronto. "We both came here with hopes and dreams for a better life," Harvey said.

This time, Junior seemed to embrace the cold climate, tempered by the warmth of his mother's love. Her main concerns were that he stay in school and make something of his life. Unlike many teenagers, he did not rebel against her strict rules and "tough love" philosophy. Junior often had friends over and they called Williams "Mom."

On Sunday mornings, everyone would go to church, including whoever happened to be living in the house. "Junior would tell the roommates, 'Get up, Mom wants us to go to church,'" she recalled. They would pack into her Toyota Corolla and drive across the top of the city on Highway 401 to a makeshift church in an industrial plaza in the northwest corner of the city.

While attending high school, Charlton started working at McDonald's. He loved to eat, and his first meal in Canada after arriving the second time was a Big Mac, a favourite. He worked his way up to manager at the food chain's outlet at Warden and Sheppard avenues. After high school he was assigned to open a McDonald's outlet at the Toronto Zoo, before taking a job with a catering firm to run a concession stand at the SkyDome. Staff loved his easy-going manner and even temperament. At the time of his death, he was planning to take his girlfriend to Disney World and wanted to return to school. "Just as he was to start his life, it was over like that," his mom said years later. His aunt Uleth would lament: "I played an instrumental role in Junior's immigration and have regrets every day for taking him to his death."

"By the Sweat of Your Brow, You'll Eat Bread"

Leonard Bell, who was called Leo by his friends, had two choices growing up in the 1960s and '70s, surrounded by drug dealing and poverty in Wareika Hills, one of the toughest neighbourhoods in Kingston, Jamaica. He rejected the choice of joining the underworld. "It was always, 'I don't need this.'"

One of eight children, he was raised with strict discipline and church doctrine. "My mother made the rules, my father enforced them. You didn't defy him." His dad, Albert, a plumber, cut an imposing figure, standing six-feet-two and weighing 350 pounds of pure muscle. When young Leo heard his dad speak "it was like thunder." But Albert Bell was also a big teddy bear, the kind of man who wasn't afraid to show affection to his children. "He'd take you into his arms and hold you," Leo recalled. What the family lacked in monetary wealth, it had in love.

Despite their modest home and sizeable brood, Albert and his wife, Loreen, a seamstress, would take in children whose parents couldn't afford to raise them. Bell accepted his father's credo: "By the sweat of your brow, you'll eat bread."

On one occasion, Bell did defy his father. He dropped out of dentistry school because, he said, "I was fascinated by building." He enrolled in an engineering program at the College of Arts, Science and Technology on the outskirts of Kingston.

Bell was 20 when a drunk driver killed his father, at 58. "I wish every day he was still alive."

Young Bell learned bricklaying, tiling, carpentry and plumbing and, after leaving school, did contract work. He also opened a small restaurant in the late 1970s, around the time Kingston was awash in violence. Gangs called the Skull Posse and Hotsteppers terrorized his neighbourhood. "When police hear the [gang] names, they run."

Bell lost count of the people, mostly young men, who died violently during that period, many of them "used" by politicians who created garrison communities by arming supporters. He knew some of the gang members, they would ask him to fix their guns: Bell had trained as an army cadet where he took a course in firearms engineering. "We learned to make weapons from scratch," he said.

Bell arrived in Canada in 1995, to be closer to a daughter who had moved here with his ex-common law wife. He brought with him "a little money to sustain" himself. It helped, since "finding work was a challenge." But he never stopped hustling, taking every job he could get.

For a spell, he worked in telemarketing, selling credit protection plans, and out-sold his colleagues. "But that wasn't for me." He sold vacuum cleaners door-to-door. He knocked on doors trying to get homeowners to sign contracts with a natural gas company. "Looking back at that time I laugh about it now," he would say more than a decade later. "It was a joke. There was no satisfactory pay."

He eventually established himself as a private contractor, doing renovations, which is how he met Valda Williams in 1998. "I was referred to her by a friend to do her floors," he said. At the time Bell was shot, he was about to embark on a new business venture with his fiancée, later his wife, providing home care for the elderly. That never got off the ground. "One stupid act can change your life completely," he told me. "If I wanted to be shot I would have stayed in Jamaica."

Bell's ordeal would not end with his release from hospital. And it would be months before he would learn that the shooters included a notorious gang leader whom police considered one of the most dangerous men ever to live in Toronto.

CHAPTER 3

The baddest seed

To be sure, the odds were Tyshan Riley would grow up to become a gangster. He was born into poverty in one of the toughest neighbourhoods in Canada; raised by an often absent and erratic mother in an over-crowded ghetto apartment; learned his lessons in the street—how to sell drugs, how to steal—not in school; came to idolize the fiercest guys on the block, and embraced a gang culture ruled by guns and fear, a culture that promised money, sex and respect.

For Riley, taking what he wanted through intimidation and violence became a physical reflex. His "I'm not scared of you" attitude was honed at a young age, when he invited older boys to punch him in the gut and barely flinched. His philosophy was not unlike that of any career criminal or Bay Street hustler—wealth is the only goal.

"I know what I want in life and anything I want I can get," he would say. "It's all called progress. Every day you wake up it's progress. I eat, sleep, shit and talk money. That's the way to live."

Tyshan Anthony Riley was born in Toronto on October 28, 1982, when his mother, Marie Riley, was 22, and his father, Wondez East, was 29. Both parents were born in Kingston, Jamaica, but met in Toronto. Marie already had twin boys, Carl and Courtney, born in 1979, with another man. Two more sons, Ishon and Joshua, would follow. Having more children meant bigger welfare cheques.

Since moving to Toronto from Jamaica in her mid-teens, Marie had lived in public housing and relied on social assistance. Combative, fiery and prone to mood swings, her ambition was limited to shoplifting and small-time fraud that lacked sophistication and led to short, intermittent spells in jail.

Tyshan's early years were spent in a two-bedroom apartment in a dingy brown high-rise in southeastern Scarborough. Seven people shared the unit: Marie, the five boys and, for a time, a boyfriend named Pete.

Marie was a clean freak and didn't want her sons' friends—or their bicycles—under foot. She tried to impose curfews yet insisted the twins, in the early days known as Drips and Drops, take their little brothers with them to hang out by the basketball court or nearby plaza. This was when Joshua, whose nickname was Benz, was still in diapers. The twins were essentially "out on the street" when they were 12, said one woman who knew the boys. In her view, "the men in Marie's life always came first, before the boys."

While attending public school, Tyshan preferred activities outside the classroom, such as catching crayfish with friends in Highland Creek, which runs through southeastern Scarborough into nearby Lake Ontario. Everyone called him "Ty," and he was a "cool" little boy who people were drawn to, remembered one childhood friend, Gary Reid, who was a few years older. He called Tyshan his "homey," or "my little bro." The boy looked up to him.

"When I first came around that area, he was the kid that was going to the store to buy some bubblegum," Reid recalled. "But he was a rowdy kid that you saw had enough emotion and stuff in him. So you wanted to talk to him. That's what I did—I'd sit down and reason with him, like 'Listen, man, there are certain ways you can go about things and there's certain ways you can't go about things.'" Reid was trying to teach the kid that even on the street there were ways and rules—not all within the law—to be followed. Reid, a talented soccer player, had his life sent on a downward spiral when he was shot in the leg at 15.

Instead of starting a career in sports, something he had the potential to do, he spent his remaining teenage years and his early 20s in and out of jail.

Not everyone was enamoured with the brash little boy. One neighbourhood mom remembered an 11-year-old Tyshan as "sneaky and devious. I wouldn't turn my back on him." She said the boy was "just like his mother," constantly demanding a lot of attention. "He was a leader," she said, "but he was a leader of wrongdoing." For fun, Tyshan and his little pals would knock on doors and run away, pull fire alarms and hang out in the stairwells in the cluster of rundown high-rises in their neighbourhood. They also played basketball at the East Scarborough Boys and Girls Club on Galloway Road. A mural of children playing is painted in vibrant colours on the exterior of the single-storey building. "A good place to be" is the club's motto.

Ian Edward, fresh out of university, arrived at the club in the late 1980s to start his career as a youth-development worker. He found a nearly empty building with no equipment, some metal shelving and a couple of threadbare couches. Over the years, the club, opened in 1956, had its ups and downs, largely because of its reliance on government grants and charitable donations. But at the time Edward started, the club was in a period of transition. It had a new and energetic board of directors that saw not only the building's potential, but also the pressing need to help kids, mainly black, living in a neighbourhood that was becoming more decrepit and more dangerous every day.

Edward and another youth worker—both enthusiastic and both white—developed programs and activities from offices that were essentially converted closets. There was a gym, a games room with ping pong and pool tables, a kitchen, lounge and a computer room where kids could play video games. The youth workers' dedication paid off. Between 60 and 100 kids were soon turning up at night, taking what Edward called "strong ownership" of the facility.

Staff also recognized they were "a pretty tough, violent group of kids" and took to asking them "to leave their weapons outside," Edward told me. "We knew they were high-needs, high-risk, involved in things out in the community. But we also knew we created an environment inside where they had enough respect for what we were doing." Still,

Roland Ellis uses a computer camera
to photograph himself circa 2003.

on a rainy day after a dance in the gym, the roof leaked because of the bullet holes in the ceiling.

Tyshan Riley and his half-brother Courtney were regulars at the club. So were some of Riley's future G-Way gang brothers, including Dwight Wisdom and Roland Ellis. (Wisdom's younger brother Jason would be a co-accused at Riley's 2009 murder trial and Ellis a crucial witness against them.) For Riley and his friends, basketball was one of the few acceptable activities on the right side of the law. This was a time when Michael Jordan was the king of the sports world, a black man who was adored, admired—and filthy rich.

But there was never any chance Riley would use the game as an escape from the streets. He was considered an "average" player and a ball hog. "Tyshan would dribble without passing to anybody," said someone who watched the games. In most cases, the boys from Galloway turned a game into just another street war. They would play what they called American-style basketball, aggressively and with full contact.

One king of the court was Kareem Brenton Biscombe, who had a mouth full of gold teeth and a wicked temper. And he didn't like to lose. After the visiting West Scarborough boys beat his East Scarborough team, Biscombe chased the other players out of the building with his gun drawn. "He was defending Galloway," said the abovementioned observer. Added Edward: "This was their place and their place only."

(In 1997, Biscombe, then 23, was sentenced to life in prison for murder.)

Riley was clearly in awe of Biscombe and the other older boys who, when not playing basketball, sold drugs, robbed people and carried guns. In particular, he idolized Norris (Bolu) Allen, whose murder in 2002 would eventually touch off the war that brought Riley down. Edward remembered Allen as "powerful, for a skinny kid." He was also fearless. "He just was in everybody's face all the time—he wasn't going to take any shit." Riley watched and learned how Allen earned respect through intimidation and refusing to back down. And none of the boys was afraid of the police.

The club earned a reputation as a hangout for gangbangers-in-training, and became a magnet for police. One time, officers came to the club looking for Courtney, whom they suspected of stealing a pager from another kid. "He got the shit beat out of him" by the police, said Edward. "They were picking him up and throwing him against a fence." Edward said he wanted to file a complaint against the officers "but Courtney wouldn't agree. He knew it would just get him beaten up more the next time."

Such heavy-handed police tactics only hardened the anti-authority views of Riley and the others. When someone would show up at the club after being in prison, he was treated like a celebrity. Doing time showed he had not been a snitch.

Ellis remembered watching the guys who gave up hoops for selling drugs. "There's guys there, if you go to them and even talk about sports, they'll look like you're crazy, like straight, get home.

"They don't care about it. They don't think it exists for them. They don't believe that they have a shot at making it anywhere in this world . . . I guess they do what they feel they're good at, what they think they're good at, at least."

It was under these conditions that club staff tried to target the kids who showed the greatest potential. Riley was not among them.

When not hanging out at the club, Riley would visit the apartments of friends to play video games—*James Bond 007* was a favourite—and watch movies such as *New Jack City, New Jersey Drive* and *Menace II Society*, tales of black urban youth standing up to the cops.

These awkward, early teen years were also when Riley became self-conscious about having two extra teeth (later removed) that ruined his smile—at a time when he became interested in girls. He and his friends would attend parties in the "recreation room" of a neighbourhood high-rise known as the Pentagon or "Pent." During these "rec room jams," a DJ would spin hip hop, R&B and reggae tunes, by Buju Banton, Beenie Man and Super Cat. Riley loved these and other dancehall artists, though a friend recalled "Ty wasn't much of a dancer."

The Pent was also a great place to learn how to "chop" (slang for selling drugs) or pick up pointers on street crime. Once, the twins, for example, had bragged about robbing a pizza deliveryman. The early '90s saw an epidemic of such robberies, prompting police to initiate "Project Deliverance" in Scarborough, aimed at arresting those responsible for the two-bit pizza heists.

One day, the 13-year-old Riley and four other boys—two of them white, from nearby Orton Park—decided to "get a little money, eat some pizza," recalled a neighbour. They placed a delivery order and "masked up." Andre Matthews—who would be slashed to death on a Scarborough street in 1996 at the age of 15—held the driver at knife-point while the others grabbed the pizza and about $30. "Tyshan didn't touch him," said the neighbour. They ate the pizza and later spent the cash on action figures at a Woolco store.

It was around this time that Marie sent her rambunctious son to live with his father, Wondez East. He had survived a 1989 shooting and robbery in Regent Park, one of the most notorious crime areas of the city.

(When I first met him in 2009, East, in his mid-50s, seemed friendly and mild-mannered, a Marlboro smoker who installed carpets and lived in a bungalow in west-end Toronto with his much younger wife and two young children.)

Tyshan returned to his mother's home in Galloway and, just before turning 14, started grade 9 at Sir Robert Borden, a high school consid-ered a dumping ground for poor students. "Before he got his timetable and attended his first class, he was kicked out," recalled a friend. That may be hyperbolic but he certainly didn't last long in school.

He was getting an education, though, watching the drug deal-ers at the Pent, where guys such as Biscombe were raking in serious cash thanks to the insatiable appetite of customers—they called them "custies"—for crack cocaine and weed. For Riley, "it was the streets or nothing," said a one-time friend. "He started making fast money and there was no turning back."

Carrying his signature red cell phone filled with the numbers of custies, Riley hustled hard and understood the value of saving, or "stacking," money. "The red phone was a start of his destiny," said a childhood friend. "He wanted to be the man. But while some want to do it and get out, Tyshan took it and ran with it." He thrived on instilling fear, wanting people to know "when they see my car, don't bother with me."

By the time he was 17, Riley would boast he was making up to $3,000 a day. He sold drugs out of a townhouse belonging to Roland Ellis' mother on Kingston Road, in a warren of two-storey, brown brick buildings. The backyard's small patch of grass backed onto a tree-lined walking path where Riley and Ellis met their customers. With only one road entering the complex, spotters (younger kids who collected a few dollars for their labour) easily signalled the cops' arrival.

Riley and Ellis would sit inside, playing video games until the phone rang. They'd take turns taking "a little walk," Ellis said in describing their routine. Their clients were the "crack heads on the streets," Ellis said, "mainly hookers and bums and anyone who walked through the lane."

When Ellis' mother "caught onto the play," she threw him out. Ellis expected he and Riley would continue doing business, but found himself alone on the street, abandoned by his friend. "He went his own way and just left me, basically," he recalled later with some bitterness. That rift healed, he said, but the groundwork for payback was laid.

Still a teenager, the dark-skinned Riley was known on the street as Nitty, a name, some believe, he adopted as a homage to Chicago mobster Frank Nitti—Al Capone's right-hand man. Riley was also known as Greeze or Greezy Money and was the leader of a young crew that called itself Bad Seeds. Their signature tattoo was a sperm cell.

While the media give the impression gang membership includes some kind of initiation, in Galloway it was more of an evolutionary process. "We were all school friends, we grew up together," said Ellis. "We were saying if we know each other for more than six, seven years or whatever, why not just link—because you know we're all together, we're probably going to be together for the rest of our lives."

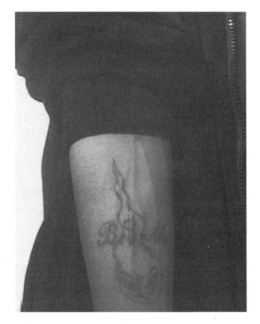

Sperm cell tattoo worn by members
of Galloway gang, Bad Seeds.

That ethos was passed on from the "original gangsters" in the area, Ellis would tell police. "They would always tell us, 'You guys are gonna be friends for life and there's gonna be stuff you guys go through. People are gonna die.'" Ellis called it "a repeat cycle, basically, that goes on in the neighbourhood."

Robberies, which they called "grimes," ripping off rival drug dealers, was the main way to grow the green, especially because these victims generally didn't call the police.

To some, it seemed, Riley's stash of cash appeared overnight. "He still has his guns and stuff but he was hurting like he didn't have money," Ellis recalled. "Then, a week later, this guy has gold teeth in his mouth, pushing a Lex [driving a Lexus], money, liquor store trips every second."

Riley had grown into a lean six-foot-tall young man who liked to wear his hair braided. In warmer months, he wore sleeveless T-shirts and low-slung jeans. On his back was tattooed the word Life. Gold chains adorned his neck. He had come of age at a time when gang members were getting younger "and more committed to making a statement through extreme violence," said Lew Golding, an addictions counsellor who grew up in the area.

In the spring of 2001, when he was 18, Riley was playing a game of pickup basketball in the gymnasium at Pine Ridge Secondary School in Pickering. He was trading trash talk with opponents that included threats to shoot each other. It escalated when Riley threw a punch. A 22-year-old named Teran Richards, who wanted to become a police officer, tried to break it up. That's when Riley's Galloway buddy, Marlon Maragh, stepped onto the court and opened fire.

He pumped three slugs from a .45-calibre handgun into Richards' back. Richards survived but lost a kidney and part of a lung during life-saving surgery. Another bullet grazed the face of a 15-year-old girl sitting in the stands with about a hundred other stunned spectators. "It's not just a bunch of kids pushing each other around. I mean, somebody's shot somebody," Tom Quinn of Pickering's parks and recreations program told *Oshawa This Week*.

Maragh, then 21, Riley and another man fled the school in a rented Pontiac Sunfire, with police in pursuit. Maragh ended up crashing the car into a van, injuring a man and his two sons. Durham Region police arrested Maragh and Riley at gunpoint. The third man got away and was never identified.

Riley pleaded guilty to assault and possession of crack cocaine found in a search after the police chase and was sentenced to nine months in jail. Over the next few years Riley would be in and out of jail on charges ranging from break-ins and breaching bail conditions to drugs and firearm possession. Maragh would later be sentenced to eighteen years in a federal penitentiary for attempted murder.

When he was out on the streets in Galloway, Riley was rolling with Norris Allen, his hero from the Boys and Girls Club, and Gary Reid, his mentor from the streets of his childhood. Both were slightly older dudes, or "niggas," as Riley called them. He had little time for those who did not share his ambition or cupidity. "Those guys could be chopping [selling drugs] out there for as long as I'm in fucking jail and they'll still not have nothing, man," he once said, looking back on his years as a teenager. "Simple and plain, you've got to save money.

I've been stacking money since I was 15 years old. These niggers are just started."

Riley solidified his control of Galloway by committing robberies and drug rip-offs, selling drugs and, when in the mood, driving around looking for enemies to shoot, particularly anyone from Malvern. He was the "big dawg" who ordered his soldiers to do his bidding.

While he always talked the talk, he had inherited his mother's mood swings and sometimes seemed unsettled by his temperament. "I don't know what to be pissed off about, I don't know what to be happy about, I don't know what to be sad about."

Riley also fancied himself a rapper and, with Ellis, booked time to record at the King Turbo studio in Scarborough. His lyrics included: "I'll fuck up your eyes like the R&B singer music / I got a gun as big as a pool stick." Some of the recordings were made under the name Throwbacks, which he would later give to his gang.

As his stature on the block and bankroll grew, so did his attraction for young women. "Money talks," a childhood friend observed, adding that while Riley wasn't the "cutest" guy he got the sexiest women.

But, ever the pragmatist, Riley had a separate standard for his girlfriends. He once told one of them, Ellis' younger sister, Christine, that he wasn't interested in "someone who's dumb or doesn't have street smarts." Riley often had advice to offer: "You got to finish school, have a career that you want to pursue and have money. If you can't do those things, I can't be with you . . . You need your head on your shoulders, like me . . . I know what I want in life and anything I want I can get it, anything I want. If I want to buy something I can go buy whatever the fuck I want. It's all about money. You've got to have money in the world to live . . . I don't have no career, okay, I make my money the way I make my money. But with you, my girl is supposed to be some legitimate person, no problems, has a career, has money, she's good. If, one day, I go flat-ass broke, she's good. You feel me?"

Riley was adept at juggling several girlfriends. But there was one who was different, who "he slept with," while he just "fucked others." Her name was Dana Lee Williams, and she was the mother of Norris Allen's two children. News of the relationship between Riley and

Williams would rock the Galloway neighbourhood after Allen was killed in 2002.

But for someone later considered a stone-cold killer, Riley also had a seemingly sensitive side that could be there for friends and family when they were hurting. "I took you in when you needed loving," Riley once told Williams. While others in Galloway viewed their romance more cynically, Williams regarded Riley as her saviour, getting her through the worst period of her life after Allen was killed. "I'm never leaving this guy for nobody," she would say. "He was the one who was there for me." He was also attentive to his grandmother, calling her and dropping by her east-end home with groceries and money.

But first and foremost, Riley reveled in his image as a fearsome gangster and it continued to get him into trouble with the law.

On March 12, 2004, nine days after the shooting of Charlton and Bell, Justice Eugene Ewaschuk sentenced Riley to two years less one day, to be served in the community, for possessing a firearm that was found in a car he was travelling in a year earlier. In hindsight, the fact that Riley wasn't sent to jail seemed to run counter to the judge's reputation for being tough on gun-toting gangsters. Defence lawyers had nicknamed Ewaschuk: "You is fucked" and "Tex," for meting out Texas-style justice.

As a condition of his release, Riley had an 11 p.m. curfew and was ordered to live with his father and stepmother. He was also forbidden to travel east of Victoria Park in Scarborough unless he was with his father. Justice Michael Dambrot, who would later preside over Riley's murder trial, would call it a "lenient" disposition, given Riley's "serious record for violence." But in 2004, with Riley out on the street, it was too late for Charlton and Bell and for other victims of shootings that would rock Scarborough.

CHAPTER 4

From Scarberia to Scarlem

By the time Tyshan Riley was born in 1982, the area near Kingston and Galloway roads and Lawrence Avenue East was saturated with public housing. The hardscrabble area is in the southeastern section of Scarborough, a vast 186-square-kilometre-borough in the eastern part of Toronto.

Named after Scarborough, England, variations of its name have over the years been used to capture something of its character. People in Toronto called it Scarberia, as a way to describe the seemingly remote location—at least as far as it related to downtown. Residents were Scarberians, or Scarbs. By the end of the 20th century, the nickname Scarlem was common, referring to the increasing number of black immigrants who settled there.

Indisputably, the Toronto borough of Scarborough in the late 20th century had evolved into a place with some serious image problems, deserved or not. Some of the blame was correctly placed on the media reporting crime. No matter where an incident took place, it happened in Scarborough, compared to when something happened at Jane and

Finch, another high-crime area, which wasn't identified as the borough of North York.

But like North York—both boroughs became part of an amalgamated Toronto in 1998—Scarborough had its share of trouble spots: places where lawlessness flourished in grimy ghettos, next to tranquil, leafy residential neighbourhoods with residents living in cookie-cutter bungalows or two-storey homes with backyards, some with swimming pools. Southeastern Scarborough provided those contrasts.

Riley's neighbourhood of Galloway was lined with strip malls, small shops, fast-food restaurants, used-car lots and places that charged usurious rates to cash cheques. Yet not far beyond the urban blight were multi-million-dollar mansions and an abundance of green space near the Scarborough Bluffs, which realtors called a "hidden treasure right next to Lake Ontario." Southeastern Scarborough was as good as any example of Toronto's widening gap between the rich and poor. (By 2009 there were signs of gentrification: a Starbucks at Kingston Road and Lawrence Avenue, and billboards indicating the construction of "luxury" townhomes was imminent.)

Just east of Galloway was Guildwood Village, or The Guild, created after the Second World War and still something of a "Pleasantville" by the time Riley was born nearby, though on the other side of the tracks. The Guild was conceived by planners who "dreamed of establishing a community that would combine quality homes with beautiful surroundings," according to a website run by residents. "Wiring was placed underground instead of being suspended from lighting and telephone poles which would spoil the look of the community." The Guild even had a coat of arms and a Latin motto, *dulce misceatur utili*, which translates as: "Let us mingle the beautiful with the useful."

Trying to uncover the history of the public housing complexes throughout Kingston/Galloway is, for the most part, futile. The Toronto and Ontario archives have some details, but not many. No one, it seemed, bothered keeping track of who built what or when.

To some children who were born in the area in the early '80s, the name Galloway seemed inextricably tied to the word gallows, though the origin of the name was much more prosaic. William Galloway was among the early settlers who owned hundreds of hectares of farmland in the early 19th century. The area's proximity to the Taber Hill ossuary, a 700-year-old burial ground for nearly 500 Iroquois, was another reason some believed the spectre of death hung over the area.

Other local lore has it that, viewed from above, Kingston Road looks like a crack pipe, the townhouses burning ash from the dirty white high-rise at 4301 Kingston Road. That building is known as "the pipe." (The view from a Google Earth satellite photograph doesn't bear this out.)

Living in one of the townhouses or high-rises in Galloway fed a sense of being geographically isolated from the surrounding area, another not uncommon feature of Toronto's subsidized housing stock. Former Galloway gang member Roland Ellis explained to police the disconnection to police: "Any way to get into that area you have to come over a bridge." He rarely left the area and had no friends in other parts of the city. "I didn't trust anybody outside of Galloway."

A Downward Spiral into Gang Warfare

A gritty section of Kingston Road near Galloway Road was key gang turf. Long ago a narrow trail winding through the bush above the Bluffs and along the lakefront, Kingston Road was widened to four lanes over the years. It would also become the nexus of two groups of young men living in two different parts of Scarborough.

At one time, Kingston Road, or Highway 2, was dotted with hotels and motels to accommodate travellers along Toronto's eastern gateway. That was before multi-lane Highway 401 stretched across the province and siphoned away a lot of the business. Left with empty rooms, motel operators in the 1980s entered into contracts with the city to house homeless families and refugees unable to find emergency shelter. The transient nature of the population further eroded the stability of the area, as did the increasing numbers of prostitutes who plied their trade in the motels on Kingston Road.

"It used to be a great area, very quiet, and a great place to raise kids. Now we've got the drug dealers, we've had one unsolved murder, and the prostitutes are hitchhiking all day in the same place," one long-time resident told the *Toronto Star* in 1992. "It's getting to a point where a decent woman can't walk along Lawrence Avenue without a car stopping and someone propositioning her." Another resident, who had lived near Galloway and Kingston for sixty years, was stricken about the condition of the cemetery where his wife was interred. "Condoms on my wife's grave, prostitutes crawling through broken fences to ply their trade on church property and vandalism everywhere is destroying the neighbourhood," he told the newspaper.

Nearby was former Scarborough mayor Albert Campbell's grave at St. Margaret's Church.

The area was fertile ground for the growth of gangs. The police response was to increase officer presence around the public housing buildings, fuelling a state of wariness and mistrust.

Ian Edward, who worked at the Boys and Girls Club, remembered police conducting community sweeps. Officers would arrive en masse, fan out, and question whoever happened to be around, he recalled. "It created absolute pandemonium. It doesn't matter if you're on your way to your job and you're now going to lose your job," Edward said. "You wouldn't tolerate that if they came into your community. But it seems to be okay for the police to do it in those communities."

Lew Golding, who became an addictions counsellor for black youth at the Centre for Addiction and Mental Health, grew up in the area and was a member of a community-police liaison committee from 1988 to 1991. He said that by the late '80s, police switched their attention to Malvern's emerging gang problems because "Kingston-Galloway was too far gone."

By then, the area had an abundance of single moms in similar circumstances: raising children without fathers. "It was a ghetto," one Galloway resident who moved away told me. That part of Scarborough joined other sections of the city synonymous with crime and ghettos.

For the first half of the 20th century, Toronto's impoverished neighbourhoods were concentrated downtown and would lead to the construction of Canada's first public housing project, Regent Park, in the 1950s. The trend of pushing low-income residents to the suburbs started to accelerate in the 1960s when Toronto was experiencing a critical shortage of affordable housing and the land on which to build it. The Ontario Housing Corporation (OHC), the provincial government agency responsible for public housing, had no choice but to look to the fringes of the city. With its large tracts of relatively cheap green space, Scarborough was particularly attractive.

By the mid-'60s, Scarborough had been transformed from a relatively quiet suburb into Canada's fastest-growing community, with nearly 250,000 residents, according to *A History of Scarborough* written in 1968 by Robert R. Bonis. The tide of young families flowing in, many of them immigrants from Europe, settled in the subdivisions and apartment buildings that had sprung up as fast as bulldozers could devour the farmland. And with the population growth came businesses and an ever-growing commercial and retail sector. For those settling in Scarborough prior to 1970, it was a relatively prosperous place thanks to the expanding economy and availability of both white- and blue-collar jobs.

But change loomed. The federal government's decision in the mid-'70s to open its immigration policy, while guaranteeing protection for refugees fleeing countries in turmoil, changed Scarborough. Arriving with young children, many of these newcomers from the West Indies, China, South Asia and the Philippines came to Scarborough and its new government housing developments. This influx of visible minorities created tensions.

Opposition to these developments came mostly from white ratepayers. Politicians, feeling the heat from their constituents, questioned why Scarborough, and its West Hill neighbourhood in particular, was receiving a disproportionate share of subsidized housing. While all of Toronto had ten units of OHC housing per 1,000 people, and Scarborough had eighteen, West Hill, by the early '80s, had about 174 units per 1,000 people.

The West Hill area, encompassing the Galloway neighbourhood, had more single-parent families, more people on welfare and more people living in high-rises than the better-known and more infamous Jane-Finch corridor in North York.

"West Hill had its fill and it is time to look elsewhere," city councillor Ron Moeser, whose Ward 9 included West Hill, said in 1992. The neediest people had been "shoved" into these townhouses and high-rise buildings and left to fend for themselves, with little in the way of social services, said former councillor David Soknacki, who represented the area until 2006. While most of their clients lived on the edges of the city, the social service agencies remained concentrated downtown.

"The best thinking of the time was: give people four decent walls and a place to live and they'll do their best," Soknacki said. The public housing developments had been built "when saving a few dollars on the short term, by putting more and more social housing units together, seemed to be the way of the future."

But as early as 1969, a task force headed by Paul Hellyer, then a Liberal MP, concluded public housing had too many "problem" families with inadequate social services for parents or recreational facilities for their children. Public housing building contracts were awarded to developers with the lowest bids, often leading to "insensitive site selection and poor design," concluded a 1973 task force on housing in Ontario. "In many areas, the design of public housing projects is incompatible with their surroundings. Marginal sites are frequently employed, in part because developers tend to reserve their prime land holdings for private developments."

Years later, John Sewell, who served as Toronto's mayor from 1979 to 1981 and briefly ran the Metropolitan Toronto Housing Authority in the mid-1980s, described public housing developments as "social disasters simply because of the way they were built." He was referring to crowding large numbers of people into buildings and townhouses cut off from the surrounding community.

The OHC's mandate to create housing that blended invisibly with the community was a marked failure and contributed to a rise in the stigma of being associated with certain buildings and areas. The YMCA raised a red flag in a 1974 memo about "the increasing alienation of OHC youth and the antagonism between OHC and non-OHC residents" in Scarborough. "These projects have literally become high-rise ghettos in the middle of upper-income families. The hostility, suspicion and fear between these two groups is worsening. The division is particularly glaring in the teenage bracket where 'gangs' complete with all the trimmings are a growing trend."

Between 1981 and 2001, there was an astonishing 136.6 per cent increase in the number of poor families in Scarborough. And Kingston/ Galloway wasn't the only area to see an increase in the concentration of poor and low-income families. Malvern, a large square area in the northeastern part of Scarborough, was, like Galloway, also isolated by geography and had limited public spaces and facilities. Locally called the "four corners," Malvern was to be a model for a suburban community that preserved mature trees, ravine woodlots and parklands. The area bordered the Toronto Zoo, Rouge River and Rouge Valley Park—just north of Highway 401.

In the late 1950s, the Canada Mortgage and Housing Corporation expropriated the area's farmland and eventually the province initiated a project called Homeownership Made Easy. The government-sponsored home financing plans allowed for the purchase of detached, two-storey, four-bedroom homes for $15,000 to $20,000 with leasing arrangements for the land.

In contrast to the mazes of townhouses and high-rises in Galloway, Malvern had a mix of single-family detached homes, semi-detached homes and low-rise garden and high-rise apartments. There were also a number of subsidized units offering rents geared to income. Malvern was supposed to be an opportune place to start a life in multicultural Canada, and predictably it became a magnet for immigrants. After years of planning and construction, the first residents moved into their homes in 1972, and for a time the experiment appeared to be successful.

But the success didn't last. Malvern, like Galloway, lacked public services. There was also poor urban planning, which meant residents generally interacted within their own cultural and racial community and had minimal contact with anybody else. Economic conditions were also not in Malvern's favour and the dream of home ownership for many was short-lived when salaries were frozen by wage controls in the mid-1970s. By 1983, Malvern had only about 13,500 residents, about half the number planners had wanted. There also remained a dearth of services, not enough shopping, schools or transportation lines. Malvern could have been a "model community" but instead was a "planning disaster," said Dave Warner, a former New Democratic Party MPP for Scarborough-Ellesmere, in 1983.

Still, not everyone considered growing up in Malvern a bad thing. Toronto-based filmmaker Sudz Sutherland, for instance, said his Malvern of the 1980s was unlike the Malvern it would become. "Back in the day, there wasn't the trade in guns or drugs like there is currently," he wrote in a 2009 article published in the *Star*. "Growing up, the worst we had to fear was that someone was going to try to beat you up."

Malvern, though, was never going to be a suburban utopia. Instead of roads designed in circles and crescents, Malvern should have been built on a grid system to allow better bus service. Families without cars were forced to rely on public transit that wasn't easily accessible, furthering a sense of isolation. Unable to venture far afield, young people stayed in close-knit gangs that took their names from streets: Empz for Empringham, C-Trail for Crow Trail and B-Way for Brenyan Way.

And, for those inclined, drug dealing was the surest way to make money. The Malvern Recreation Centre and Malvern Town Centre were popular spots to buy crack and marijuana, and the more affluent dealers with cell phones and vehicles did drop-offs outside the community.

That turned the section of Kingston Road running through Galloway turf into a battleground between the men of Malvern and those who chopped drugs in Galloway. "People would rent rooms and try and sell drugs in the area and mix in to get to know the crowd," Ellis would explain years later. "And we really didn't want people from outside the area mixing in our crowd." Galloway drug-dealing strongholds included a bar called McTaggart's, located beside a variety store on Kingston Road, as well as the walkway at the townhouse complex where a young Ellis and Riley operated.

Another Galloway Boy, Marlon Maragh, who shot the peacemaker during that basketball game in Pickering, described the friction between Galloway and Malvern while testifying at his attempted-murder trial in 2002. "People were just fighting over who can sell drugs where, who's tougher, who's stronger," he said. "One person had a problem with another person and they just turned it into one area against another."

To protect their turf, the Galloway Boys would do a "G-check," as a way to identify strangers, particularly members of other gangs. "It is like you are seeing another dog in your cage. Another dog is roaming around your neck of the woods, so you give him a G-check. You try to find out what he is doing in your territory," Ellis explained. "Then, if he doesn't want to leave," he went on, "it could turn into someone getting hurt, getting killed, getting robbed."

CHAPTER 5

Gangbanging and the art of chess

Youth gangs aren't new to Toronto or to the rest of Canada.

In 1940s' Toronto, for instance, the Beanery Boys were a rough-and-tumble group who used their fists to get a point across. One night, when one of them was refused admittance to a dance at a YMCA in the city's west end, a high school student received a thrashing because the gang member resented being excluded. "Young people are afraid to go out at night and are afraid to make complaints to the police for fear of the gang lying in wait for them," Bloor Collegiate principal W.G. Noble said in 1948 after the incident. "The situation is becoming serious."

But when much more dangerous gangs were being formed in the latter half of the 20th century, few in Canada were paying attention. One exception was Fred Mathews, one of the first professionals to study the phenomenon when the most exposure Canadians had to street gangs was from such Hollywood movies as *Warriors* (1979) and

Colors (1988), with its iconic tag line: "70,000 gang members, one million guns, two cops."

As a psychologist and program director at Central Toronto Youth Services, Mathews described the lure of gangs for young people in a 1993 report commissioned by the federal government. "They can obtain a sense of power, status, order, safety and communion with others— free from the scrutiny of the adult world," he wrote in the report titled *Youth Gangs*. "The powerful draw and influence of peers in early and middle adolescence gives these groups enormous power and influence over young people."

Mathews had first-hand knowledge. He had lived in Los Angeles, the gang capital of the United States, in the late 1970s and early '80s. When he returned home to Toronto to attend graduate school, he noticed something: graffiti. It was 1986 and Mathews began making "field notes" about it and other signs of gang activity, such as clusters of young people congregating at suburban plazas.

He paid special attention to one group hanging around the St. Clair subway station in the city's affluent midtown. They called themselves Socias, wore preppy clothes such as Polo shirts, and apparently modelled themselves on the gang in S.E. Hinton's book *The Outsiders*, turned into a 1983 movie of the same name directed by Francis Ford Coppola.

By the late '80s, youth gangs in Toronto were being blamed for "swarmings"—a downtown phenomenon where a group of kids would surround a victim and steal money or clothes. It was around this time that Mathews "realized we're on a trajectory of the American gang experience."

Others were suggesting the same. The *Globe and Mail* published an article in 1989 about teen gangs "preying on schools, subways and stores" and quoted unnamed police officials agreeing that crime by youth gangs was on the increase. "There are perhaps 40 emerging gangs in Toronto, with names such as The Untouchables, Band of the Hand, Chinese Mafia, Rude Boys, B-Boys, Posse and Massive. They distinguish themselves by the clothes they wear and their haircuts, as well as the music to which they listen. The Untouchables (mainly white suburban teens), for instance, have a clean-cut preppy look. B-Boys, by contrast, wear baseball caps, track suits and colorful running shoes."

These youth gangs augmented their wardrobes by stealing trendy clothes from the Eaton Centre and Scarborough Town Centre. Their most prized swag was Nike Air Jordans and leather jackets. Guns were mentioned just once in the article. The article ended with a warning: Toronto was "ripe" for the formation of well-organized gangs. They included Chinese, Vietnamese and aboriginal gangs defined along ethnic lines.

At the sentencing of a 16-year-old member of a Vietnamese gang in the mid-'80s, Ontario provincial court judge Robert Dnieper said gangs should be "wiped from society completely." The judge said the "only answer for him [the accused] is deportation and the suggestion that he try his gang activities in Ho Chi Minh City." He warned that a failure to act decisively would only lead to the gangs growing "like mushrooms after a rain."

Nonetheless, there remained a reluctance to see them as full-fledged gangs like those in major U.S. cities. Patrolling the seedier side of the downtown core in the late '80s—on his way to becoming Toronto's police chief in 2005—Bill Blair remembered groups "more or less loosely organized," operating in some of the low-income neighbourhoods.

"They competed with each other for drug trafficking and there were rivalries between groups in Regent Park, north and south, and Don Mount, across the river. They were competitive and occasionally violent towards each other," he told me. These gangs didn't necessarily "go under a name," but they recognized each other as part of one group or another. The names, said Blair, came later "with the cultural U.S. invasion."

The open border of the airwaves allowed rap music and hip-hop culture to be splashed onto TV screens across Canada. Music videos featured men acting like gangsters and pimps, dressed like gangsters and pimps, rhyming about guns and sex while being fawned over by gorgeous women wearing little to hide their wares.

Corporate America—and corporate Canada, for that matter—was hardly objecting to the images or lyrics of the songs. Not when there was big money to be made with "Glock squeezed in between Dom Perignon champagne and Victoria's Secret lingerie," wrote Canadian social commentators Rodrigo Bascuñán and Christian Pearce in their

2007 book, *Enter the Babylon System: Unpacking Gun Culture from Samuel Colt to 50 Cent.*

Cheap Drugs, Fast Money, Easy Sex

During the 1970s and early to mid-'80s, outlaw motorcycle and Asian gangs, for the most part, controlled the cocaine market with a more affluent clientele that could afford $100 for a gram. But crack—an adulterated form of cocaine—was geared to a low-end market. Its arrival in Canada in the late '80s was accompanied by the sound of gang gunfire.

Crack was cheap—a $5 hit bought a twenty-minute high—because it was well diluted. But it was also extremely addictive, which made it especially attractive to street dealers seeking customers coming back for more.

Jamaica was an important link in the world of cocaine trafficking. As the United States clamped down on the cocaine pathways directly from South America, traffickers turned to Jamaica as a trans-shipment point, putting a new product into the hands of the posses operating there. In the early '90s, the drugs and posse members were heading north.

"The major centres are Toronto, New York, London, Miami and Kingston," the *Globe and Mail* reported, quoting a Jamaica-based intelligence source. "They'll operate between any of those five cities and they'll have links in all of them. They have no roots, none whatsoever. The posse member is like a shallow plant, he won't own any property and everything he's got is cash."

In Toronto, police identified Jamaica's infamous Shower Posse—named for showering victims with gunfire—as one of four main criminal gangs controlling the city's lucrative crack cocaine trade. The gangs operated in the suburbs where there were large clusters of apartment buildings with many Jamaican residents, so they could blend in, police said.

Vicious turf wars broke out in the city. Members of the Shower Posse were blamed for the killing of a 25-year-old named Anthony (The Fox) Aransibia, a member of the Striker Posse. He was gunned down after being lured to the stairwell of an apartment building in

Scarborough. The killing was connected to "a territorial dispute in the crack trade," the *Star* reported.

In 1991, a peak year for violence throughout North America, Toronto had a record eighty-nine homicides, sixteen of them linked to the drug wars involving rival gangs fighting for turf in Toronto housing projects.

One of the posse leaders ran his Toronto operation from a palatial house in Jamaica. "His bases of operation [in Canada] are a music store and a modest bungalow in a quiet North York neighbourhood," the *Star* reported.

Toronto police chief William McCormack said in 1990 that Jamaican posses were a "grave concern" to his force. But he also distinguished between organized gangs and other groups of young people living in housing developments who were using the name posse as a "scare term. These are simply young hoodlums," McCormack said. This could have described some young men in southeastern Scarborough calling themselves the Galloway Posse. They were mainly involved in petty extortion, street-level drug dealing, theft and robberies at a time when Tyshan Riley was growing up.

Elsewhere in the city, gang violence in 1991 reached a deadly apex in downtown Chinatown as Asian gangs battled for control of the lucrative trade in drugs, plus gambling and extortion.

In 1997, Fred Mathews, appearing at a conference in Hamilton, Ontario, on youth violence, declared that street gangs had become "integral" to youth culture. "The problem will also get worse before it gets better," he predicted. "Before, it just involved kids on the wrong side of the tracks." He warned, "gunplay is becoming more common and young people are more accepting of others who belong to gangs."

He presciently argued that because governments failed to provide social and recreational services in vulnerable communities in the early 1990s, Canadians would likely pay a price for years to come. "We had an opportunity to lay the foundation that would have made involvement in gangs far less attractive for kids," Mathews said. "I think for the foreseeable future we'll be lucky to get it into a maintenance mode. It will be a number of decades before we can eradicate and remove the criminal elements [of youth gangs]."

By 1998, Toronto police estimated there were 180 gangs in the city with varying levels of organization. But with fluid memberships, defining and identifying them was difficult. Some—though not all—gangs were violent. A Toronto police map from that time identified dozens of territorial-based crews, posses and gangs throughout the city, largely concentrated in poorer areas with public housing complexes. Many of the names referred to a neighbourhood or specific street. In northwest Toronto, there were the Jane Finch Killaz, Trethewey Gangster Killers and Rexdale Posse. Police identified more than fifty groups in downtown Toronto, including the Regent Park Posse, Christie Boys and B-Boys. In Scarborough, the map showed a cluster of groups called "Kingston/Galloway," the Mornelle Court gang and Malvern Posse.

Some gang members identified themselves by wearing certain colours or clothing, or ball caps with the brim pointing in one direction or pants rolled up on one leg. Some were adorned with jewellery or tattoos with their gang's name or initials. Others used hand signals to communicate. Some used graffiti to mark turf.

It was around this time, in the late '90s, that Toronto police started compiling a gang-member database, the first of its kind in Canada. It included gangsters' mug shots, street names, identifying tattoos—and their enemies.

Throughout much of the 1990s and into the next decade, violent turf battles were playing out on some city streets. In Scarborough, two rival gangs made up of Sri Lankan and Tamil youth, AK Kannan and VVT, engaged in a series of shootings. Some of the attacks happened in daylight, such as in early 2001 when a car with a reputed Sri Lankan gang leader was followed to a highway off-ramp and ambushed by gunmen shooting wildly. No one was injured.

But there were casualties, not all of them gang members. Five killings linked to Sri Lankan gang wars remained unsolved a decade later, all the victims considered innocents caught in the gangs' crossfire. But the victims had unpronounceable names and shared the same ethnicity as the suspected shooters. The media—and most Torontonians—barely took note.

Luis Carrillos, a cherubic and cheerful youth counsellor with the Hispanic Development Council, started working with kids who belonged to Latino gangs in Toronto's west end during the mid-1990s. There were the L.A. Boyz, La Raza, Latin Kings and Latin Browns, "co-existing and sharing turf," he wrote in his 2000 paper, "Youth Gangs: To See Them Talk is to Hear Their Walk."

Carrillos, who immigrated to Canada from El Salvador in the early 1970s, developed empathy for the kids he grew to know, recognizing that many joined gangs because they felt invisible and alienated. Gang membership "gives security to these kids, space, it gives them power, makes them feel cool. Boys go for the girls, some go because their friends are there. Some go because they want to belong, they don't want to be judged, they have a shared cultural identity," he told me.

Carrillos answered questions thoughtfully and slowly in his office in downtown Toronto. "Gangs are a group of people who get together to do things." He said not all gangs are criminal entities and not all gang members are up to no good. "In gangs, there are kids who are bad news and kids who don't even drink." Only a small percentage of gang members commit the most serious crimes, including murder, though typically the media portray all as bloodthirsty maniacs.

Robert Gordon, a criminology professor at Simon Fraser University in Burnaby, British Columbia, concluded the way to understand why young people join gangs is to see it in terms of the activity of the particular gang. In his 2000 "Greater Vancouver Gang Study," Gordon identified three types of groups: criminal-business organizations, street gangs and wannabe groups.

The motivation to participate in a criminal-business organization, he found, "is influenced by cultural and social bonds, marginalization from mainstream Canadian society, lack of resources and employment opportunities, language barriers, and possession of few marketable job skills." Street gang membership is less straightforward, "but most kids live in poverty and are escaping dysfunctional family situations."

But perhaps the greatest allure was the money. Who wanted to work in a nine-to-five job that pays a pittance compared with the earning potential of selling drugs? The bonus was that the sexiest women flocked to Tyshan Riley and his ilk. They shared women as if they were residents of the Playboy Mansion.

Yet there was no "luxurious lifestyle" in Galloway. On the surface, the gang members stacking cash appeared as poor as everyone else in their community. "Tell me anyone who's living with a Jacuzzi in their house in that neighbourhood," Roland Ellis would comment. Asked what he spent his drug profits on, Ellis said buying clothes and more pot to smoke. He was not among those who opted for American gangsta-style trimmings, travelling downtown to Yonge Street and a jewellery store called Nellie's Custom Jewellery to buy "grills," teeth caps sported by hip-hop icons such as 50 Cent.

But money brought something else. For those who embrace the gangbanging way, "the thirst for reputation," even in death, is the purpose of gang members, Kody Scott, a former Crips gang leader in Los Angeles, wrote in his autobiography, *Monster*. "The principle is respect, a lynchpin critical to relations between all people, but magnified by thirty in the ghettos and slums."

Former California state senator Tom Hayden, the '60s radical who later married and divorced Jane Fonda, wrote in his 2003 book, *Street Wars*, that gangs create a "parallel realm, a separate nation that they have created out of nothing more than the alienation they feel from society. The real motive is to be reborn as someone, to carve out a recognition and respect that society denies."

The Canadian Gang "Problem"

By the beginning of the 21st century, many Toronto gangs identified themselves as Bloods or Crips, though there was little evidence of any association with the feared American gangbangers that originated the names. Still, in some of the city's toughest neighbourhoods, the colours of the Bloods (red) and Crips (blue) sent a powerful and perilous message. Wearing a rival's colours in some areas could spell trouble. In one incident, an undercover cop, who was black and wearing red track pants, knew better than to run after a suspect on Crips turf in a west-end Toronto neighbourhood. "He would have been shot," said a Toronto officer familiar with the incident.

In Galloway, gang members were less inclined to "beef over the Bloods and Crips thing," Ellis would explain to police. He drew an analogy to the Toronto police divisions in Scarborough. "If 41 Division wore all red suits and 42 [Division] wore all blue suits, you guys wouldn't war because you guys wear two different coloured suits—you guys are officers of the law, so you work together," he said. Just as "you guys are police officers first," Ellis continued, "we look at that—we're Galloway first, we know we're from the same 'hood. But [if] I see a guy from Mornelle [Court] or Markham–Eglinton and he's wearing red and I'm wearing blue, I'm not looking at him like, okay, we're both from Scarborough, everything's cool. It's like there's problems . . . 'Yo, you have to put that red bandana away,' or he might come to me to put my blue bandana away."

While all this was evident on the streets and in the neighbourhoods where gangs were ever-present, governments were still trying to figure out what was happening in their cities. The first-ever national statistical "snapshot" of the "Canadian youth gang problem" was released in 2004 by the federal Department of Justice. Based on data collected two years earlier, it found there were 434 gangs, with 7,071 members. It carried a warning: "Policy-makers and community leaders in Canada may wish to pay attention to the U.S. experience, which confirms that once youth gangs become established within communities, they can rapidly proliferate."

When police departments across the country were asked in 2002 to rank the criteria they used to define a youth gang, the top answers were: the group commits crimes together, hangs out, assembles together, has leaders or an established leadership structure, and members display or wear common colours or other insignia.

A 2006 federal Department of Justice report called *The Nature of Canadian Urban Gangs and Their Use of Firearms* cited a lack of consensus on what constituted a youth gang.

> Overall, there are many similarities between the characteristics of urban gangs illustrated in the Canadian research literature, and as reported by the police. However, there appear to be region-specific differentiation across Canada that includes variations in ethnic group representation, type of criminal activity, and use of firearms. Such localization might signal

the need for more city-specific research throughout Canada as the only available published literature on urban gangs was found for Vancouver and Montreal.

In any case, the report estimated that Toronto had eighty-three street gangs. The names of 3,000 people were in a police database, half classified as "at risk"—not full-fledged gang members or affiliates. To be entered into the database, a person had to meet two of seven criteria: direct/indirect involvement, self-admission, information from a reliable source, a court finding, physical evidence, observed associating with members, or symbolic gang identifiers.

Ellis offered his view of what constituted a gang. It is a group of guys who don't work, "they're not doing stuff that's sociable," he said. "It's not that there's no organization. It's just not organized—it's not organized on a mob-type status or any type of like Gambino-type family. But there is people that sit down and discuss things before they do it, so there's somewhat organization but it's not to a high degree."

The Spark that Started the Inferno

While Tyshan Riley was still a Bad Seed in 2000–01, there were two main gang leaders in Galloway: Omar Lloyd Demetrius, known on the street as O, and Gary Eunick, who in 2005 was convicted of murdering an unarmed man in a suburban nightclub over a $10 cover charge. Eunick and Demetrius were the original leaders of the Get Mad Crew, a Galloway gang that sold crack and marijuana. Their tattoo was a "mad-face." Their motto: "No fear."

For young men lacking a positive male role model, Demetrius was an influential figure who acted like Marlon Brando in *The Godfather*, prepared to step in whenever problems arose. Ellis remembered as a teenager riding bicycles with some of his friends in Malvern when "a bunch of dudes" pushed them off. "One of my boys rode off and called O," Ellis recalled. "By the time we got back to Galloway, O was already in Malvern and had a dude up at gunpoint." That time, Demetrius, who had a volcanic temper, didn't pull the trigger.

It was a different story on August 21, 1999. Demetrius was at a popular West Indian takeout restaurant on Kingston Road. Preferring not to wait in line, he started arguing with the counter clerk. Standing nearby was a man named Dave Jack. "Omar, don't get yourself in no trouble," Jack told the hothead, who shot back, "Dave, don't say nothing to me, being like you is a big pussy hole."

Jack left the restaurant followed by Demetrius, who pulled out a gun and shot him twice in the leg and once in the arm. While in hospital, Jack told police Demetrius was the shooter. An arrest warrant was issued but Demetrius had left the country and also a leadership vacuum in Galloway.

He was picked up in July 2000 coming back into Canada under his own name. At his trial, a younger G-Way member testified he—not Demetrius—shot Jack. A jury didn't buy the purported confession and in November 2001 convicted Demetrius of attempted murder. He spent several years behind bars before being deported to Jamaica in 2005. He snuck back into Canada—again—and in October 2007 was arrested for firing several shots into the air at a Scarborough restaurant.

Back in 1999, with Demetrius on the run, his close friend Norris Allen was there to step in and lead the gang. But his rule wouldn't last long. His murder would spark the war between Galloway and Malvern.

Gang Warfare: The Next Generation

By the time Tyshan Riley and Roland Ellis were teenagers, the "problem," as the beef between Malvern and Galloway was usually described—like the "troubles" in Northern Ireland—was deeply entrenched.

"I have family that live in Malvern. They don't even come to see me in Galloway," Ellis recalled. "Nobody in Galloway likes nobody from Malvern, nobody in Malvern like nobody in Gall. Like, I go see my aunt in Malvern and she'll be looking at me like, 'What are you doing here?'"

For those involved in street life, it meant never letting down your guard. Ellis described it as being like a game of chess. "It's just a plot, a game, it's like checkmate," he said. In the case of Malvern and Galloway, it meant gang members seeing their enemies as if they were pieces on a chessboard, always knowing their whereabouts. One of the reasons most of the gang members didn't have real jobs was because a rival could track their schedules—and "there'll be dudes waiting for them" when they get off work.

Asked about the history of the "war" between Malvern and Galloway, Ellis paused and replied: "It goes way back."

CHAPTER 6

Anatomy of a gang war

For Tyshan Riley and his Galloway sycophants, the final battle of the war with Malvern began on October 10, 2002. It would end when Riley was arrested on April 19, 2004. But ten people, including Brenton Charlton, Leonard Bell and others who had nothing to do with gangs or guns, who just happened to be in the wrong place at the wrong time, would be among the casualties.

On that autumn day in 2002, Norris (Bolu) Allen, one of Riley's boyhood heroes from the basketball court at the Boys and Girls Club, parked his black Honda on the tiny front lawn of his family's rented bungalow in the middle of enemy turf. It was a bright and unseasonably warm Thursday as the gunmen prepared their ambush. Apparently, they were undeterred by or unaware of the workers on the rooftop of the house beside 4 Wickson Trail, a residential street in the heart of Malvern.

After saying goodbye to his mom and sister, the 21-year-old Allen stepped down the concrete steps and got into his car, cranking the volume on its high-wattage stereo before reversing onto the street. Before he had a chance to drive off, the suburban calm was rocked by gunfire, leaving Allen slumped forward in the Honda's front seat, the engine idling and music still blasting from the speakers.

His sister ran outside, saw her brother's bullet-riddled body, and ran back inside the house, crying hysterically. She soon came back out with a phone pressed to her ear, calling 911, followed by her mother. "My son is shot, my son is shot," Janet Allen screamed, a witness told the *Toronto Sun*. A neighbour ran over to help and pulled Allen's lifeless body out of the car and onto the driveway. His mother threw herself to the ground and frantically tried to resuscitate him, while other neighbours rushed to see what had happened. There were six shell casings scattered around.

The roofers watched three young black men tear off in various directions. One was wearing a red bandana. Another had covered his face with a camouflage-print bandana. Both held handguns. A third

Norris "Bolu" Allen, a Galloway gang leader shot to death in 2002.

man was dressed in dark clothing. Dana Lee Williams, the mother of Allen's children and later Riley's girlfriend, told police the shooters had to be from the Malvern neighbourhood "because they're all on foot. Where they going to run? They had to live in the area."

It was an appalling period of violence involving young black men. Police believed all the homicides were connected to gangs or illicit drug trafficking. "What we had was a conflict that had escalated wildly out of control," Toronto police chief Bill Blair would say. Nevertheless, the public outcry was muted. Residents of the two Scarborough neighbourhoods, mainly black and poor and powerless, may have been on edge. But most people in the city had never heard the sound of gunfire.

Police investigating Allen's death had several suspects and many motives. Yet, as is customary in gang slayings, no one was willing to point fingers, let alone testify in court. One police theory was that Allen, who sold pot and cocaine, was "taxing" other dealers—demanding a piece of their profits. Allen leaned on people "he shouldn't have," so "Malvern took him out," said one investigator.

The *Toronto Sun*, quoting an unnamed police source, said Allen "went to ground after rivals began hunting him." At the time of his death, he was out on bail and wanted on an outstanding warrant for having a restricted firearm. "Norris Allen was one of our biggest problems," according to the *Sun's* source.

One confidential informant (C.I.) told police that Allen's killers went by the street names of Bannas and Victor, and were connected to Malvern gangs.

The more widely held belief was that Allen was murdered by the Malvern Crew in revenge for shooting Dwayne (Biggs) Williams—no relation to Dana Lee Williams—during a talent show at Lester B. Pearson Collegiate on February 23, 2000. It was a Saturday night and the show, called "Voices of Malvern," drew about 300 people to the school auditorium. While the young performers sang on stage, a gunman crept behind where Williams was sitting and opened fire. Hit in the back and leg, Williams, then 20, hobbled out of the auditorium, down a hallway, and into a washroom. A police officer on the scene followed the trail of blood, found him inside, and called for an ambulance. Miraculously, the only other person injured was a man who suffered cuts in the stampede from the auditorium.

Williams, treated and released from hospital, was no help to police. He told them he'd let them know if he found out who the shooter was. A few weeks later, his mother's house was sprayed with bullets. No one was injured; no one was arrested.

But, within the Scarborough underworld, many fingered Norris Allen for targeting Williams. The oft-told story was that Williams had stolen a gun belonging to a Galloway gang member, that someone had "asked" him to return the weapon and he had refused. "Basically, that's the hammer," Roland Ellis told police, "that's what started everything."

Dana Lee Williams later recalled how a Malvern Crew leader had confronted Allen one time when he was in a car with their three-year-old daughter. She said she was so fearful she slept behind couches pushed up against her front door.

To further confuse the case for police, one informant suggested Dana may have set up Allen. How else would the shooters know he would be at his mother's house at that time? This C.I. even suggested Dana wanted payback after Allen began beating her and made her have sex with him at gunpoint. And even Allen's mother, Janet, told friends she thought Dana was responsible for her son's murder. Dana strenuously denied this and police uncovered no evidence to give the theory any credence.

Stoking such speculation was that Dana, almost immediately after Allen's death, became romantically involved with his acolyte, Tyshan Riley. "He was the one who started making me come around and started to come out of my room," she said, "and doing all this stuff for me." He paid her car payments and her rent.

If Allen was executed for shooting Dwayne (Biggs) Williams at the Malvern school in February 2000, his killers had been patient, since twenty months had passed when he was ambushed in his mother's driveway. Regardless, Allen's death touched a nerve for Tyshan Riley and others in Galloway. For many of them, Allen had been an idol. He was feared but also greatly admired. Some say he had the aura of the late rap star Tupac Shakur. One police officer suggested his street name,

Bolu, derived from that of a member of the notorious Crips gang in southern California. But the name was probably pinned on Norris as a kid, after the goofy bear named Baloo in the Disney movie *The Jungle Book*, inspired by a Rudyard Kipling classic.

As a teenager, Bolu—no one called him Norris—loved making people laugh, sometimes by "hanging moons" and play-wrestling with younger kids. Born December 8, 1980, he was only a couple years older than Roland Ellis and Tyshan Riley. But he cultivated their loyalty and respect by taking them to play paintball. "Yo, if I die, would you ride for me? Like, would you defend my death?" Allen would ask.

To his family, Allen was the go-to guy, eager to listen and help when his siblings came to him with their problems. He was also a romantic who would get down on one knee and sing to Dana, who was an attractive 17-year-old with almond eyes when the two started seeing each other.

There was also a darker, vicious side. Lean and lanky, Allen didn't look menacing. But he demanded respect and thought nothing of slapping someone across the face, wrapping his arm around the terrified transgressor and threatening: "Yo, guy, I know where your family lives." He earned loyalty by offering protection. If a kid in the neighbourhood had scrapes and bruises, Allen would become an avenging angel. Years later, one of his admirers smiled at the memory of Allen settling a score, even though the kid's injuries were the result of a schoolyard accident.

So, news of Allen's murder spread quickly through Galloway. Roland Ellis took a call from an aunt, who said one of his friends— she wasn't sure who—was lying dead on a street in Malvern. "What do you mean 'you see him lying in the street'?" he asked. She explained she was watching a crowd of people and police and, on the ground, was the body of a young black man. Ellis knew where Allen's mother lived. He also knew he was a target. The call upset Ellis, though he was closer to Allen's younger brother, Marcus. (That night, Marcus slept at Ellis' house because he was scared to go to his home, still ringed with crime-scene tape and cops.)

Tyshan Riley got word of the killing as he and other gang members gathered in Ellis' backyard. Someone pulled out a bottle of rum cream liqueur. Riley poured its syrupy contents onto the ground—a show of respect for his fallen friend, taking a page from Tupac Shakur, whom Riley adored. In the late rap star's *Life Goes On* video, Shakur empties a bottle of liquor onto the ground, singing: "We poured out liquor for ya." The ritual would be repeated in the coming months.

But Riley still needed to see his dead friend for himself. "You, you, you, let's go," Riley said to three of those gathered. They jumped into his car and sped to Malvern. When he returned, Riley was crying. "Yeah, it is him on the ground," he told Ellis in tears. "I seen his shoes, his car is there, it is him on the ground."

The next weekend, at the Ogden Funeral Home in Scarborough, the chapel was packed with mourners. Some put Allen's death into the context of the staggering toll of young black men.

"We've lost another young member of our black community to violence," said friend Simone Williams. She appealed to the conscience of the killers by reciting the lyrics of "Murderer," by reggae group Buju Banton.

Norris Allen Sr. led the congregation in song. His son's children, Shamia, then three, and two-year-old Jada Lee, sat listening as their mom, Dana, paid homage to their father. "You had to know him to love him," she said. "Basically, he was misunderstood."

Years later, a friend said Allen's death was like "a grey cloud hanging over the neighbourhood." In tribute, many copied the "King Son" tattoo Allen had on his stomach. Riley had Bo Lu tattooed across his chest.

Within days of Allen's death, Riley changed the rules of engagement with Galloway's enemies. He told his crew they would now be known as the Throwbacks, "throwing back" what Allen got, Ellis would testify. Rather than focus on robberies, drug dealing and home invasions, they would form "ride squads," driving around looking for rival gang members to shoot at.

It's a concept that may have had its origins in Los Angeles. In the foreword to ex-gang member Cotton Smith's 2006 book, *Inside the Crips*, rapper-turned TV star Ice-T explained: "In the ghetto, when someone gets shot, the cops are going to let it ride. Meanwhile, children and mothers are crying, little sisters scream over the dead body. The family looks to the young men in the 'hood. The young men start riding for justice. So when someone kills someone on your side, you go to their side . . . and retaliate."

For Riley and his cohorts—who wore hoodies emblazoned with the word Throwbacks and adapted the emblem of the NBA logo, with its trademark basketball player dribbling a gun instead of a ball—simply being from Malvern made someone a target. This was street justice, and it was all about instilling fear—and benefiting from the notoriety and power that came with it. All of this to control a few blocks of community housing, the majority filled with peaceful, hard-working people already anxious and stressed about everyday events like feeding children and finding a decent job.

"Tyshan Riley, basically, started his own thing of his own hand-picked soldiers, of people from different neighbourhoods to form one powerhouse group," Ellis explained when he testified against his former friends. "That is how I see him trying to take over the neighbourhood." That meant a campaign of terror that would leave a violent and bloody trail in Scarborough.

CHAPTER 7

Slipping can be fatal

Less than a month after Norris Allen was gunned down, Eric Mutiisa
was found dead on a driveway in Malvern.

Mutiisa had spent part of the day selling crack at the Scarborough
Town Centre, a huge shopping mall just south of Highway 401. One of
his customers agreed to give him a lift in exchange for drugs. Mutiisa,
who was 23 and wore his black hair tied in twists sticking straight
up, asked to be driven to a two-storey home with a two-car garage
and large driveway. Mutiisa would not live to say why he wanted to
go there.

On November 2, 2002, Mutiisa was wearing a blue and white
baseball cap, bomber-style jacket, white T-shirt, white running shoes
and baggy jeans tucked into his socks. Stuffed into his pants were a
replica handgun, several rocks of crack cocaine and three cell phones.
Mutiisa had several aliases, including Lynx.

It was late afternoon when the two men arrived at the narrow street
crowded with parked cars lining both sides of the road. For someone
planning an ambush there were plenty of places to lie low. Mutiisa

climbed out of the car. His driver continued before making a U-turn and heading back toward where he'd let his passenger off.

As he approached, the driver heard three loud bangs and spotted Mutiisa lying on the driveway. He also caught a glimpse of a man wearing dark clothing walking quickly toward a car. He stopped briefly before driving away, shaken and frightened.

Several neighbours dialed 911 to report the sound of gunshots. It was about 5 p.m. Within minutes, as dusk folded into darkness, detectives Roger Caracciolo and Adam LeBlanc arrived at the quiet residential street.

They found Mutiisa curled in a fetal position at the bottom of the driveway, his head pointed toward the garage, his feet toward the sidewalk. There was a bullet hole in his cheek. Blood on his face. A diamond earring lay on the driveway. Three spent rounds formed a half-moon near his head. Caracciolo looked at the young man's wide-open, dead eyes. There would be no emergency run to the hospital.

The detective found a blue cell phone in Mutiisa's jeans pocket and a Champs athletic bag on the driveway, but no identification. Inside the front pocket of his jeans was a folded wad of cash, which Caracciolo left undisturbed. In his waistband was a replica firearm wrapped in a red bandana. A cell phone battery was inside his clenched fist.

Mutiisa's body was still there when homicide detectives Kathryn Martin and Randy Carter pulled up and took over. At the time, Martin was a twenty-two-year veteran of the Toronto Police Service, her last four years in homicide averaging about five cases a year. (In 2009, she was appointed the first woman in charge of the homicide squad.) They arrived to find Caracciolo and LeBlanc shivering in the bone-chilling, November evening. Martin suggested they take turns sitting in a patrol car to try to stay warm. It was a welcome if unexpected gesture from a busy homicide detective.

Officers canvassed neighbours but turned up little. Yet the circumstances led Martin and Carter to assume what seemed obvious. Mutiisa was killed in Malvern, a community plagued by gangland shootings. The fact his cash and other possessions were left behind also signalled the hallmarks of a gang execution, possibly one of revenge.

A post-mortem would show Mutiisa died as a result of two gunshot wounds to the head.

Martin figured Mutiisa must have had some connection to the house where he was found, "because by then we learned from witnesses he wasn't dumped there and he was too far up the driveway to be dumped out." There was, however, the possibility he had been chased and just happened to land where he did. "You don't want to go down one path and miss something—so you try and keep an open mind to everything," Martin told me. No one inside the house claimed to know Mutiisa or have any idea why he was there.

It took police several hours to determine his identity. With little information, Martin obliged the television cameras with some details of the victim's appearance, including what he had been wearing. A young woman watching television that evening called police to say she recognized the victim.

The Gangster Game

The worst fears of Eric Mutiisa's parents were realized when Martin and Carter knocked on their door in Pickering around 4 a.m. "It was really sad, it's always sad, but this was particularly so," said Martin, who described the Mutiisas as "lovely people."

Research suggests there are certain "best" indicators, or risk factors, that determine why young people get involved in gangs. They include the need to escape an abusive home environment, parental neglect or indifference, and family breakdown. But Mutiisa seemed an exception. His parents were decent, hard-working professionals who despaired about the choices their son had made. They tried to steer him on the right path and even thought about sending him away from Canada.

"Wonderful parents, unremarkable kid, and he wasn't going to listen to anybody," his lawyer, John Struthers, recalled. Struthers built his reputation in Toronto vigorously defending gang members and had represented Mutiisa on drug charges. He remembered Mutiisa dressing the part of a gangbanger—except, when his mother was around, he would remove his bandana.

"Eric was just into the game," Struthers told me. "He was ultimate gangster fodder. He was not highly intelligent, he was a fellow that just seemed to have a sense that the pirate was cool. That's who he was: outside the system, outside the law. His sense of self-worth was not going to be generated by the usual and standard achievements in life."

The Mutiisas were supportive of police efforts to solve the case and later referred to Martin as "our detective" whenever they saw her in the news. "They believed we were doing the best we could," Martin said. They also understood finding their son's killer wouldn't be easy.

During the investigation, Martin discovered Mutiisa had once been shot in the leg. She also learned two suspects in that incident belonged to the Galloway gang and one of them was a young man named Tyshan Riley.

Some people in Galloway suspected Mutiisa was involved in setting up Jeffrey Williams, a Galloway guy nicknamed Swift, who was shot to death in 2000. Police believed Riley and an associate later shot Mutiisa in the leg to retaliate. Mutiisa never reported that shooting to police. Two days before Christmas, Williams, 23, had spent the day shopping for his three kids at Cedarbrae Mall with his older sister before returning home. After receiving a series of phone calls, Williams reluctantly headed back out.

He was sitting in the backseat of a 1994 BMW when the driver stopped in a parking lot outside a sports bar in Malvern. Suddenly, three or four men approached, looked in the windows, opened the doors and started shooting, witnesses said.

"It appears he was brought there and served on a platter," homicide detective Mike Davis said later. Williams' "acquaintances" drove to the nearest hospital and dumped his body by the emergency entrance.

"We are begging you to come forward," his sister, Jeannette, said during a news conference weeks later at Toronto police headquarters. "My family yearns for answers." No one was ever charged with his murder.

Suspecting that Riley may have returned to finish the job on Mutiisa, Martin wanted to wiretap his phones but didn't have enough evidence to get a judge's permission to start listening in. While police "went down a bunch of investigative paths, we just weren't able to substantiate anything," she said. Riley would later deny having anything to do with Mutiisa's murder.

But Roland Ellis had a different recollection when he later spoke to police. On the day after Mutiisa was killed, Ellis remembered running into Riley as he walked out of the high-rise known as the Pentagon. They dabbed their knuckles, Ellis recalled, and he asked Riley, "What's up?" Riley told him he had "caught his first body."

Ellis knew what that meant. He then asked Riley if the person he killed was the man he heard about on the news. "Yes, Lynx," Riley replied. Ellis thought Riley "seemed pretty happy, jumpy and a little different." I asked him how did he catch him slipping, how did he manage to come across on getting Lynx in that situation? And he told me that he set it up through a girl him and Lynx were seeing at the time.

Ellis would elaborate on the concept of slipping. "It's like stepping on banana peels," he said. "You don't know what you're doing, you're gonna slide, you're gonna slip." In other words, the person caught slipping was vulnerable.

Ellis said Riley told him he was sitting in a parked car on the street waiting for Mutiisa to arrive. "He said he seen Lynx walking down the street with his hoodie on and just approached the gentleman from the side and shot him in his head," Ellis said. "He told me the reason . . . was because he had something to do with Norris Allen's death." Riley didn't explain why he thought this. Ellis said he thought Riley told him he used a .45-calibre handgun. "Then he went about his day and I went about mine."

In the coming months, Riley was acting more and more like a mafioso don in Galloway. He was the key supplier of crack and pot to his underlings, flashed a gun when he needed to get a point across, and showed everyone he was prepared to use it when necessary. It didn't matter if the target was from Malvern or if it was an old friend—not if it meant settling a score.

On December 8, 2003, Riley arrived in the alleyway at the back of the townhouses at 4311 Kingston Road with Damian Walton. Ellis was there smoking weed with some other G-Way guys. Riley warned the group "the block is going to be hot tonight," Ellis recalled when he spoke to police. When Ellis asked why, Riley replied the bullets would be flying because he intended to kill Gary Reid, his older mentor from the streets whose nickname was Pye.

Reid had moved to Galloway to be closer to the mother of his children. He was also leaving behind Jane and Finch, where he had been shot as a teenager. His mother, a hard-working, religious woman originally from Jamaica, blamed her son's descent into a life of crime on her ex-husband's mistress, believing that the woman had placed an evil spell over her house but her son wound up the unlucky recipient. When out of jail, Reid was well known for his musical talents. He was also popular with the ladies.

Riley had stayed with him at times and knew Reid's three kids. Reid, in turn, knew Riley's family. Reid said he would "bend his back over" for Riley. But Riley believed Reid had set him and Norris Allen up to be arrested at a robbery scene a few months before Allen died.

Riley told Ellis and others a place and time was picked for revenge. Ellis spent the remainder of the day outside. When the sun went down, he went home and stayed there.

Later that night, Reid ran into a young woman named Neville Badibanga at a nightclub in the city's west end. He offered to drive her and her cousin back to Scarborough in his girlfriend's Jeep Liberty. When they arrived at the high-rise apartment on Kingston Road, Badibanga remained in the front passenger seat to chat with Reid.

Suddenly, out of the darkness, two men dressed in black ran in front of the car and opened fire. Reid pushed Badibanga down onto his lap and tried to cover her from the volley of shots that blew out both the front and back windows. Reid wasn't hit but Badibanga didn't fare as well. Wounded, she got out of the car and collapsed behind the building. Reid jumped out and ran after the gunmen fleeing on foot, but stopped when he heard Badibanga screaming. "I picked her up, threw her in my car and drove her to the hospital and left her there," Reid told police. She later recovered.

The next day, people in Galloway were talking about the shooting, though nobody seemed to know any details. A few days later, Ellis said he overheard Jason Wisdom, a fellow gang member, and Riley discussing the shooting. Wisdom told Riley if he'd had a more powerful gun, "he [Reid] would've been dead. Riley was just like, 'Yeah, whatever,'" Ellis said.

Nearly a year after the shooting, on September 24, 2004, police executing a search warrant seized a loaded Glock semi-automatic pistol from a fourteenth-floor apartment at the building where Reid and Badibanga had been ambushed. Police found it inside a Reebok shoebox wrapped in plastic bags and stashed in a bedroom closet. The inside of the shoebox had a red stamp that said "Pye," Reid's nickname, and the date December 8, 2003. The apartment belonged to a young woman named Denae Nichols, a friend of Riley's who was later convicted of possessing the gun.

Reid had never reported the shooting. But in 2005, while in custody at Maplehurst Correctional Complex, west of Toronto, two Toronto police detectives paid him a visit. They said they had something to tell him and invited him to the police station. After consulting with his lawyer, Reid agreed. Once at the station, police played him several audio conversations and then asked if he knew Tyshan was involved in the shooting. Reid was stunned by what he heard. He told officers it was "crazy" that this youth, who "I'd bend my back over for," would try to kill him. On April 1, 2005, Reid gave a lengthy videotaped statement to police, implicating Riley. Appropriately, it was April Fool's Day and the joke would later be on the cops and prosecutors.

CHAPTER 8

The good kid

While Eric Mutiisa and Gary Reid were streetwise gangsters, Omar Hortley was a young man who got caught in the gunfire reverberating through the streets of Scarborough during the time Riley and his boys were on their deadly mission.

It seemed the only common link for the victims was they were all young, black and from Malvern.

After finishing supper on January 25, 2004, Hortley's mother said goodbye to her only child as he headed out into the darkness to walk the half-kilometre along the quiet snow-covered streets in Malvern bordering the Rouge Valley. Hortley was going to a friend's house to watch wrestling on pay-per-view TV. He had turned 21 in October.

The 911 call came in at 7:38 p.m. It was a cold Sunday night and Detective Constable Stuart King turned on his cruiser's lights and siren as he sped to the location where residents reported hearing gunfire. With him was an officer in training. As they approached the intersection they saw a young black male lying on his back on the road. King got out of the cruiser, walked to the victim and quickly returned to his car to broadcast a request for more officers and other emergency services. But it was too late for the paramedics to save the young man. By the time Detective Guy Colton from Forensic Identification Services—Toronto's version of the sleuths in the *CSI* shows on American television—arrived a few hours later, Hortley's body had been removed. A large pool of blood and a jacket remained on the ground where Hortley had fallen. Left behind, were shell casings and bullet fragments.

Homicide detective Sergeant Frank Skubic was the first "on call" that night. The burly, affable and well-respected veteran knew right away this would be a difficult case. There were no witnesses, no motive and little to go on. During a police canvass, two residents reported seeing a black, four-door vehicle, possibly an SUV, cruising the neighbourhood without lights. "Tail lights were seen leaving the area immediately after but there was no description of the vehicle," Skubic said the next day. "We don't have any clear direction right now. We can't eliminate the possibility that this was a random act, a case of mistaken identity, perhaps, or even a street robbery gone bad. We just don't know."

While the magnitude of gang- and gun-related violence had increased in Toronto, there was nothing to suggest Hortley "was involved in guns or gangs or bad activities. He had no criminal record," said Skubic. Yet the homicide had "all the hallmarks of a gangland slaying. But he's not a gang member, therein lies the mystery," the detective concluded.

In her post-mortem report, Dr. Jacqueline Parai noted Hortley had five gunshot wounds: three to the head, one to the neck and another to the upper arm. Ballistics reports indicated that shells found at the scene came from two different firearms. One of the bullets was fired from a .45 Witness semi-automatic.

Stop the "Genocide"

Omar Kente Hortley lay in an open casket as hundreds of mourners packed into the Ogden Funeral Home on Sheppard Avenue East on February 3, 2004. At a viewing the previous evening, his grade 12 school picture sat on an easel amid a forest of floral arrangements. A collage of coloured photographs, showed a youthful, beaming face surrounded by loved ones.

As tearful family members, friends, former school and soccer mates assembled for the service, no one could make any sense of what had happened to the decent kid who died steps from his home on his way to a friend's house. Hortley had recently been accepted at Durham College to study music production and promotion, a field he dreamed of entering after years of listening to and making music on a computer in his bedroom.

Born October 15, 1982, thirteen days before Tyshan Riley, Hortley was raised by his mom and went to St. Bede Catholic Elementary School before attending Pope John Paul II Secondary School. He had done some modelling when he was young, appearing with a group of children on the July 1987 cover of a *Toronto Life* magazine. The photo was to promote a story about a "fun-filled festival of free events to keep your children busy and happy all summer long."

As a teenager, Hortley was a "very good kid," a high school guidance counsellor told the gathering. "His deportment was always affable. You would joke with him, he was that kind of student, he never seemed to be angry at anybody or anything."

While in his final year of high school, his grandmother got sick. The cheerful young man, who wore his hair in braids, decided he needed to be with her as she battled bone cancer. So he took a break. After she died in November 2002, Hortley found a part-time job and returned to the classroom to obtain a remaining credit.

While he hadn't grown up with his half-sister Amanda, the two grew close in 2003 after a family get-together. "After that day, Omar would come down to chill with me, we would play ball, talk about whatever came to mind, and I told him things that no one else would know," she wrote in a Facebook memorial. She remembered her brother warning her about "guys who were after one thing." He loved to play video games and watch wrestling.

The day of his funeral, mourners got an earful from a 35-year-old Scarborough preacher named Orim Meikle, who told them he had better things to do than bury another young black man. While few mentioned the circumstances of Hortley's death, Meikle delivered a fiery sermon that called on the community to use the killing as a spark for change. A black man who had dabbled in crime before turning to God, Meikle spoke boldly and openly about what was well understood. "Our children carry guns like we used to carry bubblegum," he told the congregation, some of whom had spilled into a room next to the chapel to watch on a monitor. "Our children are made to feel and to believe that to be tough, especially in our black culture, somehow creates manhood and virility within you. Most of our children spend half their lives in jail."

He blamed the escalating violence on parents who failed to set rules and on "absentee fathers." He called on black people to stop "blaming slavery for everything" and to "wake up" and stop the "genocide" being committed by young people. He added that for change to come, fathers "need to step back in the home. Away with absentee fathers, breeding children as if they're racehorses. We are not racehorses," he said to scattered applause. "We need to do things differently in our community."

Meikle's hard-hitting eulogy was a call to action. "We're not working together as a community to eradicate violence. Things have got to change," he said. "We're going to kill ourselves, we're committing genocide in our own culture." The pastor encouraged other religious leaders to step forward.

"We do need to be candid, I don't think this is the season to be politically correct," he told me a few days later in his Scarborough office of Rhema Christian Ministries. "We need the church, education system, community programs working together in partnership, each serving their distinct and specific role," Meikle said. "If we can unify, we could put forth a concerted effort and you get more accomplished. And I think leaders now are sensing that."

But the pastor did not point any fingers at anyone in the community for gunning down Omar Hortley. Nor did the victim's family. Who would target this young man?

A year later, suspicion fell on Riley and his top lieutenant, Philip Atkins, when the two would be charged with killing Hortley. As of 2010, they had not faced the charges at trial.

Another Score to Settle

A few weeks after Hortley's funeral, 16-year-old Mark Jones was washing a car in the driveway of his family's semi-detached home, which backed directly onto Tom Longboat Junior Public School in Malvern.

As he went about his chore, and chatted with a friend, Jones saw an SUV pass by and then return with the passenger side facing his house. He was almost done when he looked over and saw the SUV again before it stopped three or four houses away. The passenger door opened and someone got out, he said later.

His friend ran away but Jones didn't get the chance. "Easy, easy, stop," Jones yelled as the shooter pointed a pistol and started firing. Jones would later tell police the gunman was a "cold-hearted demon" and described him as a "skinny black dude" with a skeletal face. He had a dark complexion, looked to be 17 or 18 years old and was carrying a black gun.

Students at Longboat had just been let out for the day. Some were already walking home. Teachers who heard the shots quickly ushered about seventy-five students back into the building and locked down the school until police declared the area safe. "We're lucky no students got hurt," Detective Scott Whittemore said. "That's a lot of bullets to be flying around at 3:30 in the afternoon." Ten rounds had been fired.

Jones was rushed to Sunnybrook Hospital with gunshot wounds to his lower back and legs. He was listed in serious condition that night. His mother, Violet Bernard, rushed from work to Sunnybrook. Jones was able to talk a bit and squeezed her hand. Four bullets had been pumped into his body. Doctors told her the surgery on the wounds—two in his leg, one in his side and a fourth in his lower back—went well and that the mother of five would see her only son recover.

"Luckily, the injuries are all to his lower body. Nothing hit the heart or anything like that," Bernard told reporters.

Friends of the grade 10 student didn't want to talk to reporters. Bernard said her son, who wanted to be a mechanic, kept to himself, wasn't involved in gangs and had some nice friends. He had just transferred to a new technical school. Whittemore said investigators hadn't established a motive and didn't know whether Jones had been targeted.

"I mean, ten rounds at one person, you'd think that they may know each other," Whittemore said. "But it could be a mistaken-identity thing, you know. Nowadays, we just don't know anymore."

Investigators concluded the shooters were in a black SUV with a tire mounted on the back, dark tinted windows and at least two people inside. Ten .40-calibre shell casings were found at the scene.

Inspector Wayne Pye, one of the senior officers at Scarborough's 42 Division, stopped short of saying the teenager was deliberately sought out. "I'm reluctant to say he was targeted," because that would suggest Jones was known to the gunman or gunmen, Pye said. "What we're learning," he continued, "is that all it may take is someone driving down the street. The shooter may not even know the person, and the guns come out."

The shooting of Jones was the first in the three weeks of 42 Division's task-force project called GRIT 2—for Gun Reduction Identification Targeting, and 2 because it was the second go-round for the project. While Malvern was only a small part of the sprawling division in northeast Scarborough, the area was the scene of much of the violent crime. In the first month of 2004, the division had three homicides, including Hortley, and thirteen shootings, mostly in Malvern, as well as a sharp rise in street robberies. "That's why we formed the task force, to focus on the violent crime, shootings, the guns," Pye said.

The division enlisted help from specialty units of the force, including the Guns and Gangs Task Force, and had been "saturating" the area every night, with between twenty-five and forty officers. At the time, though of course it wasn't mentioned, police were intercepting thousands of phone calls as part of Project Impact, targeting the Malvern Crew.

Faced with the code of the streets, where snitching is a sin for some in the community while others are simply living in fear, the phone was not ringing off the hook, offering tips to police. That didn't stop police from asking for help. As Whittemore said of Jones' shooting: "Someone out there saw something more, and we need them to call us."

About a month after the shooting, Jones' mom called police to say she had heard from a friend of her son that the shooters were members of the Galloway gang and that Tyshan Riley was behind it. She said it related to Norris Allen's murder "and that the Galloway gang members knew Malvern guys were in jail so they were coming to settle the score."

CHAPTER 9

Project pathfinder: the first big break

With the latest violence in Scarborough, police, politicians and a pastor were lining up to respond with solutions ranging from stiffer sentences for gun crimes to prayer.

"I never thought we would see the kind of gun violence in Toronto that we've seen over the past months," Mayor David Miller said after a March 2004 meeting with Police Chief Julian Fantino and MPs from the city. "It's not acceptable to me and it's not acceptable to our community."

Miller said that in the meeting—just two days after Charlton and Bell were shot—he had stressed the need to talk to U.S. officials about stemming the tide of guns coming across the border. The mayor had also instructed Fantino to ensure police were visible on the streets, to "reassure the residents of our city that when they walk in their neighbourhoods, they will be safe." And he spoke about the need for stricter sentences for gun crimes, "so people know that if they are caught with a gun in a crime in the city of Toronto, they will go to jail and they will serve serious time."

The sense of urgency about the violence in Scarborough brought Fantino to Queen's Park where he met with Premier Dalton McGuinty. After the private meeting, McGuinty said he had a "greater sense of confidence that we can manage this, that they're taking some important steps."

Fantino also welcomed the anti-gang task force, announced earlier by the province, that would see veteran prosecutors and police officers work side-by-side to throw gang members in jail. Fantino, characteristically thumping his law-and-order chest, speculated about special prisons for gang members caught with guns. "I don't know if throwing everyone in jail is the answer, but the really bad asses should go to jail," Fantino said. "If we were to target these individuals and give them a mandatory ten years for using a firearm and maybe build a special jail ... how long do you think it would be before they got the message? It wouldn't take too long."

The recent violence also came on the eve of Ottawa and Queen's Park announcing $7.9 million in federal funding for community-based crime-prevention initiatives in Ontario—$3.5 million of that earmarked for sixty community organizations in the Toronto area.

Yet while a wide-ranging group of Toronto-area organizations was in line to receive funding, Liberal MP Derek Lee, who represented Scarborough-Rouge River, was disappointed none was in Malvern. "We have these announcements, which are federal and provincial, and not a nickel went into the Malvern area of my riding, not a nickel."

Reverend Orim Meikle, who had delivered that impassioned sermon at Omar Hortley's funeral, called for peace on Toronto's troubled streets. The pastor said he would mobilize prayer teams to fan out into neighbourhoods in crisis, to bring a message of hope to young people. "We will be unleashing 600 prayer warriors," Meikle said. "Our message is simple: prayer works. The church has been doing it for years, but we've been just doing it within four walls ... so we're seeking to bridge the spiritual void in our community, in a non-intrusive, non-disruptive fashion." Several walks took place in 2004. After the Toronto police Project Impact gang offensive in May of that year—rounding up leaders and associates of the Malvern Crew—Meikle suggested it was "a response to our prayers on the street."

Project Impact, run by the Guns and Gangs Task Force, targeted members of the Malvern Crew. From December 15, 2003, to May 12, 2004, it intercepted thousands of calls between Malvern gang members.

Despite all the gunplay in Scarborough, including the murders of crack dealer Eric Mutiisa and innocent Omar Hortley, it took the rush-hour shooting of Brenton Charlton and Leonard Bell on March 3, 2004, for investigators to focus on a connection tying all these incidents together.

Project Pathfinder Begins

Inspector Brian Raybould, a vintage car nut who went on to head the homicide squad, had given the investigation a name: Project Pathfinder. Witnesses at the Scarborough intersection that day had described a black SUV that looked like a Nissan Pathfinder fleeing the scene and police had seized a closed-circuit-camera tape of what appeared to be a Pathfinder following Charlton's blue Neon moments before the shooting.

Homicide Detectives Al Comeau and Wayne Banks had been assigned to the case. Comeau, as a higher-ranking detective sergeant, was in charge.

Most of the tips to Crime Stoppers were dismissed as bogus. One—likely planted to throw police off the trail—suggested the drive-by shooting of Charlton and Bell involved a Malvern Crew member's initiation.

Comeau and Banks and four other investigators were working full-time on the case. Unfortunately, they had no idea that officers working on another "project"—Project Impact—had wiretap evidence that would have been crucial in the Pathfinder case, including a suggestion that Tyshan Riley and his boys were doing most of the shooting in Scarborough.

"We shared information but obviously there were some calls that didn't come out on the [Project] Impact wires until later in our investigation," Banks would explain later. In any event, he added, "people say all sorts of things on the phones—it doesn't mean it's true." Suspicion is one thing, proving it another. It would not have been grounds to arrest Riley. That would later become a much-argued point.

Nevertheless, before March had ended, Riley and the Galloway gang would be identified as key suspects in the Charlton and Bell shooting and they were suspected in several other unsolved homicides and shootings.

The first big break came by chance. On March 24, 2004, three weeks after the Charlton and Bell shooting, Constable Janice Blakely was patrolling southeastern Scarborough just before 2 p.m. when she pulled over at a townhouse complex on Kingston Road and started talking to a woman named Heather Nicole Kerr.

Kerr had a dark black complexion, black hair, brown eyes and tattoos on her arms, including a Playboy bunny. Kerr had criminal convictions for a handful of petty crimes. She also had a number of outstanding charges, including trafficking in cocaine. Her last arrest had been about three weeks earlier, two days before her twenty-first birthday, coincidentally the same day Charlton and Bell were shot. Blakely questioned Kerr about possibly violating one of her bail conditions.

Kerr had some fast explaining to do. The woman told the constable that she'd been let out of a car driven by someone named "Tyshon," and gave that incorrect spelling. She told the officer "Ty" had seen a police car behind them and had run from the car.

Then she said something that marked a turning point in the investigation. Kerr told the officer she did not want to go back to jail and had information to provide on shootings in the Malvern area. Constable Blakely called Detective Banks.

"We had just gone out for probably the first warm meal Al [Comeau] and I had in a while," Banks recalled. They left a Swiss Chalet restaurant halfway through their dinner. They knew not to keep a cooperative witness waiting with time to think that no one was interested in what she had to say, Banks explained. "We ended up going in and speaking with Heather," Banks told me, "and the information she gave us corroborated a lot of the information that we had. She was able to tie a lot of it in and say that we're in the right direction. It was a nice bonus to have in the early stage in the game, so we could focus and identify where and whom we wanted to look at—and resources."

That night, just before 7:30 p.m., after telling Kerr she would be released in exchange for her cooperation, Banks and Comeau sat down to conduct a sworn videotaped interview. It lasted two and a half hours. Kerr gave the officers what seemed a no-holds-barred account of what had been going on in the neighbourhoods of Galloway and Malvern. She gave a detailed physical description of Tyshan Riley, someone she had known "since they were little," as well as describing his family members.

Comeau asked if she had ever seen him driving a black Pathfinder. Kerr replied she heard he had sold it a day earlier to a guy named Space. (Riley never had vehicles registered in his name. He had girlfriends for that.) Kerr said she had asked Space about the deal. He said Riley had told him the vehicle was "hot," that it "had done stuff to people before" and that he should get it painted.

And she had other information. She said the sister of Mark Jones, wounded the previous month on his driveway in Malvern, told her the 15-year-old was shot from a black Pathfinder and that "Ty" had done it. Kerr said she asked Riley and he denied it.

She also described a recent incident when she was in a car with Riley and Philip Atkins. They began chasing a green van because they thought "Malvern guys were in it." She quoted Riley as saying: "I wanna pop one of these niggers." At one point during the ride, she said Riley and another gang member jumped out of the car with guns drawn. They told her one of the guns was a "nine," the other a .45. But no shots were fired that day.

When asked if Riley always carried a gun, Kerr replied, "Yes, most of the time." She said he was "crazy." She said a number of gangs operated in Galloway and Riley was a leader. Kerr said Riley told her he and another gang member, always wearing black and gloves, went to Malvern every day to see if there were people they could shoot. Riley called their targets "Malvern heads." She said she often saw Galloway gang members drive by when she was at a Malvern mall. Kerr said the G-Way guys regularly watched the TV news, to find out what the police knew.

She had other morsels. Kerr said the beef between Malvern and Galloway started with the murder of Norris Allen and that the Galloway gang had something to do with the murder of Eric Mutiisa.

Police had done a good job locking up all the Malvern guys, she said, but it had allowed G-Way gang members to shoot innocent people. And Kerr had a warning: If the police didn't get Riley off the streets there would be more blood spilled. Kerr, however, said she had asked Riley if he was involved in the Charlton and Bell shootings. He told her he had nothing to do with it, she said.

After the interview wrapped up, Kerr agreed to drive around the area to point out places of interest to the two detectives. "We couldn't be seen driving around with Heather so we hid her as we drove around checking out addresses," Banks said.

Anyone's sudden willingness to cooperate with authorities alerts any good cop to the possible motivation. For instance, was Kerr supplying information to find out what the cops knew about Riley?

Tyshan Riley, circa 2004.

"We were very careful on how involved we got with Heather," Banks told me. "But at the same time, we wanted to keep Heather as a resource." Banks was aware Kerr had been picked up for the fairly minor charge of breaching her bail conditions. "There was no big gain she was able to get. It wasn't like she was charged with a very violent offence that she was looking at [penitentiary] time by cooperating with us." Kerr never said so directly, but Banks' "spidey sense" told him she was "disgusted" that innocent people in Malvern were being shot. Kerr knew many people who lived in Malvern.

After Kerr's initial statement, the detectives talked to her about going into the witness protection program. She wasn't interested. But they kept an eye on her anyway. "We took all the precautions that we could, obviously to ensure her safety without letting her know. So, then again, she doesn't go and tell people 'This is what police are doing.'"

In fact, police later suspected Kerr was working both sides, tipping off Riley about police interest in him. Her cooperation would further be tested after she received a threatening note, purportedly from Riley. On a white, lined, eight-by-ten piece of paper, inside a small white envelope, the handwritten note read:

Lady H
Wha gwon Lady H everyting
Everyting with you. Ya you done
Know respect for the Christmas card zeen. You tell me
You have mad love
For me and that your
Praying for all of us.
But I head different
I heard your moving like
Some bird always talking to dem people da
If you have Mad
Love for Me
Tell Me it anit so
Ha Ha

you know who it
is Keep it real
A.K.A. Nikki
Please don't
Try to fuck
Me over
Mad Love

Translation: You say you are loyal and are praying for us but I hear differently. Tell me it isn't so. (She would wind up going to jail on a drug charge and never testify against any in the Galloway gang.) Still, after talking to Kerr the detectives knew Tyshan Riley was their number-one suspect.

CHAPTER 10

Takedown at the mall

A peace officer may intercept, by means of any electro-magnetic, acoustic, mechanical or other device, a private communication where (a) the peace officer believes on reasonable grounds that the urgency of the situation is such that an authorization could not, with reasonable diligence, be obtained under any other provision of this Part; (b) the peace officer believes on reasonable grounds that such an interception is immediately necessary to prevent an unlawful act that would cause serious harm to any person or to property. (Section 184.4, Criminal Code)

Detective Al Comeau called Crown attorney Ann Morgan to ask if Heather Kerr's statement was enough evidence to get an order under 184.4 to allow police to start wiretapping the phones of Riley and his associates. It was an informal chat. Comeau contended it was "an urgent situation to prevent further shootings and killings." Morgan, though, decided there was not enough evidence to constitute the emergency situation required by 184.4.

But that didn't stop police from seeking other means to nab Riley. They tried just about every legal means to keep track of their prey.

A day after interviewing Kerr, Comeau and Banks ordered surveillance on the apartment building where Riley's girlfriend, Dana Lee Williams, lived. They followed Riley every time he was seen leaving the building. But Riley proved adept at spotting cars on his tail and losing them in traffic. Still, Comeau and Banks made daily requests for surveillance on Riley, though he was never watched around the clock.

Police also sought judicial orders authorizing tracking devices be put on the vehicles Riley was known to use—all high-end imports, including a Pathfinder, Lexus, Acura and an Infinity—and on his phone. On April 5, 2004, a judge signed a warrant to track the vehicles. But no device was ever installed. "It was too difficult" to locate the vehicles, Comeau said later. So police went back to court seeking permission to use a device that could track Riley's phone—and, presumably, him—though the technology didn't necessarily pinpoint where a person was, just the general vicinity. A judge gave permission, but this didn't work, either.

Meanwhile, the Project Impact team continued to intercept calls between members of the Malvern Crew. On March 31, David Francis, one of the Malvern leaders, and another man were overheard discussing "Nitti" driving around Malvern brandishing a handgun. A few days later, the hardened gangbanger—Francis had been acquitted of attempted murder and survived a gunshot wound to his head—was overheard saying Riley was dangerous and had killed six innocent men. "It's like a joke to them," he said.

Francis said he needed to be armed. "Anybody can get it, there have to be laws, and they are breaking the code." The man on the other end concurred: "They are breaking the principle."

By this time, Comeau and Banks got wind of the wiretaps already being monitored by Project Impact. They believed something had to be done while they drafted a wiretap application and supporting affidavit to secure judicial authorization to start bugging phones. But they faced a dilemma. On the one hand, they had a duty to complete their investigation of the Charlton/Bell shootings. But they needed more evidence and didn't want Riley to know he was a suspect. On the other hand, if Riley and his boys were out there with loaded weapons, police had a responsibility to protect the public from further violence.

And there was yet another complication. Police were well aware Riley had repeatedly breached bail conditions—violating his curfew, for example—imposed on his previous firearms conviction. In other words, he was "arrestable." But Banks and Comeau figured if Riley was picked up, he might be tipped off about the homicide investigation. They continued to work other avenues.

Placing an undercover officer with the Galloway gang was not an option. There were black officers on the force. But none could simply parachute into Galloway and infiltrate the tight-knit criminal community.

"An undercover officer would be unsuccessful in gaining the confidence of any of the named gang members enough to gain the necessary evidence to prosecute the individuals responsible for the murder," Comeau would conclude. Besides, he would note, all of the people "involved in this crime have long-standing friendships, family connections and associations."

As the drive to corner Riley and the others picked up speed, Banks and Comeau had regular meetings at police headquarters at 40 College Street with Inspector Brian Raybould and Superintendent Jeff McGuire, the dry-witted head of the homicide squad, as they tried to determine the best way to collect evidence against Riley.

On Easter weekend 2004, they issued officer safety bulletins: If any of Riley's vehicles were spotted, the occupants should be considered armed and dangerous.

"Innocent people are being shot up in Malvern," said the warning.

On Easter Sunday, a drive-by shooter sprayed a townhouse in Malvern with gunfire around 10:30 p.m. Inside, a woman was lying in bed when a bullet ripped through her bedroom wall and landed in the bathtub. No one was hit.

Witnesses gave various descriptions of the vehicle. Some said they saw a red or purple SUV in the vicinity before the shooting. A week earlier, surveillance officers reported seeing Riley climb into a red Chevrolet Yukon after leaving a probation office. Police suspected he might have been the shooter. (It was later determined that Riley was likely not involved.)

At the time, public and political pressure was building for police to do something about the shootings in Malvern. Yet police could say little about all the work going on behind the scenes. The Malvern Crew arrests, stemming from those wiretaps on David Francis and others, were still weeks away though some gang members had been picked up during the course of the investigation. And while police had Riley in their sights, all that could be said publicly was that police were beefing up their patrols of the area and trying to keep tabs on known gang members by making sure they were living up to their various bail conditions.

The Malvern townhouse shooting had unnerved Banks and Comeau. Comeau was getting ready to leave for a week's vacation in the Caribbean the next day. The timing was less than ideal and he considered cancelling—something homicide detectives are often called on to do. But on too many occasions he'd made sacrifices that had taken him away from his family. This time, he decided to go.

This left Banks in charge. He was born in the northern Ontario town of Timmins. His father was an Ontario Provincial Police officer. Eventually his dad quit the force and the family moved to Scarborough, where Banks attended Agincourt Collegiate Institute in the 1970s.

Banks was just 17 when he joined the Toronto police force in 1978. From 1983 until 2000, he was posted in Scarborough's 42 Division, where he watched it go from being a relatively quiet suburban area on the edge of farmland to one of the city's busiest in terms of 911 calls. He joined the homicide squad in 2002 and had a few major investigations under his belt when Charlton and Bell were shot.

By then in his mid-40s, Banks, still youthful and good-natured, had a reputation as a no-nonsense cop who was fair and worked hard. Solving the Charlton/Bell case was something he cared passionately about. He had promised Bell he would put whoever shot him behind bars. He would also visit Valda Williams to keep her updated on her son's murder case. "I think it's very important for us, as investigators, that families be kept in the loop," he told me. "They're the ones who have lost a loved one and if we don't keep in touch, they develop that fear that the police are doing nothing." A half-hour of his time makes a victim or family member feel "like they're part of it. We get caught up on these gang murders, on any murders, but we can't lose focus."

But it seemed that time was running out. Staff Inspector James Ramer, the unit commander of intelligence services, ordered daily surveillance on Riley until midnight. If officers spotted any criminal "activity," they were to remain on watch. Yet at a senior managers' meeting on April 14, 2004, the approach to arresting Riley changed. Because of the risk and liability involved, Riley needed to be arrested for breach of his bail conditions if he was seen anywhere in Scarborough.

That same day, Riley had a 9 a.m. court appearance in Oshawa, where he faced drug charges from the previous year. Six surveillance officers were watching the courthouse. Riley arrived in a white taxi around 10:25 a.m. and passed through a metal detector as he entered the building. He was inside for only about twenty minutes. Officers watched him leave and climb into another taxi. They followed for about two hours, as the cab drove around Durham Region, before Riley got into another car. Somehow, he was "misplaced" by surveillance.

The next day, police persuaded prosecutor Ann Morgan they needed an emergency wiretap on Riley's phone. "You've got to show that you've exhausted every possible investigative avenue," Banks explained later. So, now authorized under Section 184.4 of the Criminal Code, police started tapping Riley's lines on April 15. Banks believes 184.4 was the first time it had been used in a murder investigation. The purpose was not to gather evidence but to prevent further bloodshed—the idea being police could keep track of his whereabouts and anticipate his next move. For three days, they heard nothing that caused them major concern.

But on April 19, they would see the climax of the investigation of Riley and his followers. Police would finally zero in on their targets after yet another shooting in Malvern and a frantic search that would ensue.

Nowhere Left to Run

It was a fine spring day in southern Ontario. A welcome weather system had pushed in a ridge of warm air, causing the mercury to rise to nearly 20 degrees, teasing winter-weary Torontonians. They responded by wearing shorts or parking themselves on an outdoor patio to revel in the first hint of springtime.

Riley left his girlfriend Dana's sixteenth-floor apartment on Scarborough Golf Club Road that Monday morning and headed to a silver Audi. A police surveillance team had already scoped out the Audi parked behind the building. But for some reason the officers left. By the time they came back, the car and Riley were gone.

But the cops spotted the Audi again shortly after 11 a.m. at a nearby strip mall, in front of a beauty salon on Kingston Road. Riley was having his hair braided. Riley left the salon at 12:35 p.m. The plainclothes officers, in an unmarked car, stayed back and watched Riley and another man climb into the Audi and drive away. A short time later, the unidentified passenger jumped out of the car and Riley sped away, alone.

Riley drove fast and changed lanes often. It was a challenge for police to keep up and remain undetected in the light traffic of the early afternoon. They lost him at 12:50 p.m. Two minutes later, the cops saw the car, then "misplaced" it again. At some point, Riley picked up another passenger believed to be his good pal Philip Atkins.

It was around the same time that two friends, Chris Hyatt and Kofi Patrong, both 19 years old, were hanging out in a grassy area behind Campden Green, a townhouse complex where Patrong lived with his family in the heart of Malvern. The warm sunshine also brought schoolchildren to play around this patch of grass, dotted with picnic tables, barbecues, bicycles and birdhouses.

The teens were chatting when Hyatt heard footsteps and saw a "dark image" moving slowly toward them from behind a fence that separated the park from adjacent backyards. Hyatt could make out the figure was wearing a black jacket over a light-coloured top and jeans. It was 12:52 p.m.

Suddenly, Hyatt saw a spark and heard a loud noise at the same time he felt his hand grow hot. He thought, at first, it was a firecracker, but didn't stick around to find out. He ran and jumped over a fence.

As he leapt, he felt another burning sensation in the back of his thigh and then in his toes. But Hyatt kept moving, vaulting over five more fences before banging on a neighbour's door and frantically asking the woman to call 911.

Hyatt had suffered four bullet wounds: on the left buttock, left ankle, left foot and left hand. Patrong was hit three times, in the left thigh, lower left leg and right foot. Neither Patrong nor Hyatt were gang members. They had no idea who had shot them, and had no clue as to why.

At the 911 communications centre, operators were fielding numerous calls about a shooting in Malvern. Deemed priority calls, or "hot shots," the dispatchers sent several cruisers racing to Malvern. Witnesses told officers they saw a silver or grey car, new, fairly clean and "possibly an Audi," speeding away. Within three minutes, police broadcast the first description of the vehicle, a "silver/grey car."

Officers from various units, including Emergency Task Force tactical units, canine units and traffic units, joined the search. As vehicles converged on the scene, police locked down nearby schools, including Mother Teresa Catholic Elementary School. Students were ordered to stay inside the remainder of the day.

Banks was in a meeting at intelligence headquarters when he got a call at 1:10 p.m. telling him "there had just been a shooting and there might have been a connection to our guys." Banks first called the surveillance unit, "because they were out on Tyshan," and learned they had lost him again.

And Banks got more news. There had been an intercepted call at 12:53 p.m., the approximate time of the shooting. He went into the room where Riley's calls were being monitored and listened to that recording.

Banks later explained what he heard.

"Riley was talking to an unknown male in the background about the shooting, and how 'we should have shot the one guy first,'" Banks testified almost four years to the day later. (The recordings made the day of Riley's 2004 arrest were later ruled inadmissible and were not heard by the jury at Riley's 2009 trial for the murder of Charlton and attempted murder of Bell.)

At 1:17 p.m. Banks ordered the arrest of the Audi's occupants, urging "extreme caution" to all police cars on patrol in Scarborough. It was not transmitted over radio—because criminals were known to tune in to scanners—but sent by text to computers in police cruisers. "We don't have the most secure radio bands in Toronto," Banks would later testify. "There is equipment that could be bought at any Source store, and most tow trucks can monitor police bands."

Banks then had an emergency conference call with his superiors. His orders were clear: ensure public and officer safety but Riley must be arrested immediately.

Banks asked an intelligence officer to locate Riley by tracing his phone to a cell tower. It gave police a general idea and more officers were deployed to scour the area.

The detective contacted the Emergency Task Force at 1:29 p.m.

"The ETF were in the area from previous arrangements that we'd made with them for coverage in the Scarborough area for Mr. Riley," Banks later testified.

Staff Sergeant Tom Sharkey was told his services might be needed that day. By 2004, the veteran Sharkey had responded to more than 1,000 calls to high-risk situations and was leading one of six SWAT teams in Toronto, each comprised of nine officers. (That summer, with news cameras rolling, it was Sharkey who would order police snipers to fire on a man who was holding his ex-wife hostage outside downtown Union Station. The man was killed instantly.)

As police searched for the Audi, Riley and Atkins picked up Marlon Wilson, a gang confederate.

Atkins and Wilson were so close they said they were "like cousins." Wilson was one of seven children and his mother was a close friend of Atkins' mother, Alice. She had looked after Wilson when he was young, when his mother struggled with drug addiction. His father was never in the picture. Since the age of 13, Wilson had been in and out of trouble with the law.

Atkins had called Wilson earlier that morning to say he and Riley would pick him up after Riley had his hair braided. The Audi belonged to a friend of Wilson's and he'd let Riley borrow it.

Wilson had promised to withdraw $140 from a bank machine to give Riley.

As ambulances rushed Patrong and Hyatt to the hospital, twenty-five to thirty police cars fanned out across Scarborough looking for the Audi and its occupants. Banks was directing the manhunt back in the wire room where he listened to two calls purportedly made from Riley's cell phone. The first sounded like Riley talking to an unknown man about money, Banks later explained in court.

"The second call was from Mr. Riley saying he'd like to meet the male at the Morningside Mall [in Scarborough]." That call, Banks said, came at 1:47 p.m.

At 1:55 p.m., thirty-eight minutes after Banks had ordered the arrest of the Audi's occupants, the officers on the surveillance team were given information that had just been gleaned from the wiretaps. Banks instructed the officers as well as the ETF "to use their resources to make a safe arrest."

"I basically empowered them that: 'You're the experts, you know how you prefer to do your high-risk takedowns.'"

Officers in an unmarked car caught sight of the Audi at Morningside Mall at 2:05 p.m. Inside were three men. This time, the cops weren't about to lose their target. They followed the car at a safe distance, east along Highway 401, for about thirty minutes. The Audi drove into the Five Points Mall, a sprawling outdoor shopping complex in Oshawa. Durham Region Police joined the operation. At 2:42 p.m., the word went out over police radios: conduct a high-risk takedown.

Numerous marked and unmarked police cars started flying in behind the Audi as it was steered into the parking lot.

Wilson and Atkins were arrested hiding under a truck.

Riley bolted toward a Rogers Video store located in a corner of the mall. On his heels was an officer who followed him into the store and into a back office. He noticed ceiling tiles on the floor. Riley had hoisted himself to the ceiling and was trying to get away in the crawl space—like Bruce Willis in a *Die Hard* movie. Suddenly, he came crashing through the ceiling, entangled in electrical wires—a humiliating spectacle for a young man who considered himself invincible. A bullet-proof vest was recovered in the office.

Later, Riley's and Atkins' fingerprints were found inside the Audi. A small amount of gunshot residue was found on Riley's hands. While Riley was in custody, a police officer reported seeing him trying to urinate on his own hands prior to the test.

Police told Wilson they were charging him with attempted murder and weapons offences. The seriousness of the charges combined with his lengthy criminal record could send him to the penitentiary—away from his son—for a long time, they told him. That night, Wilson gave two videotaped statements to police, starting with the shooting earlier that day in Malvern. "I wasn't there," he said in what would turn out to be one of five such recordings. "You could ask my people [girlfriend and sister] what time I left the house."

A wiry six-footer with light brown skin, Wilson had known Riley since they were kids. Wilson was known as Mardawg or Blood Money, a name he'd made up for himself and had tattooed on his forearm.

Initially, Wilson told police he believed Riley had done the shooting alone that day, that his good friend Atkins was at his girlfriend's place. Wilson later recounted that when he got into the Audi that afternoon, Riley and Atkins told him they had just caught a couple of guys "slipping" in Malvern. One ended up on the ground screaming, while the other curled up in a ball.

Wilson said they dropped Atkins off at his girlfriend's house, that he headed inside with a just-fired .40-calibre gun. (No such gun was ever recovered.) Riley and Wilson then drove to have the car washed before returning to pick up Atkins, who had taken a shower.

In a subsequent conversation with Comeau and Banks—there would be many such talks and Wilson's eventual testimony would be both contradictory and comical—Wilson explained his mindset when he began cooperating with police: "This time, I'm like 'No, I'm not going down for nobody else.' I have my son to raise. I just came out of jail. I was only on the street three months."

The day after the arrests in Oshawa, a team of officers executed a search warrant at the apartment of Dana Lee Williams. They found a bundle of money in the outside pocket of a brown suitcase in a closet in a child's bedroom. In the living room, they found two more bundles of money in a love seat, tucked behind a cushion. The total seized was $14,343.

In a night table beside the bed Dana shared with Riley, officers discovered two .45-calibre bullets wrapped in a bandana, a small glass vial containing hash oil, and Riley's bail release papers. Hanging in the closet was a sweatshirt emblazoned with the words Southside #1, Greezy Money and North Side Gunners.

But Riley's arrest was just the beginning of another critical phase in Project Pathfinder.

Safer Streets?

With Riley off the streets, Scarborough immediately became a lot calmer and safer. Since this seemed to further incriminate Riley as being responsible for most of the gunfire, he got word to some of his associates to go to Malvern to do some random shooting, an informant told police. There's no evidence this happened.

Riley would ultimately be charged with nine shootings between October 2002 and April 19, 2004, including the murders of Charlton, Mutiisa and Hortley.

But in April 2004, at the time of Riley's arrest, the public had yet to understand that the leader of the Galloway gang was probably the principal triggerman during the previous year and a half, starting with Eric Mutiisa's November 2002 murder. In fact, residents were getting the message: that the Malvern Crew—not Riley and Galloway—had been the primary cause of all the mayhem. Only a select few in the criminal justice system—and the gangbangers in Scarborough—knew better. "Malvern was the victim," a Malvern gang leader would say later.

(Yet the arrest of Riley, a man regarded as one of the most dangerous in Toronto's history, merited only a few paragraphs in the next day's newspapers.)

Then, on May 12, 2004, with great fanfare, police announced they had arrested sixty Malvern Crew members and associates on a vast number of charges, mainly drugs and firearms offences. None was for murder and only a few for shootings.

Police Chief Julian Fantino called it "one of the most significant police operations in recent memory" and cited the threat of street gangs. "Their malignant impact [was] so damaging to the communities they seek to destroy, that we felt we had no choice but to adopt a new intelligence-led, targeted enforcement approach."

For the first time, police had used new "criminal organization" legislation as a tool to dismantle street gangs. "This will set a precedent for law enforcement agencies across the country. It will help police in the dismantling of these gangs that are laying siege to communities," said Detective Sergeant Greg Getty, who was in charge of Project Impact in Malvern.

"Scarborough appears to be a changed place," said Superintendent Jeff McGuire, who took over the homicide squad halfway through 2004. "These guys [Malvern] are entitled to their day in court, but since a whole lot of people went to jail there's been a lot less shooting going on." Beyond that, said Getty, "it's improved the quality of life in Toronto and, long term, I think it's the biggest improvement I've seen in twenty-eight years [as a police officer]."

Police said it was their targeting of "gangs as groups" that was paying dividends in safer streets.

"The word gets out there ... 'The cops are looking for us, let's keep our heads down, or let's just not commit any more offences,' which is the whole point," Inspector Brian Raybould of the homicide squad said at the time.

Over the next few years, Toronto police followed with other projects targeting street gangs. Project Flicker went after the Ardwick Bloods at Islington and Finch, Project XXX dismantled Rexdale's Jamestown Crew, Project Kryptic targeted the Driftwood Crips at Jane and Finch and, in early 2009, more than 100 people were rounded up as part of Project Fusion.

In almost all those cases, press conferences followed that trumpeted hundreds of gang-related charges that invariably would be drastically winnowed down. Detractors called them public-relations exercises aimed at justifying the spiralling cost of law enforcement.

For Patricia Fough, the mother of Omar Hortley, the good kid shot dead in Malvern, the raids and arrests may have been a balm for the neighbourhood, but they did not ease her personal pain. "I know he would want me to be strong and keep going. But he's always in my heart. Always."

Throughout that spring and summer of 2004, authorities had yet to charge Riley with a single murder. They kept him locked up on two attempted murder charges. To go the distance to first-degree murder, they would build their case slowly, primarily using wiretaps to eavesdrop on Riley's jailhouse conversations and those of his family and associates.

The wire

It was apparent that police could not have cornered Riley without listening to his phone calls. Throughout the wiretapping phase of Project Pathfinder, both before and after Riley was arrested, police did their eavesdropping out of intelligence headquarters, in what was supposed to be a secret midtown location. While there were no signs outside the building, anyone paying attention knew police business was going on inside, given the number of unmarked police cars coming and going. Within the single-storey building, there were designated "wire" rooms used when an investigation was up and running.

Police and prosecutors across the country were increasingly using wiretaps to bring down street gangs, naming multiple "targets" in warrants, with the aim of capturing incriminating conversations that would lead to charges, convictions and jail terms. Defence lawyers frequently—and sometimes successfully—challenged the validity of these efforts, mostly by highlighting errors to show the police over-reached in affidavits submitted to obtain a judge's authorization.

The wire room used during Project Pathfinder was a long and narrow space painted an institutional peach. The first-floor windows were not at eye level, where they would normally be, but close to the ceiling. Anyone outside would need a ladder to peer in. The room was lined with chairs and desks with computers equipped to capture and digitally record calls from the various phones being screened. Between thirty and thirty-five people wearing headsets—all civilian monitors hired for the duration of the operation—determined if they were authorized to listen in and noted if the call was relevant, irrelevant or worthy of further investigation by police.

The room was staffed twenty-four hours a day, seven days a week. The monitors logged key information, most critically the names of the people talking based on how those on the line referred to themselves. As was often the case with gang-related investigations, the subjects mainly used nicknames. In Project Pathfinder, they were dealing with people known as Brub, Toops, Burns, C.D., L.P., Cockeyes, Pablo, Dooby, Twin, Baldhead and Brick. Surveillance photos, mug shots and lists of nicknames and "expressions" were tacked on bulletin boards to aid the monitors. It's expected that much of what's said is either in code or slang.

In multicultural Toronto, the people hired spoke a variety of languages. In both Project Impact and Pathfinder, a qualification for monitors included an ability to speak and understand Jamaican patois and the slang of the streets.

The wire room was a sterile work environment, and that's just the way it was meant to be. No newspapers or personal phone calls were allowed as they might distract the snoops from concentrating on their task. The ability to pay close attention was paramount. "There's a difference between what you think you hear and what they're saying," Staff Inspector Steven Izzett, the intense unit commander of intelligence services, told me.

With Riley behind bars, Banks and Comeau, back from vacation, were breathing easier and now believed they had reasonable grounds to persuade a judge that wiretaps were needed to pin the murder of Charlton on Riley and the Galloway gang. Preparing an affidavit to make that happen was a laborious and tricky process. It had to be carefully constructed and bulletproof—to withstand constitutional challenges once the case went to court.

Working closely with prosecutors, Comeau continued preparing the material in support of the wiretap application, including the affidavit to submit to a judge. "Other investigative techniques cannot be employed to reach the goal of this investigation which is to collect evidence of the murder of Brenton Charlton and the attempted murder of Leonard Bell," Comeau wrote in the introduction to the affidavit. "I believe that there is no reasonable alternative to solving this murder investigation." Riley and other members of the Galloway gang were responsible and the "motivation was the ongoing retaliatory shootings between the Malvern Crew and the Galloway gang," Comeau wrote. He went on to underscore the tragic consequences for an innocent like Charlton: "This murder was a case of mistaken identity."

Comeau explained that other investigative procedures had been tried and failed. Up to that point, confidential informants, undercover officers, Crime Stoppers reports, surveillance, interviews, forensics, witness identification and videotapes had all been used without nailing Riley *et al*. Comeau discussed why the techniques had not produced sufficient evidence for murder charges and why additional wiretapping was needed while the suspects were in custody.

The affidavit named several targets, including Riley, other gang members, family and associates.

It summarized the information police had against them, including what investigators had gathered from six confidential informants.

One C.I. had "identified Riley as someone who was moving up the ranks of the gang and who wanted to be the big man of Galloway." Another, facing charges, was permitted to "stay out of custody" after telling police Riley was the biggest money earner in the Galloway gang and that he had an arsenal of guns. Three more informants made damning allegations against Riley and the rest of the Galloway gang "in the hope of obtaining consideration" on charges they were facing.

Another C.I. went further, providing a sworn, videotaped statement, including information that the shooting of Dwayne (Biggs) Williams, at the school in Malvern, was the origin of the dispute between Malvern and Galloway and that Riley was "the main Galloway guy doing the shootings." There was also information that the Galloway Boys got their guns by breaking into homes.

But that same C.I., "unlike many of the other informants," said "Bolu [Norris Allen] was killed by Riley and Atkins because he had stolen marijuana from Atkins. After the killing, Riley became involved with Bolu's girlfriend, Dana Williams."

Some of the informants linked Riley to numerous other shootings and murders.

As well, the affidavit contained a synopsis of Heather Kerr's statements, including Riley's denial to her that he was involved in the March 3 shooting of Charlton and Bell. Also, there were portions of Marlon Wilson's statement, given at 3:35 a.m. on the day after he was picked up with Atkins and Riley in Oshawa, where he said "they do it when they're bored, go up to Malvern and pop someone, doesn't matter who. Just anyone in Malvern because of Norris Allen."

In his affidavit, Comeau also threw in examples of wiretap chatter picked up during the separate Project Impact investigation suggesting Riley was a gun-toting maniac.

On June 7, 2004, Justice Nicholson Duncan McRae granted an authorization, valid for two months, to intercept calls from various residences and locations, including a beauty salon called Head to Toe, owned by Dana Lee Williams' mother; three other locations in Scarborough; three phones at the Metro East Detention Centre, described as the "temporary residence" of Riley and Atkins; and any police vehicles used to transport the suspects. In addition, interceptions were permitted from four vehicles, ten cell phones and "any other stationary, mobile or portable place in Canada that any of the named persons attended, resided at, resorted to or made use of." In an era of disposable cell phones, known to be well used by drug dealers, Galloway gang members seemed a bit old school—they kept numbers they'd used for months.

The authorization also contained "minimization clauses," essentially a list of rules when listening had to cease, such as if a lawyer was on the line. And so they started listening.

Here's what they heard: explicit sex talk, lovers' spats, gossip, crying babies, death threats, drug deals, a robbery in progress and a bevy of young women fawning over Riley. On one occasion, Riley sang (rapped) to a spellbound devotee. Several calls captured Riley in not-so-subtle fashion arranging to have a gun concealed, later alleged to be one of the guns used in the Charlton and Bell attack.

They also heard plenty of evidence to suggest Riley was still calling the shots back on his turf.

When Jason Wisdom—who would go on to stand trial with Riley and Atkins for the murder of Charlton and attempted murder of Bell—couldn't pay an outstanding debt of $250, Riley told him to "make it" by doing a crime.

"I need my money, I want my money," Riley told Wisdom, who had not yet been arrested.

"You gotta make money somewhere. You get welfare? Bro, I need $250. You owe me $250, remember?"

"I remember," Wisdom replied.

Riley offered him a break. Make a down payment and then pay up in full in two months. And no "sob story."

"Give me two bills, don't make it sound like it's hurting you. Brother, brother, brother, fuck man," Riley said before suggesting: "Do a grime, man up, and do a grime." Selling drugs won't earn enough money to pay the debt, according to Riley.

"I need my two bills. At the end of the month. I don't want to hear nothing else."

During the month of July, the monitors also picked up conversations that revealed how gang members were reacting to news that Marlon Wilson had been talking to police. Dana Lee Williams, who was out on bail after being charged as a result of police finding money and other evidence in her home, had read prosecution documents submitted to her lawyer as part of disclosure requirements. She discovered Wilson had given a statement implicating Riley in the Hyatt and Patrong shootings. Gang members were soon burning up the phone lines with talk of Wilson's betrayal—all as the cops listened in.

"Greeze is foaming" and threatening to "slew him," Atkins said of Riley in one conversation intercepted by authorities. "I would fucking break [Wilson's] face," Riley fumed during a conversation taped July 13, 2004. "You have to smash him though, man," replied the friend. "Of course, dawg," Riley shot back.

Riley devised a plan. It was hatched in a conversation he had with Damian Walton. Small-framed and bookish looking, Walton was referred to by some Galloway Boys as "Greeze's accountant," meaning gofer. "He just has to do what the man says, or get slapped," Riley's brother Courtney once said. Walton's nicknames suggested the ludicrous and dim-witted side of these young men with little education. He was often called Burns, other times Smithers. But he was obviously much more like Waylon Smithers, the sycophantic assistant to Montgomery Burns on *The Simpsons*. Riley once told Walton: "You're my little peoples."

With Riley, there was always a pecking order. "The way he would tell Philip Atkins to do something would be totally different from the way he'd tell Damian Walton how to do it," Ellis said later. With the more taciturn Atkins, he'd "try to use his head a little more and be on a more of a friendship level with it."

So that summer, with Walton not in custody, Riley told him what to do: "Call him [Wilson] downstairs tomorrow." Riley went on: "I'm gonna make ray ray and you go with...you come with ray ray and some. Yow call him down, eh." Translation: Riley wanted to confront Wilson face-to-face in the downstairs visitors' room at the jail.

Riley then brought his girlfriend in on the plot. "Yo, fucking bring Burns," he told Williams, "so he can holler at him and bring [Wilson] down." Riley, perhaps remembering the possibility that his call was being monitored, then appeared to back away from the threat to harm Wilson. "I'm not, I'm not doing nothing like that, man."

Dana Lee Williams and Damian Walton were also overheard arranging their visit to the jail the next morning.

On the way down to the visitors' area, Marlon Wilson bumped into Riley. "That was fucked up. I can't believe you did that," Riley spat.

"You're the one giving those people against me," Riley said.

Later, Riley continued his harangue on jailhouse phones after he and Wilson were housed in different sections of the facility. "Yo, Greeze, I'm sorry, dawg," Wilson replied, promising to make things right by going to court and "switch it up." Riley told him that is what he had to do. "I'm rolling with you out of the chosen few on the block, you feel me?"

Wilson murmured agreement, interpreting Riley's message to mean "that out of everybody that he knows he's hanging with me" and that basically he's the big guy in Galloway and "taking food out of people's mouths by having him in jail."

As long as Wilson went along with the plan, Riley promised not to spread it around that he had "flipped," the biggest sin of all. Atkins picked up the receiver and threw in his two cents': "I still love you but you disappoint me."

Inmates in provincial institutions use jailhouse payphones and must call collect. Frequently, their loved ones and friends have conference call capability so they can patch in another person without giving police a traceable number. The result, during a wiretap operation, is a confusing array of voices for anyone listening in.

Wilson promised not to testify against Riley or Atkins. He said he would tell the judge that police forced him to lie. A day later, Wilson apologized again to Riley for giving a statement and reiterated his promise to change his tune. But doubts, for good reason, remained.

* * *

A few months later Riley and another G-Way guy, Ernesto Gayle, discussed how they needed to keep Wilson close. "You know, some people are going to die," Gayle said. A week later, Atkins said he wanted to "kill that guy," that the man he considered a cousin should "catch some hot ones" for informing.

Meanwhile, Riley's mother, Marie, was out for Wilson's blood. "I'm going to deal with it. That boy has to die, or run away, trust me," she told Riley's girlfriend. "I'm going to fuck him up."

She also told her son Carl about Wilson. "He's a pussy! That boy should go away. Marlon, that came into my house, ate my bun and cheese, that boy has to die. I don't care what nobody has to say, he's not going to make my son go to prison."

Marie added later that she wouldn't stop fighting for her son, and that she better not be in the courtroom "to see him [Wilson] talking because then they'll lock me up ... He might not make it to court, too.

That boy there can't lock up my son. Anything I have to do to destroy that pussy, I'm going to do it, and then ask for forgiveness."

If "Ty goes down, he [Wilson] can't live around here. He is dead, because I'm setting up somebody to murder him."

An adherent of Obeah, folk magic practised in Jamaica, Marie mentioned her pastor was "fucking him up wicked." Marie, in her husky growl, added: "Police will have to change his name and send him away because he's gonna—he's gonna get stuck, eh?"

As the expiration of the wiretap warrant approached on August 5, Comeau prepared a second affidavit. It included numerous references to interceptions made by police during the first authorization as well as indications of how police planned to "stimulate" discussions, possibly by holding news conferences or instructing Heather Kerr to stir the pot, telling Riley and others that police were asking questions about the Charlton/Bell shooting.

Justice John Hamilton granted the second authorization, also valid for two months, beginning August 5, 2004. Both authorizations sought evidence of murder, weapons trafficking, robbery and accessory after the fact to those offences. Some targets were dropped, others added, including Roland Ellis. And police weren't just bugging phones.

In mid-July, Banks and Comeau held a news conference to release a Crime Stoppers re-enactment of the Charlton/Bell shooting. Its dual purpose was to generate tips and stimulate phone chatter among suspects.

They also took turns visiting some of the same people whose conversations they were intercepting. Banks and another officer visited Dana Lee Williams just before 8 a.m. on August 31, as she was getting her daughters ready for the day.

Banks said he wanted to ask her about the death of Norris Allen, the father of her girls, and about another shooting, one at Finch Avenue and Neilson Road, where a black Pathfinder was used. An anonymous caller had indicated a black male using the name "Nid" and maybe someone named Burns or Barnes, had committed the murder, he told her.

Williams said she had no idea who those people were. "I don't know anyone who drives a Pathfinder," she said. Banks apologized but said he had to ask another question: Had Williams set Allen up to be killed?

She started to cry. "I don't know what to say, my name is in there. It hurts for people to say I would be involved." What really stung, she said, was that one of the people initially pointing the finger at her was Allen's mother.

Williams detailed the day Allen was killed, that she was at college, in a criminal justice class. She recalled how she and Allen had broken up two weeks earlier, after she told him she would no longer sleep with him. She said she had found out he was cheating on her. Williams said she told Allen he wasn't "allowed to come to my house," which was why he was staying at his mother's home in Malvern. "The last year was really rough, I was trying to make him straighten up his life," she said, sniffling.

The interview ended after about an hour, with police no further along. Similar interviews, with others on the periphery of the Galloway gang, also turned up little. After four months of eavesdropping there wasn't a single utterance that put Riley or any other Galloway gang member at Finch and Neilson on March 3.

As the second wiretap authorization period came to a close, investigators believed they had evidence of weapons and drug trafficking, fraud, as well as "evidence obtained in regards to another murder investigation," referring to the Hortley and Mutiisa homicides. It was time to take the next step.

Comeau and Banks prepared two thick volumes of material to obtain numerous search warrants—for eight residences, cars, jail cells and inmates' property bags. The items police were looking for included ammunition, spent shell casings and weapons, newspaper articles pertaining to shootings, letters, telephone records, cell phones, pagers and vehicle permits. In addition, they were hunting for gas and car maintenance receipts as well as hair and fibre samples from a seized 1988 Nissan Pathfinder.

On September 30, 2004, a justice of the peace signed off on the warrants that allowed police to start busting through doors of Galloway gang members and associates. They had only forty-two hours to complete their task: from 6:00 a.m. on October 1, 2004, to 11:59 p.m. on October 2, 2004.

CHAPTER 12

The cucumber in the freezer

It was several hours before dawn on Friday, October 1, when about 100 officers, including the Emergency Task Force in its trademark military-style jumpsuits, met at 42 Division in Scarborough.

"We had a debriefing at 3 o'clock in the morning with everybody," Banks recalled. "Nobody was told ahead of time any information. Secrecy was obviously paramount." The raids would be simultaneous so nobody could tip off others named on the search warrant.

"When you do the search warrants," Banks explained, "there's an obligation to knock on every door and announce you're there. But there are grounds in the statute that says that if you believe evidence is going to be destroyed or a danger element is there, then you can ask the judge to bypass." In the majority of these cases, police had a judge's permission to do a "dynamic entry," meaning they didn't have to knock or announce themselves in any way.

By 6 a.m., everybody was in place, poised to invade the homes of their Galloway targets. The sun would be up in fifteen minutes. It was time to move.

Casting the Net Wider

Marie Riley was sleeping in her seventh-floor apartment on Lawrence Avenue when officers crashed through the front door with guns drawn. She screamed as they dragged her out of bed, handcuffed her and told her she was under arrest.

Her youngest son, Joshua, then 12, was roused from sleep and also handcuffed as officers started tearing the place apart, looking for drugs and weapons. They found shirkas—throwing stars—a prohibited weapon, under the Criminal Code, used in martial arts. They took a special interest in a cucumber, wrapped in tinfoil, in the freezer. Inside the foil was a piece of paper with names on it—names of police officers, correctional officers, a Crown attorney and a judge involved in her son Tyshan's case.

Police ushered a sobbing Marie out of the building, leaving Josh in the care of the building superintendent. When she got to the police station, she called a friend.

"My life is ruined, my life is fucked," she was overheard telling her friend. "I'm a good person—I don't get involved in shit like that." Police had charged her with conspiracy to commit murder, she said. "I've been good all my life. Cops fucking ruin people's lives."

She really started wailing when she mentioned Josh. "My baby's only 12," she cried. "I need a fucking smoke. Jesus Christ, I can't cope. I can't cope."

Police were spreading the net to include more people, besides Riley and Atkins, in the Pathfinder investigation.

That morning, they kicked down the door of a Kingston Road apartment where Frances Newby lived with her eight-year-old son, Javon. The night before, she had reluctantly agreed to let the boy sleep beside her—a decision she said later was a blessing when officers crashed through her bedroom door, pointing their guns at her bed. Stunned, Newby jumped on top of her little boy, saying later that she feared police might shoot him.

Police scrambled to corral her somewhat ferocious dogs, including one named Hennessy—the name of the brandy favoured by gangbangers—that had belonged to Norris Allen. She called it "the last piece of Bolu" she had left.

Police seized a photo album and numerous newspaper articles and letters referring to Galloway's gang war with Malvern.

Prior to the search, what most interested police was a black 1988 Nissan Pathfinder registered in the name Frances Jane Newby. That summer, Banks and Comeau had twice visited Newby, asking about the SUV's whereabouts. Newby said she had no idea and suggested it had been stolen. Taking her into custody on the morning of October 1, officers told her she was under arrest for attempting to obstruct justice for the benefit of a criminal organization. Her father took her son, Javon.

Newby was also given access to a phone at 42 Division and spent more than four hours sharing news of her plight. One of the people she spoke to was her son's father. She told him "the vehicle" was the reason she had been picked up.

Before the suspects were hauled in, news outlets had been tipped to the operation. TV cameramen were posted outside 42 Division, where most of those rounded up were taken.

That afternoon, at "The East," as the Toronto East Detention Centre was known, Riley tried to find out who was in and out of custody.

He had been asleep in his cell that morning when police appeared yelling, "don't move, don't move."

Corrections staff moved Riley to segregation while police armed with a warrant seized all of his pictures, mail and phone book. Riley somehow knew, within hours, that police were employing the "criminal organization" umbrella to cover most in the roundup.

Around the same time, at police headquarters, Chief Fantino was announcing another police triumph over gangs. He said officers had executed thirteen search warrants and arrested or issued warrants for sixteen people.

The police P.R. machine was now ready to acknowledge what its detectives had known for months, that the shooting of Charlton and Bell was a major chapter in the city's recent gang warfare. Fantino reiterated in the news conference that "nothing in this investigation suggests that Mr. Charlton and Mr. Bell were anything other than hard-working members of our community who were on their way home to their families." He added: "The investigators soon learned this shooting was related to ongoing gang activity in the Scarborough area. It was believed that members of the gang known as the Galloway Boys were responsible."

Fantino also announced that 21-year-old Tyshan Riley had been charged with the murder of Charlton and attempted murder of Bell. Until that point he and Philip Atkins, 22, had been charged only with shooting the two teenagers in Malvern on the day they were arrested. Riley also faced numerous other charges relating to alleged gang activities, including instructing and participating in a criminal organization and conspiracy to commit murder.

Leonard Bell, upon hearing the news, said he felt some relief. But, he told me, "there's nothing that can be done to bring back Brenton—a good soul, gunned down in the prime of his life."

Detective Banks called Charlton's mother, Valda Williams. "When I made the phone call, I asked her where she was. I said to her, 'I just want to let you know we made an arrest in Brenton's murder,' and for about five minutes all she did was break down and cry," Banks recalled. "If she said thank you a hundred times, she said it a million times." Reflecting on that day, Banks said: "This is what we're doing it for."

The next day, Riley was brought to the same courthouse he first saw when he was 13 years old.

The Ontario Court of Justice at 1911 Eglinton Avenue East, west of Warden Avenue, was commonly known as the "Scarborough court." Built in the 1970s within a retail plaza, it contained fifteen small courtrooms. The building was surrounded by "superstores," discount fashion retailers and fast-food outlets. The courthouse was only three stoplights from The East where Riley and the others were being held.

The courtroom was filled with a couple dozen mothers, wives, girlfriends and other family and friends as the suspects were brought in for arraignment. Also there was Valda Williams, who faced her son's accused killers in court for the first time. She started to sob and was led from the courtroom by relatives.

Most of the sixteen suspects were silent and stoic as they were led in and out of court. Riley's mother, charged with conspiracy to commit murder and possessing a prohibited weapon, was not. "I didn't kill nobody," Marie Riley, 44, her hair tied back in pigtails and wearing an orange jumpsuit, shouted from the prisoners' box. Her son, and most of the others, were not granted bail and were taken back to jail.

The male prisoners were all sent to The East, which meant corrections staff had their hands full trying to control the shenanigans of Riley and the rest. At the beginning, there was also the issue of keeping members of the Malvern Crew apart from the new Galloway arrivals.

At the time, about 15 per cent of the Scarborough jail's 475 inmates were classified as belonging to a "security threat group," including members of street gangs and outlaw bikers. A few years earlier, there had been a growing recognition that this new breed of prisoner was "going to be challenging the system because naturally they're predatory and controlling," said Deputy Superintendent Dave Mitchell.

To combat this, staff had implemented a system to keep track of gangbangers, to prevent one gang from establishing a power place within the jail. Mitchell called it "in your face management," designed to keep gang members in line. Rivals were forced to live together to ensure there was no "numerical superiority" in a housing unit, he told me. That eliminated one gang from declaring: "There's four of us and two of you. I can do what I want."

All of this may have prevented an all-out gang war at The East. In fact, Riley and the Malvern leaders seemed to get along just fine. Nonetheless, in no time, Riley had established himself inside as a "bullet maker," a nickname for someone who is calling the shots.

During the previous summer, wiretaps had picked up a bunch of mysterious references to shoes. It turned out people wearing hollowed-out running shoes were literally walking marijuana and other contraband into the facility. On October 15, corrections authorities issued an alert to staff: Pay special attention to Nike Air shoes; check to see if the soles had been slit and hollowed out to create a compartment. It was also suggested that a truckload of Nike shoes had been hijacked somewhere in Toronto exclusively for the purpose of smuggling contraband into correctional facilities. Riley and his fellow Galloway inmates had lined up someone on the outside who was charging $250 to outfit a pair of shoes.

Arrested in May, some of the Malvern men were already pleading out. One of them, Jamol Johnson, described as a "mid-level" figure in the

Malvern Crew, apologized in early October "to the community, and to my family," after pleading guilty to participating in a criminal organization. He was sentenced to "time served in pre-trial custody"—five months plus one day. It was said to be the first conviction in Canada involving a street gang under the recently enacted criminal organization law.

The flood of charges and arrests in Galloway by no means brought the Project Pathfinder investigation to a conclusion. The bulk of charges was still months away. And Marlon Wilson, despite having assured Riley he was on his side, would become a significant player in the police investigation.

CHAPTER 13

A rat takes a road trip

On October 25, 2004, Comeau and Banks went to see Marlon Wilson in jail at the Toronto West Detention Centre, where he had been transferred to keep him apart from the G-Way guys at The East.

The detectives told him they were investigating a homicide on March 3, 2004, and asked him if he would sign a consent for a judge's order to bring him to a police station to listen to some wiretaps.

Two days later, Banks and Comeau brought Wilson to a police station in the west end of the city. But they had barely settled into their seats in the interview room when Banks was called away. (Banks was back in rotation with the homicide squad and had to respond to a murder in North Toronto. It turned out to be one of the city's most high-profile cases that year. The victim was the owner of a downtown gay bar. His longtime live-in boyfriend was charged with first-degree murder. A largely circumstantial case, the man was acquitted by a jury in 2008.)

In any case, the job of taking a videotaped statement from Wilson fell solely to Comeau, who told the prisoner he was investigating a "homicide and attempted murder that took place up at Neilson and Finch Avenue on March third this year." Did Wilson know anything about it?

But first, Comeau played a number of intercepted calls for Wilson. He listened as Riley and Atkins were discussing "slooing" him, which meant to harm or kill. Wilson also heard Riley's mother talking on the phone about killing him. Wilson was already upset that he was still in jail, sore that Riley and Atkins had not stepped up and told police he was nowhere near the scene of the Hyatt and Patrong shooting. As the detective hoped, hearing the tapes put Wilson over the edge.

Wilson told Comeau that Riley had called him in the early evening on March 3 and told him to buy some liquor to celebrate, since they had killed "Ross," a Malvern Crew member. They agreed to meet at the Galloway-area apartment of Maxeen (Smokey) McPherson and Derrick (Junkie) Corbette. It was a favoured hangout, where the gang frequently gathered to smoke weed, drink, listen to rap and gossip.

Riley told Wilson that he had shot a Malvern Crew member called Ross P. "I got there and they told me they caught him at the legs in the purple Neon. They shot him," Wilson said. But later, when they watched the news on TV, Riley realized they had killed someone else. Wilson said Riley had been driving a black Pathfinder.

He said there were at least eight people at Smokey's that night—they always called it Smokey's, as in "see you later at Smokey's"—though there could have been more. He remembered getting there around 5 p.m. and leaving about 7:30.

When Comeau asked if Atkins had ever told him he was involved in the shooting, Wilson said no. But Wilson did implicate Tyshan Riley in the murder of Omar Hortley and the shooting of teenager Mark Jones in his Malvern driveway.

A couple of months later, firearms charges against Wilson were withdrawn. Just before Christmas, he was released from jail. But before Wilson was let go, Detective Constable Darryl Linquist came to talk to him about the possibility of entering the province's witness protection program.

While his life might have been in danger, cooperating with police wasn't a concept Wilson was keen on. Having been in and out of jail since he was 13, Wilson felt no kinship with the police. In any event, he wasn't planning to stick around.

Two days after his release, on December 22, 2004, Wilson, his friend Hertzel Shamilov, who police described later as a gangbanger wannabe, and Wilson's cousin headed west in the same silver Audi that had been seized at the Oshawa mall the previous spring. Police, for some reason, had released the vehicle to Shamilov when he asked for it back.

A Trans-Canada road trip can be especially perilous in winter. There were some white-knuckle moments, such as when the car did a 360 in the middle of the highway.

But they eventually got to Vancouver, where Wilson's girlfriend joined them. He tried to establish himself on the West Coast, which meant smoking a lot of weed, recording a rap album at a friend's home studio and hanging out with prostitutes. He would deny being a pimp, though he had no problem with his girlfriend stripping or turning tricks as a prostitute to support him. After a short while, Wilson's girlfriend returned to Toronto to look after the couple's young son. Wilson remained, living the low life in apartment-hotels in Vancouver's bustling west end.

Meanwhile, staff sergeant Dean Burks, a former homicide detective who had come on the case in late 2004, was trying to track down Wilson. "I started to feel worse. The more I read, realizing all the work that had to be done," he said. One of his duties was keeping track of witnesses—though, in reality, there never were that many. So Burks zeroed in on Wilson, looking for more information and trying to ensure he would be around to testify in Toronto.

The two would spend a lot of time together over the next few years. They were a very odd couple: the rock-steady white cop from the Prairies and the erratic black kid from the streets of Scarborough.

Burks had moved to Toronto from Kindersley, Saskatchewan, in 1987, to become a police officer in the big city. He was devoted to his wife and two children. He was known as a straight shooter—his partner described him as a cop who "calls it the way he sees it, even if it's the unpopular point of view." His frustrations with the onerous paperwork and glacial pace of the justice system, especially in this case, would surface on occasion. One of his biggest challenges would be handling Marlon Wilson.

Burks tracked down Wilson's whereabouts in Vancouver and repeatedly called his cell phone. Wilson never returned his calls. So Burks obtained a material witness warrant, which allowed Vancouver police to arrest Wilson. They collared him on February 8, 2005.

Burks and Detective Darryl Linquist flew out the next day to deliver Wilson the bad news: He was about to be brought back to Toronto in cuffs. The detectives met with Wilson at a police station in Vancouver. The interview was videotaped.

"I don't want to go to Toronto," Wilson says. "You're basically using me so these people go to jail . . . This is bullshit . . . I'm in jail 'cause I helped you guys . . . You guys don't care if I get killed. If a guy like me dies in the street, police are happy."

The tape shows a tough guy turned to mush. Wilson, wearing a baggy black T-shirt, rubs his hands over his closely shaved head, which he hangs so low it can touch his shoes. He shifts and squirms in his seat, at times pleading.

Burks takes the lead while Linquist takes notes. Burks, wearing jeans and a casual shirt, his leather jacket hanging on the back of a chair, plays good cop *and* bad cop throughout the interview. But Wilson at times is sparring with the detectives.

"I didn't do nothing to get arrested," says Wilson, waving his arms in the air. "You guys really think—if you guys keep doing this to me—I'm going to help you guys?"

"We're not going to keep doing anything," Burks says, before Wilson cuts him off.

"Well, you did it. Now I have to go back to Toronto and go to jail there. That ain't right, man. You guys want me to work with you, then you guys are just treating me like garbage, putting me in jail."

Burks plays bad cop: "Treating you like garbage? You didn't call me back. How many times did I call and leave messages for you? How many times?"

Wilson backs off. "You guys can do what you want ... Now I'm going back to Toronto for what? Then what's going to happen to me?"

Burks, the good cop, confides that when Wilson didn't return his calls, "we thought you were dead."

"There's nobody on the street to kill me," Wilson responds.

Burks offers Wilson a place in witness protection. "It depends on whether or not you're suitable for the program" by cooperating or "fuck off again." (Burks did not know Vancouver police would be videotaping the interview and would appear to cringe when excerpts were played in court.)

More good cop: "I have to be in a position where I can say, 'Yeah, you know, this guy is a valuable witness and you know what? Yeah, he is going to come back to court and testify and cooperate.'" Burks reassures Wilson he'll return to Toronto as John Doe. "We don't want these guys to know you're in custody."

Burks also suggests something he knows at the time isn't true: "Don't think everything on this case rides on you."

Over the two-hour interview, Wilson vacillates. One minute he has no intention of cooperating with police. The next, he tells Burks he has "a lot more information" police can use against Riley. Wilson also reveals he has a personal grudge against Riley: "He tried to have sex with my 'baby mother' [girlfriend, mother of his son] ... He's not a true friend. I hate him." One thing about Wilson: he would always be consistently inconsistent.

"If you guys don't help me, I'm not going to come [to testify]," Wilson says.

"Right," Burks responds.

"If you guys help me, I'll come."

The next day, at 3 a.m., back in Toronto after the four-hour flight, a weary Wilson gives another statement in a first-floor police video room in Scarborough. He tells an equally exhausted Burks about Riley's role in the shootings of Charlton, Bell, Hortley and Jones.

"I don't like this piece of shit, Ty," Wilson says, sitting across a table from Burks. "I don't like none of these guys no more, you know what I'm saying? So I will be happy to do it. Like a grudge thing for me, now." This time he also gives up Atkins, the childhood friend he considered family. "I can't believe I'm doing this to my cousin," he mutters. "It's crazy."

A couple of weeks later, after a bail hearing, Wilson was released from custody. He was the one witness police and prosecutors were counting on. But he would soon be joined by another turncoat—a much more reliable witness—from the tough streets of Scarborough.

CHAPTER 14

A sinner comes clean

On February 22, 2005, police got their biggest break yet. That's the day they first interviewed Roland Ellis, a convicted thief, crack dealer and Galloway gang member. Ellis would provide not only evidence in this case but a look into the world of Toronto's violent street gangs. Burks would compare him to Salvatore (Sammy the Bull) Gravano, the biggest rat in Mafia history.

Born in Toronto on December 7, 1982, two months after Riley, Roland George Ellis moved to Galloway when he was five, along with his mother, two sisters and brother. His Jamaican-born mother was a stern disciplinarian who tried her best to shield him from negative influences, drilling into his head "if you don't hear, you're going to feel."

They lived in a government-subsidized townhouse complex on Kingston Road when Ellis was going to elementary school. After the bell rang, he did what a lot of other youngsters in the neighbourhood did: he headed to the Boys and Girls Club. There he met Riley, Riley's twin brothers, Carl and Courtney, Philip Atkins, Norris Allen, Ernesto Gayle and others destined to become Galloway Boys.

The childhood hangout at 100 Galloway Road of Tyshan Riley, Roland Ellis and other members of the Galloway gang.

Ellis stood out from the other kids, who were a tough group "living on the fringes," recalled someone who worked at the club in the early to mid- '90s. "Roland was good-natured and wide-eyed and looked out for his younger brother and sister." On the basketball court, Ellis handled the ball with skill and played by the rules. It was also clear he was "straddling" two worlds, but managed to exist in both.

Around the age of 12, "we were just into sports. We weren't really into those type of activities as yet," Ellis said as an adult, adding, "we later on turned into a bunch of thugs."

When Ellis got older, unlike most of his contemporaries, he had part-time jobs, working when he was 15 at Fran's Restaurant at St. Clair Avenue and Yonge Street, and, when he needed quick cash, at his uncle's car wash in Toronto's west end. He also did some construction work and painted houses as part of a youth jobs program. But, by the time he started grade 7, Ellis was losing interest in what was going on in the classroom. "I was focusing on a lot of girls at the time, so I couldn't focus with the schoolwork."

His waning enthusiasm for education got him "shipped" to Sir Robert Borden with many of the other boys from the neighbourhood. He remembered it as "a dead-end kind of place," where he started smoking a lot of pot and became more immersed in gangbanging. In grade 11, Ellis was kicked out of Borden after he got arrested for stealing a fellow student's $800 Rocawear jacket, a popular brand with urban youth. A few weeks later, he and a couple of friends took another kid's pot and Walkman.

For a while, he attended the Scarborough Centre for Alternative Studies, taking high-school credit courses, but the streets eventually became more attractive. With no father at home, some of the older guys in the neighbourhood, those no longer enamoured with gang life, tried to send a message: "Stay in school and don't end up like them, basically don't follow their path-type stuff," Ellis recalled. "But it went in one ear, out the next."

He was known on the street as Sledge. (Explaining the origin of the nickname in court later would elicit a lot of salacious laughter.) Ellis had OG—standing for Original Gangster—carved into one arm. He also had a KG tattoo for Kingston/Galloway. In his late teens he took over as leader of the Mad Soldiers, a small group of youths from the south side of Galloway.

He got away with some robberies—mainly ripping off other drug dealers—and at various times carried guns, which some gang members gave nicknames. Using a webcam, Ellis snapped a photograph of himself posing with one. Underneath, he wrote: "Me and Little Breezy."

By 2002, at age 20, he had been convicted of two counts of robbery. In 2003, he was locked up for several months after being convicted of failing to comply with a condition of his probation.

Uneducated, Ellis turned to the only skill he had, the only one that would make him money: selling drugs. He had learned the trade watching the way the older guys did it.

"I would learn the sizes of each piece [of crack], how to tie the bags, where to hide it, stuff like that, who usually buys what, what to look for if it is an undercover [cop]." This came in especially handy when he and Riley were selling drugs out of Ellis' mother's townhouse.

He also rapped and recorded music under the name Ambush, apparently an homage to his modus operandi as a robber. He smoked a lot of pot. He sold it, too, to buy more. If there was money left over he was something of a clotheshorse and liked to dress his lanky six-foot-four frame in baggy urbanwear bought at a nearby mall.

Asked at one point if he ever felt he had a chance of being able to succeed in straight society, Ellis said no. "We set high goals but we just didn't know about how to reach the goals properly, I think."

Through much of his teens and early 20s, Ellis was, in his own words, "gangbanging hard."

He explained the distinction: "Gangbanging hard [means] you're defending something, like you'll stand up for what you believe in. If you're just gangbanging you're just a follower basically."

He went on to explain the life of a hardcore gangbanger: "Carrying guns, selling drugs, running every time you see the police, organizing criminal activity."

But Ellis said there was a difference between his Galloway crew on the south side of Kingston Road and Riley's boys on the north. He noted both gangs did G-checks, including at McTaggart's bar, where a lot of drug dealing took place. "I was like really ignorant at times," he said years later. "People would come there and drink and want to sell their drugs and stuff and we'd be telling them—members of the south side, even north side as well—we'd tell them they can't sell their drugs here." Ellis and the Mad Soldiers would be smoking pot in the alley, while gang members from the north side would be "thirty yards away in the park, selling crack and pot. They always had a lot of money and they always had a lot of drugs."

Years later, as Riley's case moved through the courts, defence lawyers would try to discredit Ellis by suggesting he had pumped himself up and was really a wannabe leader of south side. "Were you calling the shots in south side?" challenged one lawyer. "The shots in what?" Ellis replied sarcastically. "We didn't really do anything on the south side. We didn't really hurt people or anything like that, so there wasn't really shots to call."

Nor was there planning, he said. "Stuff just happened spontaneous in south side. There was not 'we're going to sit down, okay, the next person who walks through there, we're going to jump them.' It wasn't like that." The north side, however, was where "they would sit down and plan on what they would do before they actually do it," he explained. "They would be talking about different grimes that they have planned for the upcoming days, what they would do that same night."

Gang leadership wasn't a popularity contest, nor was it determined by a vote. It was based on "who gets the most attention, who's calling the shots, who has the most brains in the group," Ellis said. For the longest time, in Galloway, that person was Norris Allen. But things changed after Allen was mowed down in the fall of 2002. That's when Riley launched his "rides" of revenge and asked Ellis: "Are you rolling with us or not?"

Am I going to jump in cars and shoot people? Ellis thought. He told Riley to forget it. "I am my own person doing my own thing."

The relationship really went downhill after Riley was arrested in Oshawa and jailed in the spring of 2004. While Riley could no longer "really affect" people on the outside, he continued to use "his mouth to threaten people from the inside or have one of his little goons do something for him," Ellis recalled.

That summer, Ellis continued to deal dope—called tree, ganja, sees, dro (hydro) or herbs—and crack to the "bums in the slums," as he described it. He was pulling in up to $300 a day, $400 on Fridays, when people "partied . . . harder."

Ellis and others in Galloway also continued to spend time smoking weed, drinking, listening to rap and gossiping at Smokey's apartment hangout.

On one occasion, Smokey handed Ellis the phone.

"Greeze wants to talk to you," she said, using one of Riley's street names.

Ellis picked up the receiver and asked the jailed gang leader, "What's up?"

"What's up, family," came Riley's reply. "Can you do me a favour?" He wanted Ellis to take the rap for what was found—the more than $14,000 in cash, plus bullets and some hash oil—when police first searched his girlfriend Dana's apartment. Ellis continued to listen.

"Just say that it is yours and I will give you money for it," Riley told him. He made a vague offer of paying Ellis $10,000.

"I was like, okay, yeah," Ellis responded. "I will do that for you, that is 'soft.'" Translation: whatever.

But by the time Ellis got home he was boiling. Why should he go to jail for this guy? What had Riley ever done for him? "He treats everyone like a piece of shit, in my eyes, including me." He decided not to be one of Riley's "little puppets you can throw around." He would tell Riley to forget it when Ellis was summoned for a pow-wow at the jail.

"I gave your name to Dana's lawyer and the lawyer is going to call you," Riley told Ellis on the jailhouse phone, their faces separated by a pane of bulletproof Plexiglas.

"Call me what?" Ellis replied.

"Yo, bro, stop fuckin' around," Riley shot back. "Like you said: You are going to do that for me." Ellis said he hadn't agreed.

"I am going to give you a week to think about it," Riley threatened. "If you don't do it for me, yo, you already know what is going to happen."

Ellis shrugged: "All right, whatever."

A few days later Riley was calling again from jail.

"Who is this? What's up?" Ellis asked.

"So did you think about what you were talking about?" Riley said.

Ellis repeated he wasn't going to take the fall.

"Okay, you are getting dumped," Riley said. Ellis knew what that meant. Riley would order a hit.

"Do your thing," Ellis said.

Ellis knew Riley was someone to fear. Ellis also knew loyalty, for Riley, was a one-way street. Hearing Riley threatening to kill him wasn't something Ellis would brush off.

He told some friends about it. They told him not to worry, that Riley was in jail. Ellis wasn't reassured. "I took upon my own actions to do what I had to do to defend myself." Ellis acquired a .38-calibre revolver and a bulletproof vest. He kept both with him at all times. He spent much of the summer of 2004 "looking over my shoulder."

Still, even with a death threat hanging over Ellis' head, the ties from the neighbourhood were strong. Riley again wanted to test Ellis' loyalty when he asked him to toss some marijuana over a wall and into the yard at the detention centre. Ellis reluctantly agreed.

"He [Riley] sees me as a person lower than him. He looks at me as a person less than him."

Later, when questioned why he would toss the marijuana for someone who wanted him dead, Ellis' response showed how tight the bonds were for these young men. "We were all friends," Ellis replied. "We're all from the same neck of the woods." Still, Riley's threats preoccupied Ellis.

And the animosity between Ellis and Riley was evident to those listening in the wire room. It was an area with potential to exploit.

On February 22, 2005, Ellis was staying at a friend's place playing video games when he picked up the phone.

"It's Detective [Roger] Caracciolo from Toronto police." Ellis thought it was one of his friends playing a prank.

"I'm not bullshitting you. I'm a real officer," Caracciolo said.

"Yeah, okay, whatever," Ellis replied.

"Toronto police want to speak to you."

"Am I in trouble?" Ellis interrupted.

"No, you're not in any trouble. We just want to speak to you and then we'll let you go. We'll come and get you."

"No, I don't want you guys coming to the house." Ellis agreed to meet at Morningside Mall. He told Caracciolo what he would be wearing. But, before leaving for the mall, Ellis called his probation officer to see if she knew what was up. She didn't, and told him to meet the officers to find out.

Caracciolo might have been out of uniform, but Ellis knew a cop when he saw one. He got in the unmarked car, drove to the station and was directed to an interview room. He sat down with Caracciolo and Darryl Linquist, the detective who, a few weeks earlier, had travelled to Vancouver with Burks. At 5:56 p.m., a video recorder was turned on.

Inside a windowless room, the three men were seated at a small, round wooden table.

Ellis, wearing a blue and yellow bomber-style jacket, jeans and a black stocking cap, faced the camera and seemed braced for the worst.

Caracciolo introduced himself. Linquist did the same, though the camera only captured the detective's knees beneath the table and his fingers occasionally tapping away at a laptop.

Caracciolo read Ellis a "waiver," spelling out the consequences of giving a sworn statement, including the possibility that he might one day be a witness at a trial. Ellis said he understood and swore on a Bible "to tell the whole truth and nothing but the truth." Caracciolo then explained he was involved in the investigation of a shooting at Neilson and Finch in March 2004, and that police had since been using wiretaps on suspects.

"You're familiar with the takedown that happened in the Galloway area? What is your understanding of what happened?"

Ellis replied it involved "gang activity" and the people who were arrested posed a threat to the community.

"Who would you know that was apprehended?" Caracciolo asked.

"I know all the individuals that were apprehended," Ellis said, including Tyshan Riley.

"Was he a friend?" Caracciolo asked.

"Nah."

Caracciolo said he would get to the point. "The investigation brought to light some people who want to harm you, and when I say harm, if I was to say the word dump, what does dump mean to you?"

Ellis snickered. "To get rid of the person, kill them."

Caracciolo told Ellis police were "concerned for your safety," and asked if he wanted to hear the calls "intercepted during our investigation that talk about dumping you." Ellis said yes.

On his laptop, Linquist cued up a recording made the previous summer. Within seconds, Riley's angry voice filled the tiny room. At first, he is heard berating his lackey, Damian Walton, for not complying quickly enough to Riley's order to toss drugs over the wall at The East—as Walton and Ellis had done following previous orders.

"You see a fucking fence you see a fucking wall, you see wires on top of the fucking wall, bro. How hard is it?" Riley ranted. Ellis buried his head in his arms on the edge of the table. He continued to listen.

"Who you with? Who you with?" Riley snarled at Walton, who told him Sledge, Ellis' street name, was there too.

"Put him on the phone, tell him I want to talk on the phone, eh?" Ellis then listened to himself receiving instructions from Riley.

"What's going on. Listen bro, throw the shit and fucking leave, bro. As soon as the phone cuts off, throw the shit and fucking leave, bro. That's all it is, eh? It's all it fucking is, eh." Ellis and Walton were on a cellphone, in a car, a few minutes away from the detention centre.

Riley wouldn't let up, lecturing his now recalcitrant courier for being too obvious on his last delivery over the jailhouse wall.

In the police interview room, a disgusted Ellis shook his still-bowed head as he listened to Riley continue the tirade.

"Last time, I can't believe I seen you. Everybody fucking seen you. No one's fucking supposed to see you, bro. Listen, when the phone cuts off and you get a call, right, you guys come up here right now, man, park now."

This time Ellis wasn't backing down. What did Riley do for him after the last drug toss? he asked.

"What do you want for this, man? You kids are pissing me off, eh," Riley shot back. "You guys want me to come out of jail and get wild on you kid? What do you want, what do you want for this? Do you want money for it?"

Ellis replied "teeth," meaning bullets.

"Brother, those are hard. I got to make a call, brother. It's hard, bro. I tell you it's hard."

Riley then told Ellis to put Walton back on the phone and continued his harangue.

"Everybody's pissing me off. Yo, what are you guys still doing on turf, bro? You guys are doing shit while I'm in jail? Listen, brethren, drive the fuck up here and come on time."

Atkins, who took the phone from Riley inside the jail, had the final word.

"You guys are coming, like, you guys hurry up. We're getting, ten minutes, man. We're going to call you back in fucking seven minutes, man. All right, hang it up."

With that, Ellis raised his head and made a throat-slashing gesture. He'd had enough.

"Why don't you tell me about that day and what that situation was?" Caracciolo asked Ellis.

"He wanted a package," Ellis responded with an uncomfortable grin, appearing in a daze.

"And what was in the package?"

"Just like weed and shit, weed, lighter and all that shit."

Walton, he explained, was Riley's "little run-around kid."

"I didn't really wanna do it. I was just like, 'fuck just leave me alone,'" Ellis said, letting out a sigh.

"And what's your feeling if you didn't do it? What would happen if you just said 'No, I'm not doing it?'"

"Well, see, he'd probably try to send a hit on me, call somebody, to do something to me or do something that would affect me."

Ellis told the officers he was warned "those guys are plotting to lick you down." What did Riley mean by "lick you down," Caracciolo asked. "To kill me," Ellis responded.

During the interview, Caracciolo alternated between leaning back in his chair with his arms folded or sitting forward, occasionally fiddling with the drawstring on his blue hoodie. A black man, with a shaved head, Caracciolo cut an imposing figure even sitting down.

For Ellis, the calls brought back all the anxiety of the previous summer. He told the officers how he had taken precautions, and how nobody could just walk up and kill him, that it would start a war. Caracciolo then asked, "Why do you think Tyshan Riley would want to kill you?"

"Well, in his brain he wants to control all of Galloway, he wants to be known as the head man like, 'I'm the man who runs Galloway,'" Ellis said. "With him being incarcerated right now, he knows that the block is all divided up right now and it's making him mad and he feels that I'm controlling one piece of the pie. So, in his brain, if he can take out the people that he feels are controllin' pieces of pie, he contains the whole pie."

Throughout the interview, Caracciolo stoked Ellis' resentment of Riley. "How does that feel, knowing that Riley's planning to kill you?" he said at one point.

The detective also tried to boost Ellis' ego by asking him who at that time was running south side, which was Ellis' turf. Ellis paused before answering. "South side is not really run by anybody, we're just like family, like we all grew up together and there's not really anybody who's like saying, calling the shots, or telling anybody to do certain things."

Caracciolo pushed further. The detective reminded Ellis that when Riley had been running the north side "everything gravitated to him." But wasn't that also the case with Ellis on the south side? Caracciolo asked, adding: "Am I looking at the perceived leader of south side, is this why you're dancing with me here?"

"Not really, well yeah, like the people would come to me and talk to me and stuff," Ellis responded. He was a reluctant leader, but agreed when Caracciolo suggested Ellis had a reputation for being a "calm person."

Caracciolo continued to ask questions about who was who in Galloway and how things were organized. For a hardened gangbanger, Ellis answered politely and agreed to listen to another wiretapped call. This time, Riley's voice was introduced with his trademark phone greeting: "Holler," which sent Ellis' head sinking again. On that occasion, Riley was on the line dissing Ellis and threatening to "box [kill] him when I get out of here [jail]."

After playing the call, Caracciolo asked: "So why is Riley so angry with you, man?"

Ellis mumbled an inaudible response.

The detective pressed: "I'm looking at you and your mind looks like it's racing a hundred miles a minute right now."

Staring ahead, Ellis said, "Just' chillin, man; I don't know, man."

The detective played more wiretaps, including one where two gang members were discussing how "Sledge has to get dumped." There was also talk about how they were to "put a word out that Keys [Sheldon Nugent] is supposed to get dumped."

Ellis explained it was part of a "cover-up." Nugent was one of Riley's right-hand men from the north side. "If they were to dump me it would start a war between north and south side," he explained, clearly chagrined. If word spread that north side was prepared to kill people from their own side, then it doesn't look like "a north side south side type 'B' flick," he said, apparently using a movie analogy.

Caracciolo asked Ellis how it felt knowing Riley's "planning to kill ya?"

"I don't fear him like everybody else," he said. "I have boys right now that tell me every day they hope that he beats his charges and it's not for the sake of him coming back out and us partying or something like that."

He was referring to street justice and the fact Ellis wasn't alone in his dislike of Riley.

"What I'm saying so it goes both ways. I guess, man, like he wants me gone," Ellis said. He paused, then added: "I guess, you know, there's people that want him gone too."

Caracciolo stuck to the theme: Since Riley wanted Ellis killed, was Ellis not interested in payback? "If a guy's trying to kill me—I'm gonna go and tell everybody I think I know about him and everything he's done."

In other words, there was nothing wrong ratting out someone who was planning to have you killed.

Caracciolo asked, "Is there anything you know about him you want to tell me right now?" He added with a chuckle, "I mean I'm putting it all on the table for you, man, I'm hitting you with a lot of stuff." Caracciolo then added the zinger: "Do you know much about the murder at Neilson and Finch?"

At first, Ellis said, "Not really. Ah, like I wasn't there or nothing, like I just heard."

But Ellis had more to say about what Riley and others were up to the day Charlton and Bell were shot.

"They went up there, they musta staked out some houses and shit—the dudes came out of the house, they followed them and just drove up beside them and basically dumped the car and just drove off."

"Who was 'they' that you heard," Caracciolo asked.

"I heard C.D. [Jason Wisdom] was in the car and Tyshan Riley," he said. "I don't even know who was driving or what, I just know those two were in the cars, though."

The shooters were in an SUV, he said, but did not identify the make or model. Caracciolo asked him to clarify: Who was in the car?

"Jason Wisdom and Tyshan Riley," Ellis said, "but there was probably more but like I don't know who else was in there."

"Who told you about this stuff?"

"This is just news like carries around the block. Like these dudes, when they do stuff, they're not smart," he replied. "They'll call up people, 'like everyone come to Smokey's tonight' and like 50 people [will be there] and everyone's watchin' the news seeing what's going on—maybe like smoking weed, drinking like—celebrating type of shit."

Ellis said he had nothing to hide regarding any shootings.

"I don't really do that type of shit, I'm not with them on that."

Ellis had some additional thoughts on what motivated Riley and "his wild shooters."

"They do it and let everyone know like, 'Yeah! I just killed that guy' and to get stripes, everyone to try and respect this guy."

By now, Ellis was more at ease with the detectives and, at times, became animated as he opened up about the secret life of the Galloway gang. No more so than when he was fingering Riley as someone who did a lot of "dirty dealing," with a propensity to order followers, when necessary, to "bust their guns" on the south side to deflect heat from Riley's north side.

They covered more ground over the next hour, with Ellis implicating Riley and Wisdom in a shooting ambush where the victims survived, before Caracciolo returned to Nielson and Finch, telling Ellis police believed Charlton and Bell were victims of mistaken identity.

Ellis concurred. And divulged some more. The targets, he said, were supposed to be "Biggs' affiliates," referring to Malvern's Dwayne Williams. Charlton and Bell were clearly "not affiliated to Biggs in any sort of form."

As Wilson had done previously, Ellis corroborated that the motive behind the drive-by shooting was to avenge the 2002 death of Norris (Bolu) Allen which had been a defining moment in Galloway.

While there had been stabbings and shootings back and forth between Malvern and Galloway, it was a shock, at least to Ellis, that "someone would actually die."

"When B died it was like ----, like that really hit like Yo! This is reality."

Ellis said he thought Riley had something to do with Allen's murder.

A week before Allen died, Ellis recalled hanging out with a group that included Riley and Allen, who seemed to eerily predict what was to come.

"He was saying to everybody like 'Yo, if I die, would you ride for me?'" Ellis translated: "Like 'would you defend my death?'"

Ellis, without hesitation, told Allen yes, but recalled Allen was more interested in how Riley would respond. Ellis recalled that Riley said nothing.

From that night on, Ellis said he believed Riley was a "dude" who had to be watched. "I always had the thought in my head, when I talk to my boys. We always saying if you find this dude has something to do with B's death—it ain't gonna be good," he continued. "This stuff—I don't wanna be involved really, man, it's too crazy for me."

When Caracciolo, again, returned to the March 3, 2004 shooting, Ellis was more forthcoming.

Ellis said he, Wisdom, Riley and a bunch of other people were at Smokey's when a TV news report came on that said two guys in their 40s had been shot at Neilson and Finch.

"And then what did Tyshan say?" Caracciolo asked.

"He was just mad," Ellis said, because the victims weren't members of the Malvern Crew.

"But you were sure Tyshan did the shooting?"

"Yeah," Ellis said. Wisdom, he added, "said that they drove beside the car and started shooting and just took off."

Before the camera was shut off, Ellis told police that Riley was responsible for other shootings.

But one of the problems that police faced in dealing with gang members was that most officers didn't know the lingo of the streets.

For example, Ellis referred to everyone in his community by their nicknames, not what he called their "government names"—the ones on their birth certificates. When he said that Riley and Wisdom shot Pye and a woman, Ellis was talking about Gary Reid and Neville Badibanga. Or when Riley boasted "he caught his first body," a guy named Lynx, he was talking about Eric Mutiisa.

"Did Tyshan tell you why he murdered Lynx?" Caracciolo asked.

"In revenge of the death of Norris Allen," he said, adding, "a.k.a. Bolu." Riley and his guys called themselves Throwbacks, he said. "It's basically for retaliation for B [Bolu]. They're throwing back to what B got."

Ellis said Riley told him a girl both he and Lynx were seeing had "set it up for him." He died in a driveway, after being shot in the head, Ellis correctly reported. "I don't think he gave the guy a chance to even look at him."

As the three-hour interview came to an end Ellis also had a couple of questions. If police overheard Riley making death threats the previous summer, why were they only contacting him now, more than six months later?

Caracciolo paused. "Ah, a natural progression in an investigation, I think, um, sometimes you weigh things and . . ."

Just after 9 p.m., Caracciolo asked a bunch of questions about drug dealing and whether gang members committed "any frauds or anything like that?"

"Just crack dealers, that's it," Ellis replied. "Basically ghetto. Just a bunch of crack dealers and gun carriers, that's it." Most of the robberies committed by G-Way members were of low-level drug dealers selling weed and crack, just like themselves.

Caracciolo then reminded Ellis: "What you've told us has been under oath and is there anything else that you want to change at this time?"

"I wish I could change my life but I can't do that. No, there's nothing I'd like to change."

But Ellis immediately regretted what he had done. During the police interview, Ellis had told Caracciolo and Linquist he did not want enter the witness protection program. It hadn't yet sunk in that he might actually be called to testify against his friends in court.

About a week later, Ellis told his mother what he had done. It was an emotional discussion and they decided he needed to try to undo the damage. They called Caracciolo. Ellis cried as he told the detective he didn't want to be involved in the case and was worried that when word got out he'd be a dead man. He also asked him to destroy the videotape, which was, of course, not going to happen.

Ellis said he needed some time, that he was taking a brief trip to Jamaica, where his mother was getting married. Over the next few weeks, he ignored police attempts to contact him and tried to keep a low profile in Galloway. But he was growing more worried for his safety, especially since the word on the street was that police had little other evidence against

Riley. Then, on April 18, on his way to see his probation officer, Ellis saw Caracciolo and Linquist waiting in the parking lot. They handed him a subpoena to come to court. Ellis knew then he needed to go into witness protection. Otherwise, he decided, he would be a "sitting duck."

He would be relocated and could not have any contact with family or friends. "There was no turning back," Ellis said later. He went to the witness protection office to prepare to disappear from Galloway, to begin life under a new identity.

Staff Sergeant Dean Burks, who had dealt with Ellis during his days patrolling some of Scarborough's meaner streets, remembered what he said to Caracciolo when he heard Ellis had agreed to come in for an interview: "This guy's not going to tell you anything." Burks said of his previous dealings with Ellis: "He was never ignorant, but I'd never describe him as a nice or cooperative guy."

Nor would any Toronto police officer expect cooperation from someone like Ellis. The "no snitching" code of the streets was well established as Toronto police, over the years, watched its homicide "solve" rate drop from 80 per cent in the 1980s to between 50 and 60 per cent in the 1990s and beyond. Homicide detectives frequently made public appeals for witnesses to come forward, saying silence only emboldened the gangsters. Still, few answered the call.

Burks was shocked when he learned Ellis had not only talked, but was willing to share his insider's perspective in court. What was Ellis' motivation? Burks said he would be guessing: "He was smarter than these guys. Growing up, he had rules. And he had a falling out with Riley," Burks told me. "Shooting and killing innocent people, not gangsters, the rules of engagement, as friggin' screwed up as that sounds, there are rules of engagement and he [Riley] broke them."

By the time Ellis gave his first statement, Riley and Philip Atkins had been charged with the first-degree murder of Charlton and the attempted murder of Bell. Police had also established a link between Riley and the Pathfinder allegedly used in the drive-by shooting. Police now had Wilson's earlier statement and the new one from Ellis. The moment had come to start preparing the final instalment of charges.

On April 29, 2005, Chief Bill Blair, who had recently replaced Fantino as Torontos top cop, stood up in the media studio at police headquarters. An "unrelenting" joint investigation involving units across the Toronto Police Service had resulted in 108 new charges against nine men "in the second round of Project Pathfinder," he announced.

Because of Ellis' sworn statement, Jason Wisdom was now charged with first-degree murder and attempted murder in the Charlton/Bell shooting. Atkins was also charged in the case as a result of Wilson's cooperation. Atkins and Riley were additionally charged with killing Omar Hortley, the kid who was simply walking to a friend's house to watch TV. Riley alone was charged in the 2002 murder of Malvern drug dealer Eric Mutiisa.

"A number of our neighbourhoods have been plagued by random acts of violence and gunplay in which innocent men have lost their lives," Blair said. "We have seen a tremendously positive impact flowing from the results of this work, in which a very small number of people have been taken out of the community and incarcerated. The impact on public safety has been dramatic and, I believe, long lasting."

Blair, naturally, didn't mention the former drug dealer and robber who helped crack the case. Publicly, police were the saviours of the community. But they couldn't have done it without Ellis.

On August 2, 2005, Ellis was in a downtown hotel room, giving police a longer, more detailed, statement that offered greater insight into the workings of Toronto street gangs. Caracciolo was there but this time it was Burks, the officer now in charge, asking the questions aimed at gathering evidence to help prove G-Way fit the legal definition of a criminal organization.

Asked about the targets of their robberies, Ellis told them about life on the streets—and in jail.

Drug dealers typically rob other dealers, sometimes their own sources, he said. "The dudes, when they get down and they're hungry and they ain't got nothing, all the guys have firearms to their name, they get hungry and they do a grime. They'll rob a dealer or whatever."

They also asked him about what was going on inside Toronto jails, particularly the detention centre called The East, which many Galloway Boys were calling home.

"People get extorted and people sell drugs and stuff," Ellis said. "Just for living on that range, you gotta pay people ... It's fucked up in there."

"Pay them cash?" Burks asked.

"Yeah, like I was in the Don [jail] one time and a dude was paying like two [hundred] bills, three bills, just to stay on that range."

"How would he do that?"

"His people would wire the money in dude's account on the street."

Was it protection money? the officers asked.

"Most of the time happens to people who, it's like their first time in jail and they don't know what's going on ... Like a bull [tough inmate] will come to him and go 'Yo, if you don't want to get hurt in here, just tell your people to put money in my account ... So it's like a protection thing basically. It's fucked, but it's crazy."

Switching gears, Burks was trying to gather evidence to support the charge that the Galloway Boys were a criminal organization. He asked about how control of drug selling worked, zeroing in on McTaggart's pub on Kingston Road.

"Who was dealing crack out of there?" Burks asked.

Ellis said Riley and others.

"Okay, let's try to be a little specific, can you maybe just walk into McTaggart's and start selling crack out of there?"

Ellis said no.

"Why not?" Burks asked.

"Guys in the area wouldn't allow that," he said. Anyone trying such a gambit would be approached and asked, "'What are you doing?' They'd probably be robbed," Ellis said with a chuckle.

Sometimes the answers weren't clear-cut.

"Okay, who controlled the crack dealing out of the bar?" Burks asked.

"Well, it's not really who controlled it because everybody ..."

"I don't mean a specific person," Burks interjected.

If he didn't get the answers he was looking for, Burks believed he was on course to support the criminal organization charge. Ellis was sometimes vague and his gang slang not always comprehensible, but by then Burks knew he had helped build a case.

But Ellis still had to say it all again—and again—in court.

CHAPTER 15

The Crown's sledgehammer

The preliminary hearing at the Scarborough courthouse began September 5, 2005. It was optimistically predicted the proceeding would last a minimum of six months. Even on the first day, there were signs that wasn't to be.

Preparations had been going on for months. No case like it had ever been heard in a Toronto courtroom. There were seventeen co-accused facing more than 100 charges, ranging from first-degree murder to robbery, weapons and drug offences. Binding all the charges together was the allegation that most of those charged were members of a criminal organization (Galloway Boys) and that the offences were alleged to be the product of that organization's criminal activities.

"To establish an evidentiary foundation that the individuals constitute a criminal organization is difficult and the prosecutorial efforts to mount such a prosecution are massive," noted the presiding judge, Justice Paul Robertson of the Ontario Court of Justice. For the court, he added, scheduling for a case of this magnitude would be "nothing short of a Herculean task."

"I know of no other case in Canadian history of criminal court proceedings involving as many defendants or a case involving twenty-five lawyers."

Security was a major concern. The Galloway Boys and their cronies were considered a ruthless and unpredictable lot. There was no telling what might erupt inside or outside the courthouse. A possibly combustible complication was that members of the Malvern Crew were being prosecuted in the same courthouse. There was concern about supporters of the two gangs congregating in the courthouse at the same time. That couldn't happen. But it would be a logistical nightmare to ensure the cases weren't being heard on the same dates.

Months earlier, there had been a meeting involving representatives of the Ministry of the Attorney General, Toronto police, who are responsible for security in the city's courthouses, court staff and judges.

At that meeting was Detective Phillip Devine, whose duties sometimes included conducting threat-vulnerability assessments for "internationally protected" people, such as the Pope or world leaders, when they visit Toronto. An overall security plan was developed for the Galloway preliminary hearing, calling for several modifications to the courthouse.

A tall, wooden fence and concrete barriers were installed in front of an entrance on the east side of the building, blocking the view from the roadway of witnesses entering the courthouse. At the other end of the building, the eleven defendants in custody would arrive with a phalanx of guards from the detention centre just a few blocks away. Everyone entering the courthouse had to pass through airport-style security. Once inside, heavily armed police officers would be stationed at the door to Courtroom 405. Others would patrol throughout the building.

Anyone wishing to enter the courtroom, including lawyers and court staff, first would be scanned by a security officer equipped with a metal-detector wand. In addition, court security officers were instructed to search for potential weapons or "escape implements." This involved going through briefcases, purses and, in some cases, leafing through legal textbooks.

"It would take very exceptional circumstances being made out to the court to justify such an exceptional procedure as the searching of Crown and defence counsel," Ralph Steinberg, then president of the Criminal Lawyers' Association, told me at the outset of the hearing. He added: "Even in that case, file materials must remain confidential."

Obviously, the security measures were unprecedented.

Defence lawyer Emma Rhodes, who wasn't involved in the preliminary hearing but was later part of the defence team, described the setup as akin to the way Hannibal Lecter was restrained in the 1991 movie *The Silence of the Lambs*. She was referring to Courtroom 405, which was altered to include three bullet-proof prisoners' boxes—fully enclosed from the sides and top. They were locked from the outside to prevent those inside from opening the door. Most of the spectator seats were removed, replaced by several rows of long tables and padded blue chairs filled with a revolving cast of defence lawyers, plus up to eight Crown attorneys.

Not allowed in the courtroom were members of the public, including relatives of the victims and accused. They, along with members of the media, watched the proceedings on a single closed-circuit monitor in a courtroom next door. They too would be searched and wanded by a court officer, with a quick scan across the bottom of their shoes for good measure.

Defence counsel made it known "in the strongest possible terms" they weren't happy being wanded before entering the courtroom. A group of them challenged the requirement, bringing the proceedings to a halt in mid-September as the judge heard arguments.

"I object to being searched upon entering a courtroom. I consider it an affront to my own personal dignity and an affront to the administration of justice," wrote one unnamed defence lawyer in an affidavit filed with the application.

Toronto police submitted evidence to show why this was all necessary, including seventeen intercepted phone calls that "clearly establishes that a number of the accused actively conspired or discussed the necessity to murder one of those Crown witnesses and have taken steps directly or indirectly to get Crown witnesses to change their evidence."

Police would later submit to court a thick book of "in-custody occurrences," which included dozens of alleged infractions by the defendants including smoking in cells, lighting fires and numerous threats against court officers.

Less than a week into the hearing, the judge adjourned court early in the afternoon. After he left, Dwight Wisdom, who was facing a murder charge, started shouting at court officers. "Get me out of this fucking box" and "open this door and I'll knock you pussies out" as he punched the Plexiglas and kicked the prisoners' box. Wisdom was handcuffed and shackles were secured around his ankles before officers escorted him back to the main cell area at the courthouse. There, Riley said "gun shots, gun shots" and made a gun gesture with his hand and pointed it at the officers. There would be more outbursts as the proceedings dragged on. Once, Riley started yelling and punching the Plexiglas in front of him. He then turned around and punched the plaster wall behind him, leaving a fist-sized hole.

Much later in the proceedings, Riley was found to have "contraband in his rectum," according to a handwritten report filed by a correctional officer. A metal detector wand began "alarming" near Riley's backside, it said. Riley was placed in a holding cell to wait a further search when correctional staff saw him repeatedly flushing the toilet. Staff retrieved a six-inch folding knife, silver and black in colour made by Smith and Wesson, from inside the toilet.

Riley ended up pleading guilty to various offences relating to these incidents.

The rantings of Riley's mother, Marie, were the most egregious examples that police presented. In addition to multiple calls where she threatened to have Marlon Wilson killed or kill him herself, one recording captured her telling someone to "make sure you murder both the judge and the Crown." Then there was the cucumber found in her freezer, with names written on pieces of paper. The list included police officers, correctional officers, a Crown attorney and a judge. Beside some of the names were the words "death bitch," "death liar" and "enemies—death."

Defence lawyers suggested her calls were evidence of nothing more than an angry mother venting. They also noted that nothing had happened to anyone since the calls were recorded in July 2004.

Still, the judge ultimately accepted the police view of security. "It is clear from the intercepts, Marie Riley's moral and religious beliefs hold no impediment to her committing murder," Robertson wrote in his September 22 ruling. He also concluded it was "appropriate that all counsel, Crown and defence and court staff would be subject to wanding before entering Courtroom 405. All boxes and other items would also be subject to search."

Four days later, defence lawyers appealed the judge's decision. But ultimately it would stand, though the proceedings had been knocked off track for three months.

At the start of 2006, nearly two years after the arrest of Atkins and Riley, and sixteen months after the takedown of all the other defendants, the case was ready to proceed.

On January 14, the court clerk took an hour to read out more than 100 gang-related charges. Listening were about twenty-five lawyers, a dozen police officers and seventeen defendants. About a dozen members of the public and several journalists—though in Canada they are banned from reporting on preliminary hearings—watched next door via the video link.

The relief inside the courtroom was palpable when the first witness was sworn in. "I think all the parties involved, whether it be the Crown, the police or the accused, are just happy to have everything commence," one defence lawyer, Geary Tomlinson, told me outside the courtroom.

The First Move

The Crown opened its case asking that a large-scale map of Scarborough be made Exhibit 1.

Detective Constable Roger Caracciolo was the first witness called to testify about the Mutiisa homicide. Caracciolo had been one of the first officers to arrive at the scene in Malvern that cold late afternoon in November 2002.

He described finding the drug dealer's body and grisly photos of it were introduced into evidence.

But cops would not be the star witnesses in this case. On February 9, the Crown announced Roland Ellis was about to take the stand.

Because of disclosure requirements, defence lawyers had a sense of what they were up against. They had copies of Ellis' videotaped statements. They also knew Ellis would be well prepared and "present well" as a witness. They hoped to make the point that Ellis was getting something in return for his testimony. But they knew there were no outstanding charges against Ellis, thus eliminating one avenue to exploit—that he had cooperated to get reduced jail time or have charges withdrawn.

Defence lawyers had requested copies of Ellis' "contract" with the witness protection program. But they now knew that Ellis was no longer in the protection program because of "various behaviour problems." What had he done?

Before Ellis walked into court, all the defendants sitting in the prisoner boxes stood up in a show of solidarity and, hopefully, intimidation. The judge ordered them to sit down, which they did.

Once Ellis was sworn in, the lead Crown attorney, Suhail Akhtar, speaking with a distinct British accent, began by asking Ellis to identify his childhood friends sitting in the dock.

"Do you see Tyshan Riley?"

"Yes, I do," Ellis replied. He would use virtually the same inflection as the other names were read out. If Ellis was at all rattled, it didn't show.

For seven days, he answered questions about the different gangs in the Galloway neighbourhood, their membership, their activities and other symbols of gang culture such as tattoos. He testified as to the organization of the groups in Galloway and how each was connected to every other gang in the neighbourhood. Ellis then moved on to how they did things, their terminology, how they protected their turf from "rival gangs that posed a threat, [and] other individuals from other neighbourhoods who would try to come in and sell their drugs—and especially the Malvern Crew."

When questions turned to some of the specific charges against Riley and the rest, Ellis expanded greatly on his previous statements, including that on the night Charlton and Bell were shot he saw Philip Atkins with a gun at Smokey's apartment. He described how the violence had escalated after Norris Allen was killed and how Riley had exacted payback with his "ride squads."

During some of Ellis' testimony, Riley and the others sneered from inside the box. Yet Ellis never lost his composure and, as time went on, appeared more relaxed and confident on the stand.

Some of the defence lawyers, through their line of questioning, tried to portray Ellis as a hanger-on, a nerd who wore glasses and rode a bicycle—he didn't have a driver's licence—who had no real power, no access to insider knowledge and therefore couldn't be believed. They also questioned him on everything from his marijuana smoking to his nickname, Sledge, short for sledgehammer.

"It's referring to a part of my body," Ellis said.

"It was given to me from a female."

Defence lawyer Liam O'Connor, a skilled cross-examiner, later acknowledged Ellis was a truly tough nut to crack. Unlike many "rats" lawyers face, Ellis hadn't given police information to get out of jail or have charges against him tossed. Nor had he been paid some princely sum of money to come to court. But he did have a reason for wanting these men in prison.

"His motivation to say a whole bunch of bad things was that it was in his best interest for these people to remain in jail," said Atkins' lawyer, Andy McKay, an ex-cop who took a lot of flack from former colleagues for representing a gang member.

Soon it would be Marlon Wilson's turn. Defence lawyers couldn't wait to get at him.

CHAPTER 16

The bizarro world of Marlon Wilson

Marlon Wilson was 25 when he took the stand on April 5, 2006. Crown attorney Maureen Pecknold, an army reservist who also prosecuted soldiers in courts martial, began by going over his extensive criminal record, trying to air all his dirty laundry as quickly as possible.

Wilson had been convicted of assault, break and enter, escaping custody, theft, robbery and mischief. He also had convictions for weapons possession and assault. Since returning to Toronto from Vancouver fourteen months earlier, Wilson hadn't managed to stay out of trouble. Nor was Vancouver the last place Burks had had to track him down.

The previous year, Wilson was charged with committing aggravated assault in Toronto. He left town, this time heading east for Montreal, which is where Burks went to get him and return him to Toronto in August. Over the next few months, Wilson was in and out of jail for various reasons. More recently, he was convicted of obstructing a peace officer and breaching his bail conditions. He served thirty days. And, true to form, Wilson, while on the stand, was in custody on charges of aggravated assault and assault with a weapon related to drug dealing.

Despite his familiarity with the justice system, Wilson had never testified in court for the simple fact he had always ended up pleading guilty. Now, here he was in the spring of 2006, sitting in the witness box.

He was a reluctant witness, telling Pecknold and Burks before the preliminary hearing began that he felt he was in a no-win situation. They assured him whatever he said in court couldn't be used against him.

For seven days, Wilson was on the stand, amplifying his original statements to police, though with several inconsistencies. He recollected some things, forgot others, then remembered when passages of his statements to police were read back by the Crown. For instance, Wilson had told police that both Riley and Atkins had confessed to killing Omar Hortley, the good kid in Malvern who had no connections to gangs.

Turning to the Charlton/Bell shooting, Pecknold asked Wilson about the significance of a Neon being the target of the attack.

"That's the car that those guys—the Ross P guy was driving."

"How do you know that?"

"'Cause I'm the one who told them about the car." Wilson had a beef with Alton Reid (Ross P) when the two were in jail together.

"Okay, what do you mean you told them about the car?" Pecknold asked.

"I saw this guy [Reid] driving the car and I told these guys."

But when she asked "Who did you tell?" Wilson said he couldn't remember—leaving the judge confused.

"What do you mean by 'I don't remember who I told'?" Robertson asked.

"I don't remember exactly who I told."

Robertson pressed further, asking Wilson if he could narrow it down to a few people?

"I know it was either Brub [Atkins] or Tyshan, one of the two guys when I said it but I don't remember exactly who else was there."

Getting Tough on Crime—and Guns

While the sometimes sensational hearing in Scarborough—filled with tales of violent gangbangers—was being conducted under a publicity ban that winter, politicians from near and far were making public pronouncements. Both the federal and Ontario leaders ramped up the rhetoric while the gang-related murder of a 15-year-old white girl named Jane Creba in downtown Toronto the previous Boxing Day was still raw in the public's mind.

Conservative leader Stephen Harper used it as a campaign issue that helped get him elected prime minister in February 2006. And Ontario premier Dalton McGuinty, a Liberal, took the stage to announce the province was giving "police and prosecutors the tools they need" to combat street gang violence. McGuinty said he was committing $51 million to hire additional Crown attorneys and ensure the "justice system has the resources it needs to bring people who commit gun crimes to justice." There were plans to establish courts to handle large-scale prosecutions, including courts equipped with high levels of security capable of dealing with multiple defendants. It was an attempt to reassure the public that more cops and courts would make a difference. Press releases also mentioned, but played down, how the McGuinty government was "being tough on the causes of crime." They announced, for example, plans to expand a program that places youth from high-risk neighbourhoods in summer jobs.

But guns were the real focus, the enemy of the people.

CHAPTER 17

Year of the gun

The gun nuts in the United States like to say that if the government took away their weapons, only the criminals would have guns. Here in Canada, it's always been different. There is no right to bear arms enshrined in law. People don't routinely walk around with a .45 holstered on their hip, a Glock in their glove compartment or an assault rifle slung over their shoulder when Barack Obama comes to town. As a result it often seems that, besides those in law enforcement, only the criminals have guns. And lots of them.

"There's always guns around," Roland Ellis told police. "I've been living there for seventeen years [and] there's never a day where there was no gun in Galloway."

He and his fellow gang members even gave their guns nicknames. Ellis once posed for a picture with a revolver he called Little Breezy. Riley's pet name for his .40-calibre Glock was Faughty. He liked to brandish it before rival gang members, or even his friends.

Once, Riley fired his gun, for no apparent reason, near a basketball court where kids were playing. "I don't know why he did it,"

Ellis said. "He could have been mad, he could have been happy, sad, I don't know." On another occasion, Ellis recalled arriving at King Turbo, the recording studio where they went to make rap music. Riley was already there standing at the front door with a firearm, smiling, Ellis recalled.

The G-Way guys used street slang—burners, toast, piece, straps and strizzy man—to describe their guns. G-Locks were Glocks, Neen was a nine millimetre, Maggie was a .357 Magnum. Bullets were grains, teeth, shells or slugs. "Lick you down" meant to shoot someone.

(Gang members in Malvern also had their own slang for weaponry. Candy was ammunition, G-17 a Glock, Ninos a nine-millimetre handgun. To "roll heavy" meant being armed.)

Along with the communal parlance in Galloway was the practice of sharing firearms among gang members and storing them in a central location so they were easily accessible, and hidden from police. One such place was in a townhouse belonging to a gang associate in the complex where Ellis lived. In the basement was a clothes hamper where gang members hid their guns.

Gary Reid, who made no secret of the fact he was a "criminal," told police in 2005: "Every street kid has a burner." (In March 2010, Reid, 35, was arrested on gun possession charges in his old stomping ground of Jane and Driftwood.)

Back in 2005, he told police most street kids don't know how to handle firearms properly and could benefit from target practice.

"Four-five [.45 calibre] has too much kick for them. They think it's a movie, the wild, wild, west or something. You just point and squeeze. They don't understand that every bullet has a different projectile and some curve to the right, some curve to the left. That's why you officers go and train downstairs with your own firearm to know where your bullets go when you fire them."

Toronto police noted the "inextricable link between gangs, guns and drugs," in a 2004 report prepared for its civilian oversight board. "These individuals use illegal firearms as their source of power, whether it is to establish or maintain their criminal enterprise or to resolve disputes with others."

The following year was a watershed that made civic boosters cringe. In 2005, firearms were responsible for fifty-two of Toronto's seventy-nine homicides, far more than ever before. Media proclaimed it "The Year of the Gun." In response, illegal guns rose to the top of the political and police agenda. Vote-hungry politicians jumped on the tough-on-crime bandwagon. There were promises to increase prison sentences for crimes committed with firearms. Crown attorneys were designated as specialists in prosecuting such offences. Gun amnesties were established. The Toronto Raptors offered free basketball tickets to anyone who surrendered a weapon. (A few did.)

The U.S. Bureau of Alcohol, Tobacco, Firearms and Explosives (ATF) opened an office in Toronto to coordinate with local authorities. For the next five years, that office was staffed by one person.

None of the measures quieted the gunfire.

"There are two main sources of illegal firearms that are turning up on the streets of Toronto—smuggled firearms from the United States and firearms lawfully in Canada but illegally diverted for use as crime guns," the 2004 police report said.

At the time, police said members of the Malvern Crew and G-Way turned to both sources for firepower in their ongoing conflict. In some cases, gangsters followed legal gun owners home from target ranges and later broke into their houses. In others, weapons made their way north across the border, stashed in big transport rigs or even mixed in with the belongings of returning snowbirds.

As the Malvern-Galloway war heated up, three improbable people—all apparently respectable members of white society—became entangled in the warfare between black gangs. They included a former firearms instructor in his early 70s; a down-on-his-luck retiree and sometime blues performer who lived in Barrie, Ontario; and a twenty-something woman, a college graduate, described in court documents as "dependable, reliable and sincere."

An Unwitting Source

Mike Hargreaves, who once taught police officers how to shoot, stored his $40,000 weapons collection in an 800-kilogram concrete and steel safe in a seventeenth-floor apartment he rented—but didn't live in—at 31 Gilder Drive in Scarborough. (Investigators were stunned to learn that kind of firepower had been stored in a government-subsidized apartment in an area rife with gang violence.)

Over the Christmas holidays in 2003, Hargreaves was visiting his son in Orlando, Florida. That's when police believe his apartment, No. 1707, was broken into by thieves, armed with sledgehammers and blowtorches, who had lowered themselves from a balcony above. Apparently, such daredevil criminal acts were not uncommon at 31 Gilder. Neighbours recalled hearing a loud thud coming from 1707 but no one called police. The thieves made off with about thirty-five guns, including military assault rifles, machine guns, semi-automatic pistols, a bullet-pressing machine and dozens of rounds of ammunition.

"I'm shattered to know that my guns are out there being used by people with no training and no morals," Hargreaves, a white-haired, bearded former bouncer in his native Britain, told me in his modest, two-storey stucco home in Orlando.

The high-rise on Gilder was well known to police and in early 2004 they received a tip that an illegal handgun had been seen in an apartment. Officers went to the unit, which turned out to be a crack den, a floor above Hargreaves' cache. Police found a Beretta semi-automatic handgun they traced to Hargreaves. (All of his weapons were properly registered, Hargreaves said.) After contacting Hargreaves in Florida and getting permission to enter apartment 1707, police found the large gun vault open, scorched and empty.

In April 2005, along with all the other charges against the Galloway gang, Philip Atkins was slapped with a burglary rap in connection with the theft of Hargreaves' arsenal. The evidence rested on some grainy surveillance footage, allegedly of Atkins, at 31 Gilder. While that charge was later dropped, police still believed Atkins, and perhaps Riley, broke into Hargreaves' safe and used those guns to commit various crimes. In fact, Toronto police chief Bill Blair later told a Senate justice committee in Ottawa: "Nine of those handguns were subsequently used in murders in the city." He went on to suggest, without citing any evidence, that the stolen arsenal helped tip "the balance of power" for the Galloway Boys against the Malvern Crew.

"By the time we were done, there were a dozen killed, and several dozen people have been shot."

An Unwitting Gun-Runner

At about the same time as the break-in at 31 Gilder, the Malvern Crew was stockpiling weapons for the war with Galloway. "Guns and drugs were sold and delivered to members of the Malvern Crew, who sold them on the street or used them to commit other offences in Malvern," court documents said. "They protected their territory from rivals, such as the Galloway Boys, by intimidation, threats, assaults and homicides."

Unable to access a safe full of weapons, the Malvern Crew acquired most of its munitions through the tried-and-true method of cross-border smuggling—selling drugs in the United States in exchange for cash to buy guns legally or otherwise. And, besides sending its own people across the border, they recruited two unlikely gun-runners: a depressed, white-haired widower from Barrie, Ontario, and an academically high-achieving young woman who managed a fitness facility and had previously worked as a supervisor for the Children's Aid Society in Hamilton.

John Butcher, a native of England, was an amateur blues singer who performed under the name Rockin' Johnie B. He had lost his job as a financial planner and all of his retirement savings while caring for his wife, Iris, who had multiple sclerosis. She died in 2001. He was out of work and money when he was approached in a Barrie pub by a man he didn't know—later identified as an associate of the Malvern Crew.

They worked out a deal. Butcher would drive across the border, go to a specific bar—in Buffalo, Niagara Falls, New York, or Detroit—and wait to be contacted. He would be paid a couple of hundred dollars for his effort. He apparently asked few questions about the purpose of such trips. He made his first of about ten cross-border runs, in his 1991 Pontiac Sunbird, to Niagara Falls in December 2002.

His last trip was on March 22, 2004. It was just after 8 p.m. when Butcher drove his Sunbird through the tunnel connecting Detroit to Windsor. He was pulled over by Canadian customs officers, who searched the car. They discovered twenty-three guns, including semi-automatic handguns, in the wheel well of the trunk. Butcher was arrested and charged with numerous counts of conspiracy to import firearms.

When Butcher pleaded guilty in 2006, the court recognized he had been guilty of "wilful blindness," that he did not know of the lethal cargo in his car. It was suspected that a woman who approached him in a bar in Detroit swiped his keys and that an accomplice secreted the guns in the trunk before Butcher returned to the car for the trip home.

At his sentencing, Butcher, then 62, said he was appalled to learn he was responsible for handguns making their way into the hands of teenagers on the streets of Scarborough.

Had he known "those obscenities" were in his car, he said, they would have been "at the bottom of the Detroit River."

He threw himself "on the mercy of this court," was sentenced to two-and-a-half years in prison, but served only four months, because he had been in custody since his arrest.

Gun-Running for Love

Sara Villella, however, was no unwitting mule. Young and pretty, the former honours student from Hamilton was the girlfriend of a man involved in gun-running for the Malvern Crew. She was also in Detroit the day Butcher was arrested—and may have been the woman who approached him in the bar.

She too was pulled over by Canada Customs, and subjected to a strip search. In Villella's yellow bra, officers found notes which detailed the gun-running operation. Villella was later arrested and charged "in connection with the exportation of marijuana into the United States, where it was sold and the proceeds used to purchase firearms, which were then imported into Canada," according to court documents. In 2006, Villella, then 27, was convicted of a number of offences, including conspiring to import firearms, and sentenced to two years in jail.

Of course, there were still a lot of guns on the streets of Toronto. And echoes of years of recent gunfire were being heard at the preliminary hearing in Scarborough.

CHAPTER 18

Wrapped in time for Christmas

One of the most interesting witnesses at the hearing was Gary Reid, Riley's older mentor from the neighbourhood. Riley and Jason Wisdom were charged with attempting to murder Reid and his woman passenger in an SUV in that late-night ambush on December 8, 2003.

Ellis didn't know Reid that well—he was "an older dude" whom he only knew as Pye. But he had told police Reid had been "clapped up in his car," beside a Kingston Road apartment. He called it "a big set up."

"They told everyone from the south side basically not to be out that night because they're gonna do their thing. It just happened they wet up the car but the dude (Reid) was wearing a (bullet-proof) vest so the dude didn't die."

Ellis had also told police Reid knew he was ambushed by Riley and Wisdom and was thinking about getting a worker he knew at The East detention centre to poison Riley's food.

Prosecutors entered the hearing armed with a sworn videotaped statement Reid had given detectives Roger Caracciolo and Darryl Linquist on April 1, 2005.

Reid described how, just before Christmas 2003, he had been at a nightclub with his friend, Neville Badibanga, whom he called Monique.

He was dropping her off at the side of her building when out of the corner of his eye he noticed two shadows approaching his vehicle.

Reid said the shooters were less than a metre away when they started shooting.

"I'm looking right at them and they're squeezing off these shots point-blank at me," he told the officers. The shots blew out the windows in the front and back of the SUV. Reid wasn't hurt, though a bullet went through his trouser pocket and his jacket. (He did not confirm Ellis' contention he was wearing a bullet-proof vest.) Badibanga was struck multiple times in the legs.

Reid said he jumped out of the vehicle as the assailants ran away, before driving Badibanga to the hospital.

"What did you see?" Linquist asked. Reid said he recognized Riley and was told later that the second shooter was Jason Wisdom.

Linquist asked Reid how he was able to identify them.

"In my line you work, at night time, everybody comes out in black," Reid said. "So you obviously get to know a person's build and the way he runs or his walk that makes, you know, that's the person."

Gangsters always wear hoodies to hide their faces, he added.

"So, they don't really get to see too much face at night time ... but the build, the walk, that's what gives you away."

Caracciolo asked him if he saw Riley's face? Reid said no.

"But when you know someone, you know someone," Reid said.

Asked if he'd ever seen Riley with a gun, Reid said "of course."

Just as they had with Ellis, the officers prodded Reid by asking him how it felt to be shot at by Riley. It made him have "butterflies," he said.

Reid went on: "You know how you would feel when you're going out for that test, the big test? That sweat coming in like you're—you've been questioning yourself. You're like, yeah, this is the answer but no I got to check it again.

"I felt lost within myself. I was like yo, this guy shot me, I know it's him but I'm trying to find every other excuse to say it isn't him." After he gave his statement, the detectives took Reid to a roti place and bought him a pack of cigarettes. He "hooped" the pack and was brought back into Maplehurst Correctional Complex.

But at the preliminary hearing, facing Wisdom and Riley, Reid changed his story. It was a shock to prosecutors and foreshadowed things to come—others from the streets of Galloway would also change their tune.

Reid insisted that until the police came to see him, he didn't know who had shot at him. Reid also insisted he had exaggerated because he wanted to "make it sound believable," hoping he'd get a get-out-of-jail-free card. He did admit he had a grudge against Riley, for taking up with Norris Allen's girlfriend, Dana Lee Williams. Reid and Allen had been very close before they brought young Riley into the fold.

At one point, Reid, who had made a recent conversion to Islam, held up the Qur'an. "I'm telling you the truth," he said. To support this assertion, he explained that his beliefs included the doctrine of an eye for an eye, that he would have killed Riley if he thought he was the triggerman. "You beat me up I'm gonna beat you back up; you hit me I'm gonna hit you. I live by the law of Qur'an." (Years later, when their paths crossed in jail, Riley sucker-punched Reid and ran away.)

As the hearing wound down, Judge Robertson called on the lawyers for written submissions on whether the cases should go to trial. Defence lawyers argued the evidence from Ellis—and to a lesser degree Wilson—was entirely hearsay, unsupported opinion. The Crown, of course, said it had made its case. On December 18, 2006, after sixteen months of arguments, delays and tense testimony, the judge announced his ruling.

Riley, by then 24, was subdued as Robertson committed him to stand trial on thirty-nine charges, ranging from robbery and weapons offences to conspiring to obstruct justice and three counts of first-degree murder: for the shooting deaths of Malvern crack dealer Eric Mutiisa and the two innocents, Omar Hortley and Brenton Charlton. Riley was also ordered to stand trial on three counts of attempted murder. The judge also sent Riley to trial on charges he "instructed others to commit indictable offences for the benefit of a criminal organization," as well as for committing first-degree murder for the benefit of a criminal organization, the first time a gang member had faced that specific charge.

Atkins and Wisdom were also committed to trial for the murder of Charlton and the attempted murder of his passenger, Leonard Bell. Atkins was additionally charged with first-degree murder in the death of Omar Hortley. The Crown dropped the charges against Riley and Atkins for attempting to murder Mark Jones, the 15-year-old shot in his driveway in Malvern. Charges in the attempted murder of Reid and Badibanga were also dropped.

The judge said he found Ellis and Wilson to be credible, since they were both in a position to know what was going on in Galloway. "Mr. Ellis and Mr. Wilson both testified extensively as to their experiences as gang members and/or to their association with many of the accused," Robertson wrote. "In some cases, that experience was clearly based on daily contact with some of the accused over an extensive period of time."

While the threshold test for evidence at a preliminary hearing is much lower than at trial, the judge found the phone intercepts had provided "strong evidence of the relationship between the parties, their connections in the carrying out of their criminal activities, and their committing of crime in general." Fourteen others were ordered to stand trial on various lesser charges.

On that December day, just before Christmas, court officers led the handcuffed prisoners out of Courtroom 405 for the last time.

It was a long time coming for Charlton's mother, Valda Williams, who had attended court when she could. It had been a rough year, made worse by some unpleasant confrontations in the Scarborough courthouse, she told me. On one occasion, a mother of one of the accused accosted her in the corridor. "My son didn't kill your son," the woman spat. Recalling the event later caused her eyes to widen. "She didn't know how mad I was. I was willing to die right then and there. But I had Junior in my head telling me 'Mom, let it go.' He wasn't as aggressive as his mother," she explained, with characteristic brio.

What she wanted to say to the woman was: "Yes, we both lost a child in different ways but you can go see your child even if they go to prison for one million years. All I have is his grave."

Over the next year, many of the minor cases were settled. At first, none of the accused had pleaded guilty, a sign, some suggested, of the group's solidarity. But, over time, some copped pleas.

Marie Riley would admit she threatened a witness to protect her son. Having already spent eight months in jail on this charge, she was put on twelve months' probation and ordered to have no weapons or contact with Roland Ellis or Marlon Wilson.

Dana Lee Williams would eventually plead guilty to conspiracy to intimidate a witness and doing so for the benefit of a criminal organization. She spent more than two years in jail, during which she lost her job as a corrections officer at a youth facility just north of Toronto.

It was perhaps inevitable the preliminary hearing, with seventeen co-accused and a battalion of lawyers, had taken more than a year to run its course.

But it would still be years before jurors began to hear the murder case against Riley, Atkins and Wisdom in a trial that would climax in spectacular fashion and raw emotion.

CHAPTER 19

Tuco v. the House of Lords

By the time the case from Scarborough moved to the downtown courthouse in February 2008, all the characters in this legal drama were in place.

Presiding over the proceedings would be Superior Court Justice Michael Dambrot, a former federal Crown attorney before his appointment to the bench in 1996 by the Chrétien government. In his late 50s, of average height and build, Dambrot wore glasses and sported a mop of greying hair and a moustache that, while sitting in court, he played with frequently. Born in Toronto, Dambrot attended Osgoode Hall Law School and was called to the bar in 1974.

As a federal Crown attorney, one of his most memorable cases was the 1984 prosecution of two Toronto police officers. In his opening address to the jury, Dambrot said the pair had been caught red-handed setting up a scheme to import more than a thousand kilograms of marijuana per week into Canada. The plot went south when the officers tried to recruit customs agents at Toronto's Lester B. Pearson International Airport, who went to the RCMP.

"Most people, I think, realize that police are human beings," Dambrot told the court. "Some are honourable and some, perhaps, are not. This case must not become a contest between these two points of view."

The two officers were convicted and sentenced to five years in prison.

Dambrot was running the Justice Department's prosecution office in Toronto when he was transferred to Ottawa in 1988. There he became general counsel for the Competition Bureau, doing anti-trust and price-fixing cases, and then spent three more years with the Department of Justice, part of that time as director of the national strategy for drug prosecutions. He returned to Toronto before rising to the bench.

Dambrot's courtroom demeanour was more relaxed than that of some of his colleagues, as he interjected humorous asides into often dull proceedings and offered dry commentary, even in his rulings. In one instance, he understatedly illustrated how a bank suing its security firm undermined its own argument.

The case involved a security firm employee, whose job was responding to bank alarms, stealing more than $1 million from ATMs in eleven branches. The bank sued the security company, claiming it was liable for its employee's actions. But the judge noted the bank openly displayed a manual with the combinations to the ATMs. Dambrot dismissed the bank's claim, commenting: "I do not need an expert witness to assist me in reaching the conclusion that this practice, which was utterly unnecessary, amounted to negligence on the part of the bank."

Within the Toronto defence bar, Dambrot had a reputation as a judge who would listen to their arguments and ask questions in a friendly, non-confrontational manner. But that didn't stop many from believing his rulings were often pro-Crown. Some even called him the "smiling assassin."

"He's a smart guy but can be patronizing," one defence lawyer, who had appeared before Dambrot, told me.

The suggestion that Dambrot was "Crown-friendly" would surface over the course of the Riley/Atkins/Wisdom murder trial—most often and audibly by Riley's lawyer, David Midanik, who made many references, both in and out of court, about the judge's pedigree as a Crown attorney.

But Dambrot had often taken the Crown to task as well. In 1999, a federal prosecutor threw out the case against an alleged drug trafficker after Dambrot's sternly worded decision ordering the Toronto police to disclose all prior complaint records against officers involved in the case. "The attorney general has asked for the records. The police department has refused to turn them over," he said in his ruling. "This is no mere fishing expedition."

During a 2002 murder trial, Dambrot remarked that the prosecution's case looked "shaky." The second-degree murder charge was ultimately withdrawn. Dambrot had presided over many murder trials by the time he was assigned to the Galloway Boys case.

The married father of two would require all his experience to meet the intellectually rigorous demands of interpreting constitutional arguments in the trial of Riley, Atkins and Wisdom. (He would, over the course of the trial, write twenty-seven rulings that were, piled together, the size of a big-city telephone book.)

But—and perhaps even more challenging—he would have to manage the egos and divergent personalities of the lawyers who would soon be gathered before him.

A Hardliner Heads the Prosecution

Crown attorney Suhail Akhtar came downtown to lead the prosecution team as he had in Scarborough. He had appeared late at the preliminary hearing, after his honeymoon with a fellow prosecutor.

"We needed a senior person in charge who had homicide experience," said his boss, Tony Loparco, head Crown attorney at the Scarborough courthouse. "He was that person. I had confidence in him to conduct that kind of prosecution."

In his mid-40s, Akhtar had been a barrister in England—meaning he had courtroom experience. After moving to Canada, Akhtar was called to the Ontario bar in 1998, and joined the Crown office in Scarborough where he prosecuted many run-of-the-mill suburban cases, with the oddball crime-fetish thrown in. In 2001, he sent away the "Ryerson spanker." The 26-year-old Ryerson journalism student "would, without warning, pull his victims over his knee and spank them," Akhtar told the judge. The "spanker" received a sixteen-month sentence.

Taking over as the lead prosecutor in this mammoth case was a potentially career-making—or breaking—job for the tall, ambitious lawyer, whose imperious and often condescending manner (he was not known as a good listener) rubbed many the wrong way. Some called him "Lord Akhtar."

A frequent panelist at legal symposiums, offering opinions on everything from organized-crime legislation to impaired driving, Akhtar also had a reputation as a hardliner, even to lawyers on his side of the courtroom. He was also known as a man's man, turning up at the Toronto Police Association's controversial Fight Night charity event. In 2006, standing ringside after Crown pugilists beat their police opponents, he told a newspaper reporter: "Don't forget to put that in your story." Akhtar wanted to make sure it was clear the Crowns had triumphed in the boxing ring.

Midanik on Defence

The Crown's main foil in the coming months would be David Midanik, who became Tyshan Riley's lawyer in 2007 after the preliminary hearing.

Midanik looked like an aging hippie. In court and out, he often sounded like a political activist from the 1960s. He would sometimes cut his own grey hair, but never above shoulder length. It tumbled onto his suit jacket. One of the court security officers at the courthouse told me Midanik reminded her of a "pilgrim on the *Mayflower*."

Midanik would have hated the comparison. He was proud of his Jewish heritage and made no secret of his antipathy toward what he called the "WASPish Toronto establishment and conservative criminal defence bar." Midanik often mocked one member of the prosecution team, Scott Childs, saying he spoke like a member of the House of

Lords. At one stage of the proceedings, Childs, in turn, said the trial had become "the world according to Midanik."

Born and raised in Toronto, David Morton Midanik was called to the bar in the late 1970s and for a time practised in Alberta before returning to his hometown.

He also, by his own admission, was someone who didn't work well with others. He said he identified with the character Tuco in director Sergio Leone's 1966 Italian spaghetti western classic, *The Good, the Bad and the Ugly*. Midanik told me the loutish outlaw Tuco (The Ugly) said in the movie: "I like big men because when they fall, they fall hard." (The actual line is: "I like big fat men like you. When they fall they make more noise.") In any event, noise is what Midanik was known for making, prompting Dambrot, in one of his numerous pre-trial rulings, to refer to him, with considerable understatement, as "no shrinking violet."

Midanik, who turned 57 that spring, was also in a less-than-good headspace as the trial got underway, making his sometimes volatile temperament even more so. In mid-January 2008, the former tennis coach had had a hip "re-surfacing" operation, which initially delayed the proceedings. It had been a painful recovery that forced him to use crutches during the early stages of the trial. At times, it seemed as if he needed some R and R on a beach rather than a lengthy court battle.

But he relished a fight. He had successfully defended one of the men accused in the murder of a 23-year-old white woman who was sitting in the trendy Just Desserts restaurant in Toronto's upscale Annex neighbourhood on April 5, 1994, when it was held up by four black men. The victim, Georgina (Vivi) Leimonis, died after being hit at point-blank range by a shotgun blast fired by one of the robbers.

Midanik's client, Emile Mark Jones, walked free before a jury was picked. In giving his reasons for staying the charges, Superior Court Justice Brian Trafford criticized the Crown for basing its case against Jones on testimony from a single "unsavory character," and the police for erring when they took a statement from the witness.

The Just Desserts proceedings would go on to become "a metaphor for everything that can go wrong in a criminal case," the *Globe and Mail* said at the time. Trafford said the delay in bringing the case to trial was "largely explained by the relentless efforts of defence counsel, particularly Mr. Midanik, to scrutinize and attack every component of the administration of justice." Asked by the *Star* in 1998 about the judge's criticism, Midanik said it was unfair, unfounded and that he had been "relentless in the pursuit of his client's interests."

While representing Riley, Midanik remained unrepentant—a word he liked using—and would allude to the Just Desserts case. "Cases like this have a tendency to spin out of control," Midanik told Dambrot in the early days of pre-trial motions. "I don't think any of us want another spectacle of Just Desserts, even if I was an alleged part of that."

If Midanik's approach to advocacy made him unpopular with many colleagues, it made him a hero for others, mainly young black men accused of crimes. (After this trial, he represented one of the young men charged with manslaughter in Jane Creba's murder. The Crown called no evidence and Midanik's client was acquitted before his case got to trial.)

Fighting for the Cause of Wisdom

Not all the lawyers involved in the case had such supersized personalities.

Maurice Mirosolin, who represented Jason Wisdom at the preliminary hearing, was back at his side. One of only two black lawyers involved on the front lines of the case, Mirosolin, who was in his mid-40s, grew up in west-end Toronto but moved to England when he was 27 to study international relations. He changed direction, and went to law school in Britain. He hung up his shingle and practised there for several years while playing semi-pro baseball for the 1999 British champion Brighton Buccaneers. "It sounds more impressive than it really was," he later joked, recalling his time as an outfielder and third baseman in the English seaside town.

He returned to Ontario where he was called to the bar in 2003 and went on to join the well-known Toronto firm of Lockyer, Posner and Campbell, a largely criminal law practice where he represented an assortment of clients. One of his biggest victories was in Kingston, Ontario, where his client was charged with second-degree murder.

At the preliminary hearing, the judge stayed the proceedings against Mirosolin's client, due to a lack of evidence. The charge was "based on hearsay and rumour, nor was there any physical evidence against my client," Mirosolin later explained.

Mirosolin also represented two men whom the Crown sought to have declared dangerous offenders. In both cases, he prevented the designation and the life term that can go with it.

One of his best-known cases occurred between the Galloway gang preliminary hearing and trial, when a judge acquitted a Toronto man of assaulting his girlfriend. The case was in the headlines because she was a pregnant teenager jailed to force her to testify against her boyfriend. She wouldn't, and the charges were dropped.

Prior to representing Jason Wisdom, Mirosolin had represented Wisdom's older brother, Dwight, on a gun possession charge. Mirosolin challenged the cops' version of events and the judge acquitted.

Good-looking and affable, Mirosolin managed, for the most part, to remain on good terms with Midanik, mainly because he went along with almost everything the other defence lawyer said in court. "I adopt Mr. Midanik's motion," he would say time and time again after walking to the podium, facing the judge.

He and Midanik played tennis together—Midanik remained a formidable opponent—but before the trial was over Mirosolin would make a decision that demonstrated just how tenuous the bond was between them.

Initially, the defence team got on well, sometimes socializing after hours. The lawyers would often visit each others' offices in the courthouse—space was provided for them—for friendly post-mortems, sometimes over a beer. But a split in their ranks over trial strategy would become obvious over the course of the trial.

Defending the Third Man

Seated between Midanik and Mirosolin was a genial lawyer named David Berg, hired to represent Philip Atkins on a recommendation of Andy McKay, the former-cop-turned-lawyer at the preliminary hearing.

Born and raised in Montreal and in his mid-50s, Berg had taken anything but the regular route to practising law. After obtaining a doctorate at the University of Toronto in Egyptology in 1987, he did archaeological work in southern Egypt. In the early 1990s, Berg became a probation officer in Canada "due to the fact that there were no academic jobs in my field anywhere that I wanted to live," he told me.

As a probation officer, he had to appear in court on occasion. He decided to apply for law school one day after being cross-examined by a defence lawyer who tried to make him look stupid in front of the judge. Berg, in response, subtly gave it back to the lawyer, making fun of him with his answers. The judge and a police officer assigned to the case caught on but not the defence lawyer. At any rate, it got Berg thinking: "I can do that job."

After he was called to the bar, he gravitated toward clients with mental health issues, who tended to be challenging, sometimes scary and often showed an indifference to personal hygiene. But Berg liked the work because he felt he was doing some good. Berg would have nothing but positive things to say about Atkins, with whom he got on well.

That was more than he would eventually say about Midanik, though Berg was circumspect about their falling out. "As the saying goes, 'a trial is not a tea party' and a murder trial of this kind is a real boot fight. Emotions run high, personalities are writ large."

Mirosolin offered this assessment: "I can't imagine a case with more complicated personalities."

As the proceedings kicked into gear, it would be apparent Midanik and Akhtar were the heavyweights. Throughout the courthouse, there was talk that the stage was set for a clash of gigantic egos.

But, for those wearing their black robes, when the lawyers finally moved inside Courtroom 2-7, the first order of business would be security.

CHAPTER 20

The cuffs come off

Like the preliminary hearing in Scarborough, the courtroom in Toronto became ground zero for the justice system's fight against street gangs. Fear was in the air. And accommodating the defendants without making them look like hoods became a preoccupation.

How do you safely transport Riley, Atkins and Wisdom from Toronto's infamous Don Jail (nicknamed for the nearby Don River) to the courthouse? Where do they sit in the courtroom, where they can't be a threat to the lawyers, judge and spectators? Do the shackles ever come off? Is everyone involved to be surrounded by pistol-packing police officers?

Before the trial began, Justice Ian Nordheimer, in his position as administrative judge for the Toronto court, had visited the Scarborough courthouse to check on the renovations made before the preliminary hearing. He apparently wasn't impressed.

Nordheimer decided he wanted more "invisible" security arrangements "to make sure the accused are treated with the utmost dignity and respect." He didn't want cops with guns in the courtroom, or even seen in the hallway, and preferred the emphasis to be on airport-style screening of all those involved in the proceedings.

As a result of Nordheimer's concerns, a committee was formed to come up with recommendations. A "security plan" was developed and measures adopted for the commencement of the trial.

There would be extensive renovations inside the second-floor courtroom, Number 2-7, one of the largest in the Superior Court building. The three prisoners would be separated by Plexiglas, but nothing like the sealed human containers in Scarborough. Six closed-circuit TV cameras would be installed in the windowless courtroom, permitting the proceedings to be monitored from a nearby room by heavily armed Emergency Task Force officers. (They would never be called into action and the sounds of TV shows and video games could be heard coming from the room.) As well, anyone entering the courtroom through the public door would be scanned with a metal-detector wand, and all briefcases, purses and lawyers' file boxes would be searched for anything that could be used as a weapon or "escape implement." Up to eight unarmed court security officers would be posted inside the court whenever the defendants were present.

The security arrangements would also be extended to the transportation of Riley, Atkins and Wisdom from the jail to the limestone courthouse. The three would be in the usual Court Service's cube truck, but it would be escorted by an armoured car filled with a machine-gun-toting SWAT team. Riley, Atkins and Wisdom would be kept in three separate cells in the basement of the courthouse, apart from other prisoners.

On the first day of pre-trial motions, Riley, then 25, shuffled in wearing what prisoners call a "three-piece suit": a metal chain around his waist attached to shackles around his ankles, and handcuffs. Atkins, also then 25, and Jason Wisdom, 22, came into the courtroom in handcuffs.

As they had done at the preliminary hearing, defence counsel let it be known they weren't happy with the "extraordinary" security measures in and outside the courtroom. The lawyers forcefully argued the security arrangements created an oppressive atmosphere and violated the rights of the accused to a fair trial guaranteed under the

Charter of Rights and Freedoms. How could jurors do anything but conclude the accused were dangerous men if all these precautions were needed? they asked. Judge Dambrot agreed to hear arguments.

One police witness testified the three men were members of a dangerous street gang, with many of their confederates "still active in shootings, homicides and other violent clashes." The officer said the three "had been associated" with threats to witnesses. He also said Riley had twice been found with closed pocket knives concealed in his rectum.

Emma Rhodes, one of Wisdom's lawyers, argued that 2–7 was the only courtroom in the building with a security station outside its doors, something a juror might notice, and that there was no evidence of specific threats and that the concerns of the police were fanciful. She called the security measures overkill. Midanik argued there wasn't a scrap of evidence that anyone was planning an escape attempt.

Sean White, supervisor of security at Superior Court, was among those who took the stand. Midanik asked why Riley was sitting in the box in handcuffs, with a belly chain, his feet in shackles?

"I have fear for everyone's safety around your client," White replied.

"I'm not worried about my safety," Midanik shot back.

Defence lawyers also argued Riley and Atkins should be permitted to wear glasses in the cells at the courthouse. They scoffed at the suggestion their clients might use the arms of the glasses to fashion a weapon and injure someone or themselves.

After five days of arguments and testimony, Dambrot agreed the security arrangements would remain, though an X-ray machine was placed outside the courtroom so court staff would not have to rifle through lawyers' papers. "The security measures here are not an affront to the dignity of the accused at all," the judge wrote. "A juror might infer that the authorities are being cautious of the possibility of someone dangerous entering the courtroom, but little more."

Riley's shackles, however, would come off. He and Atkins would be permitted to wear glasses in the cells. But security was just the first in a long list of issues raised during more than a year of pre-trial arguments.

Arguing About Arguments

When the lawyers gathered for the first time on February 19, 2008, Dambrot joked: "I'm occupied for the next four to 4,000 months." At times, during pre-trial motions, it seemed he might not be far off.

Over fourteen months, defence lawyers tried to win arguments on everything from challenging police wiretaps to demanding that the Crown prove the Galloway Boys were part of an identifiable organized-crime group, like the Mafia or the Hells Angels. In almost every instance, the defence lawyers were trying to exclude evidence that would prejudice jurors against their clients and make them look like a bunch of scary black gangsters.

Pre-trial motions are not unusual in murder cases. For some defence lawyers, knocking out as much evidence as possible is an essential part of their strategy.

With the security motions out of the way, the lawyers got down to the legal wrangling.

In the matter of whether jurors would hear evidence that Galloway was an organized gang, the Crown argued it was important and necessary for the jury to understand the motive behind the shootings of Brenton Charlton and Leonard Bell, that it was the reckless consequence of a gang war. Midanik was adamant that the defence should never concede a gang even existed. In the end, the judge ruled that the Crown could adduce its gang evidence. Midanik took this as a sign the judge was pro-Crown. "There's not a lot of evidence on the homicide— that's why Dambrot let all of this gang stuff in," the lawyer told me.

While it was obvious to anyone listening to police wiretaps that the Galloway Boys considered themselves gang members, the exclusion of some of this wiretap evidence was where the defence won its one and only major victory. It all went back to police being allowed to obtain warrantless emergency wiretap powers under Section 184.4 of the Criminal Code, to the time when detectives wrestled with the dilemma of simply arresting Riley for violating bail conditions and potentially blowing their murder case.

Dambrot concluded that by intercepting the private communications of Riley and Atkins, police had violated their rights under Section 8 of the Charter that provides for people in Canada to be secure against unreasonable search and seizure. Dambrot found that rather than using 184.4, police should have arrested Riley, despite concerns it would have undermined the murder investigation. "Of course, all things are possible. But it was far more likely that an arrest would have taken Riley off the street for a considerable period of time and so would have been more effective than intercepting his communications in preventing serious harm," Dambrot wrote in a thirty-five-page ruling released on July 21, 2008. While the judge didn't find 184.4 itself unconstitutional, he wrote there were problems with the section that Parliament could fix with some legislative tweaking.

Midanik then brought an application that all the evidence flowing from those warrantless wiretaps be thrown out. The request was "sweeping in scope," Dambrot noted. Midanik was permitted to call evidence to support the motion. For days on end, the lawyer questioned witnesses, almost all of them police officers—sometimes raising his voice, frequently clearing his throat—and made legal arguments as he leaned forward on the wooden lectern, his reading glasses perched on the edge of his nose.

On one occasion, when I needed to attend to some business outside the courtroom, I asked one of the court officers what was taking place inside. "They're arguing about what they're going to argue about," she replied, rolling her eyes.

In the end, the only evidence Dambrot excluded was the $14,330 in cash, two .45-calibre Winchester bullets and hash oil seized in the 2004 police raids, from Dana Lee Williams' apartment. Virtually all the other evidence that stemmed from the wiretaps would be admissible, the judge ruled. Dambrot dismissed virtually every other defence motion.

As the months dragged on, it was easy to forget that three young men were on trial for first-degree murder. They sat slumped in their seats, heads leaning on the Plexiglas as they tried to stay awake.

Wisdom had asked that he be allowed to read in the courtroom. One of his lawyers brought him several books, including Scott Turow's novel *Presumed Innocent* and Truman Capote's true-crime classic *In Cold Blood*.

On March 3, 2009, Leonard Bell, whose name was rarely mentioned during any of the arguments, sent me a text: "At approximately this time, same day, in 2004 I was shot. Brenton died."

But the end of the pre-trial stage was near. Though before a jury could be picked, there was a defence application to challenge prospective jurors "for cause," a common occurrence in murder trials.

The Ontario Court of Appeal opened the door to race-based challenges of prospective jurors in a groundbreaking 1993 ruling known as the Parks decision, saying anti-black racism is a notorious fact that must be confronted. In that case, the accused, Carlton Parks, a former drug dealer charged in a 1988 stabbing death in Toronto, was black. The victim was white. After Parks, it became a routine practice that prospective jurors in Toronto and the surrounding area would be asked whether their view of the case could be shaped by the race of the accused.

Dambrot agreed potential jurors could be asked the following questions.

First, "Would your ability to judge the evidence in the case without bias, prejudice or partiality, be affected by the fact that the persons charged are young black men?"

Second, "There has been some media coverage of this case. Have you read, seen or heard anything about this case in the media, whether in the newspaper, on television or the radio, or on the Internet. You need only answer yes or no to this question." For those who answered yes, there was this follow-up question: "Would your ability to judge the evidence in the case without bias, prejudice or partiality be affected by what you have read, seen or heard?"

And finally: "Would your ability to judge the evidence in the case without bias, prejudice or partiality be affected by what you have read, seen or heard in the media or elsewhere about street gangs?"

From Ballroom to Courtroom

"Good morning, ladies and gentlemen. My name is Michael Dambrot," the judge told prospective jurors on April 17, 2009. Some 600 of them were gathered, not in front of him but seen on two large screens on either side of the courtroom.

"We need a large pool of people and there is no courtroom large enough," Dambrot told them via closed-circuit television.

Jury notices had gone out weeks earlier, instructing prospective jurors to assemble across the street in a drab, grey high-rise that was once a hotel called The Colony, now a University of Toronto dorm and conference centre. The prospective jurors now sat, row upon row in the second-floor Colony Grand Ballroom, a large, windowless room with giant glass chandeliers. Court staff checking in the arrivals had posted signs laying out the ground rules: turn off cell phones; no food, drink, or gum-chewing; no talking while court is in session, even though the actual court was across the street.

The jury pool faced their own large screen, which fed images from three cameras: one showing the judge, another the three defendants, and a wide shot of the courtroom. All 600 of them watched as Riley, Atkins and Wisdom were arraigned. "Not guilty," Riley said three times. Atkins and Wisdom did the same.

Unlike during the proceedings to this point, when the three young men wore their street clothes (hoodies and other sweatshirts, baggy jeans and prison-issue running shoes), they were dressed up for court. Riley wore a blue-and-white-striped shirt; Atkins, a white sleeveless sweater-vest over a striped shirt; and Wisdom, a grey button-down oxford cloth shirt. They looked like preppy college students.

Dambrot introduced the lawyers, beginning with the Crown. Akhtar stood up, walked to the front of the court, and turned to face the camera. "Good morning," he said with a slight smile. One by one, counsel followed, making the proceedings feel more like a school play or the opening of a TV variety show.

Dambrot had told those gathered across the street that no jurors would be picked that day and that the process could take weeks. He also warned that the trial itself could last several months, well into the summer, which prompted a collective murmur in the ballroom. With that, the court clerk reached into a wooden drum and started pulling names. There were teachers, lab technicians, social workers, hair stylists, salespeople, secretaries and one croupier. During a break that day, I visited with Atkins' lawyer, David Berg, in his temporary office around the corner from the courtroom. Berg dismissed the notion that jury selection is a "science," the idea that a favourable panel can be somehow pre-ordained, like in a John Grisham novel. Berg did, however, request an advance list of the jury pool with postal codes, with an eye toward excluding those from Galloway and Malvern. "If they live there, I don't think I want them. It was very, very close to home. Why deal with that issue if you don't have to? They remember that time on an emotional level."

Mirosolin, sitting nearby, said it's "folly" to assume black defendants are more likely to "get a break" from jurors of colour. "Black people are just as alarmed as everyone else with gun violence," he said. "And the community that feels this [gang violence] more than any other is black."

Jury selection went faster than expected; it took only a week. The twelve picked were a technician, a retired librarian, and working librarian, an assistant manager, retired professor, social worker, personal support worker, operation technologist, telecommunications supervisor, technical support worker, historian and bank analyst. Two were black: one woman in her 20s and another in her late 50s. The jurors were told to return to court after the weekend for the Crown's opening address on May 4.

But there was some court business going on without them. Midanik had brought an application to have Riley released from segregation at the Toronto Don Jail and let back into the "general population" of about 600 inmates. Another judge, Justice Harriet Sachs, would hear arguments in the same downtown courthouse.

Since January 23, more than three months earlier, Riley had been locked in a tiny cell at the Don Jail for twenty-three hours a day. No TV, no radio, no interaction with other prisoners.

"I'm not comfortable releasing him," Jim Aspiodis, acting deputy superintendent at the jail, testified during a day-long hearing. While there was no specific incident of misconduct—not one that could be proven, anyway—the primary concern was Riley's ability to "influence, incite and direct inmates not to eat, to throw food," he said. As a member of a "security threat group," Aspiodis noted there were limited places where Riley could be put. But he conceded the proper procedures had not been followed to keep Riley in "the hole," as inmates call segregation.

The lone spectator in court that day was Riley's father, Wondez East, upset that his son had been locked up in a "dungeon." "I love my son and want to support him," he told me during a break. Sachs ruled Riley be released from segregation. What Sachs didn't hear was that jail staff suspected Riley had severely beaten a member of the Malvern Crew who was in jail on firearms charges. No charges were ever laid.

On the eve of the trial, Valda Williams was filled with emotion. "A fresh wound has opened," she told me after meeting with Crown attorneys. It had been five years since her only son was killed, the motive as perplexing and bewildering as ever. Now a full-time nurse working at a retirement home, she had booked off the month of May to attend court. "I have to be there—otherwise who is going to be there for him?"

CHAPTER 21

Roland Ellis makes a grand entrance

May 4, 2009, was a bright Monday morning and the courtroom was packed.

Dana Lee Williams brought her two girls to attend her boyfriend's trial, evidently pulling them out of school. Pretty and well-behaved, their hair was swept up in buns and they wore tiny gold hoop earrings. Sitting behind them was Riley's father, his wife and their young son. Scattered throughout the spectator benches were other friends and family of the accused, including one of Riley's brothers wearing an Obama T-shirt. The Crown was ready to open its case.

Journalists from the city's major news outlets were in court, though media interest would soon taper off considerably. It was tough to sustain headlines when the victims were black men gunned down in a high-crime neighbourhood, not a pretty white girl killed on a busy Toronto street.

(Ten days earlier, a 21-year-old named Jorrell Simpson-Rowe was the first person sentenced—to a minimum seven-year term—in the Boxing Day 2005 shooting death of Jane Creba. In handing down the sentence, Justice Ian Nordheimer said: "The events of Boxing Day 2005 have become a seminal event in the history of the City of Toronto—a touchstone against which all subsequent events of gun violence in this city are measured.")

It was in this environment that Justice Dambrot opened the trial of Riley, Atkins and Wisdom. "You're going to hear a lot about street gangs, violence and guns," Dambrot told jurors once they had taken their seats. But, he cautioned, the defendants were being tried for murder, "not being tried for their lifestyle or any other conduct you hear in the course of the trial." Before turning things over to the Crown, Dambrot added the usual caution a judge makes to jurors: "Please keep an open mind."

With that, Akhtar carried a black binder to the podium and, with a short introduction of his co-counsel, began his opening address—a preview of what was to come.

"What's this case about? It's about two gangs in Scarborough," he told jurors. Riley, Atkins and Wisdom belonged to one of those gangs, which set out to avenge the death of a respected leader, Norris Allen, whom they believed was killed by rivals from Malvern. In fact, Akhtar noted, the victims—Charlton and Bell—were innocent men gunned down in a case of mistaken identity.

"It is the ride squad that forms the backdrop to the offences that you're going to hear about and decide," Akhtar said. "You see, members of the jury, the Crown alleges that what happened on March 3, 2004, was a ride squad mission involving Mr. Riley, Mr. Atkins and Mr. Wisdom, a mission whose objective was to kill another rival gang member," he said. "They thought, mistakenly, that [Charlton's] Neon contained a member of the rival Malvern gang, a man they called Ross P."

He previewed the Crown's case, occasionally waving his right arm for emphasis. Jurors would hear from two witnesses affiliated with the gang, Roland Ellis and Marlon Wilson, about what they saw and heard the night of the shooting. And there would be wiretap evidence played during the course of the trial. One series of calls would involve Riley and two others discussing how to conceal a firearm, Akhtar said.

"The Crown alleges that the conversation is about one of the guns used in the shooting of Mr. Charlton and Mr. Bell: a Glock .357." He added: "DNA tests conducted on the gun revealed the presence of DNA of Marlon Wilson and Philip Atkins."

There would be other wiretap evidence to demonstrate the existence of a criminal organization, Akhtar said. "Crown's case is a jigsaw puzzle with many, many parts, and I would ask you to be patient in receiving those pieces and to listen to all the evidence carefully," he said in conclusion.

The Crown called its first witness. Leonard Bell, wearing beige trousers and matching shirt, a trim beard and glasses, walked slowly to the witness box and took his seat. Bell, who was now 48, described himself as a self-employed renovation contractor. He was married and had seven children and nine grandchildren. He had never been in trouble with the law.

Crown attorney Lesley Pasquino asked what happened on March 3, 2004.

"I was shot in a drive-by shooting," he said, almost matter-of-factly. He had been hit eight times.

"How is your health?" she asked.

"Not too bad," he said. He said he had "little episodes," which included respiratory problems and numbness in one leg.

She asked what he remembered about the day he was shot.

That afternoon, Bell said, he was doing some renovation work at the house of a friend, Valda Williams, when her son, Brenton Charlton, asked him to come along for a drive to a mall. They stopped at Bell's apartment before continuing north to the mall and visiting a bank, then headed home. They were driving southbound on Neilson Road "when Junior, as I called him, applied the brakes on the amber before it turned red," Bell testified. He said he teased his friend, "You could have gone through the amber."

And then came the explosions. He described how he had pitched forward and saw Charlton jump out of the car. "At this point, I realized it was gunshots." He described pulling the handbrake to stop the Neon from rolling forward, and feeling a burning in the centre of his back. "I couldn't move," Bell said.

"Did you see who shot you, sir?" Pasquino asked.

"No, I did not."

"Were you able to tell us how many shots were fired?"

"I couldn't say; it happened too rapidly."

After a break for lunch, Pasquino used an overhead projector—lawyers call it an "Elmo," because it's made by Elmo Company Limited—showing Bell still photos taken from surveillance cameras at a factory north of the intersection minutes before the shooting. The Crown said the photographs showed three vehicles, the first a Neon, followed by a Pathfinder and a Chevrolet Impala, which the Crown would later tie to the case. Pasquino asked Bell to identify the first vehicle. The image lacked definition and neither the driver nor any occupants could be identified.

Bell said, with some assurance, it was the Neon he had been riding in. Others identified the images as a Pathfinder and Impala.

Once finished answering questions from the prosecutor, Bell faced Midanik, whose first questions would be fuzzy, but soon come into focus.

"Good afternoon," the lawyer said. "I take it you didn't have dreads on March 3?"

Bell did not.

"What was the length of Charlton's hair?" Midanik asked.

"Short."

"Pretty hard to mistake you for a Rasta-man," the lawyer said.

Wasting no time, Midanik was trying to undercut the Crown's theory that his client had shadowed the wrong target. Ross P, whose name was Alton Reid, had dreadlocks and was sometimes referred to as the "Dred." How could anyone confuse these two older clean-cut men, dressed in casual clothing, with gang members?

(Police knew Alton Reid as a leading member of the Malvern Crew who had been in and out of jail for drugs and firearms offences. He disputed his gang involvement, telling me in early 2008: "Police target people because of where they live." Reid said he didn't drive a Neon, and that he and Riley got on fine when they were in the same range in jail. He did, however, refer to Marlon Wilson as "a rat.")

Neither Berg nor Mirosolin had any questions for Bell, who left the stand and would not return again to the courtroom during the trial.

An Insider Takes the Stand

It was soon time for the Crown's star witness to take the stand. But his entrance would be elaborately choreographed and out of sight of the jury, an extraordinary practice since witnesses usually come in the front door—not the back.

"Make sure the jury is in the room with the door shut," Dambrot instructed court staff.

Moments later, the same door the judge used to enter the courtroom opened. A police officer wearing a bullet-proof vest came in and scanned the courtroom, the way Secret Service agents would before a U.S. president shows himself in public. She was followed by Roland Ellis, who wore a lime green dress shirt and dark trousers. Lanky and broad-shouldered, Ellis looked even taller than his six-foot-four as he passed in front of Dambrot and took the stand.

It had been three years since Ellis was kicked out of witness protection, but he continued to live outside Toronto at an undisclosed location, where he now worked and paid income taxes. But while testifying, Toronto police were looking out for him, putting him up in a hotel and escorting him to and from court.

Ellis was already in place when the jury entered. He fixed his gaze either down or straight ahead, nowhere near the three young men who appeared agitated in the prisoners' box. Atkins was rocking back and forth. Riley puffed up his cheeks, blew a blast of air and didn't look at Ellis. Wisdom wore a grim expression and kept his head down.

Glancing at the jury, Ellis swore on the Bible that he would tell the truth. The Crown was confident he would be a strong and persuasive witness, despite the fact he had once sold crack and been enamoured with guns and gangbanging. It was still the early days—just Day 2 of the trial—and prosecutors knew they still had jurors' full attention.

Akhtar began by asking Ellis some biographical information. He was now 26, had lived in Galloway for most of his life, and had a KG tattoo—signifying Kingston Galloway. The prosecutor then asked Ellis about his criminal record, a pre-emptive strike that lawyers on both sides typically make.

In addition to earlier convictions for robbery and failing to comply with probation conditions, Ellis had added to his criminal record since testifying at the preliminary hearing. The previous year he was convicted of trafficking in crack cocaine—he'd sold a rock to an undercover cop—and sentenced to two years' probation. More recently, he had been convicted of drunk driving and spent ten days in jail.

Akhtar moved on to the meat of his case. He was ready to establish Ellis' credibility as someone who knew all the key players in the Galloway gang, particularly the three men on trial. Ellis said he first met Riley when they were in grade 4 or 5, and later, "mutual people in the neighbourhood" introduced him to Atkins. He met Wisdom in high school.

"Now, we talked about a gang that you were a member of, and you say that these people were members of. What is that gang?" Akhtar asked.

"G-Way."

"Does it have any other names?"

"North Side and South Side. Then it got broken down even more. There's many names, G-Way was what we went by, Galloway Boys."

The prosecutor then asked him to define the word "turf" and describe Galloway turf. "If someone called my phone and asked if I'm on turf, I'd tell them: 'Yeah, I'm on South Side.' It just means are you in the area or not."

Akhtar approached Ellis in the witness box and handed him a street map of Scarborough, asking him to put a blue line around the area where the Galloway Boys "operated" and then asked him to delineate the area of Malvern.

"Do you want me to mark the area we had problems with people, or the whole area of Malvern?" Ellis asked.

Akhtar suggested "the area you had problems with."

The street map, which Ellis signed and dated, became Exhibit 13.

After Ellis said he had been the leader of a South Side G-Way group called the Mad Soldiers, Akhtar asked him how many robberies he had committed.

"About fifteen, twenty robberies," he replied.

"And you were caught for two of them?"

"Yes."

"What type of robberies were they?"

"People. Stores."

"And what sort of money were you making with these robberies?"

"Probably like anywhere from $2,000 to $5,000 off each one."

In total, Ellis testified, his robbery career netted "no more than 30 grand."

Before the day was out, Akhtar touched on the heart of the Crown's case, asking Ellis about the beef between Malvern and Galloway, the death of Norris Allen, and the formation of the Throwbacks to take revenge.

Finally, Akhtar told Ellis he would play some recordings and ask him to listen carefully "to see if you can identify with them." His ability to identify Riley and others would help corroborate the Crown's evidence on the tapes. After a series of calls were heard in the courtroom, most of them impossible to understand, the judge interrupted to say he wanted to explain to the jury what this "tedious" process was about. "Don't worry about the fact that it doesn't make a huge amount of sense to you right now," he advised.

Ellis came to court the next day wearing a blue striped shirt and black pants. He lowered the microphone, clasped his hands and kept his eyes down before the jury came into court.

It was another day of listening to wiretaps, and again, none of the conversations seemed to have anything to do with the shooting of Charlton and Bell. The judge concluded that 75 per cent of the wiretaps were "incomprehensible," though he said he understood the exercise was "voice identification."

One spectator seemed to hear the evidence more clearly than others. Riley's mom, Marie, had arrived in court that afternoon wearing a yellow-plaid jacket and long false eyelashes. She'd walked over from the nearby take-out restaurant where she worked, but left court abruptly after hearing her son's voice on the wiretaps.

With a couple of exceptions, Ellis identified all the voices played in court. Once the tapes stopped rolling, Ellis began to reveal the secrets of the gang culture to jurors and a public that had been unaware of his previous testimony or statements to police. For the first time,

Torontonians heard about the roots of the gang war in Scarborough, and the campaign of vengeance unleashed after Norris Allen's murder.

"We didn't know exactly who did it, just that people from Malvern did it," Ellis testified. "We didn't like them, they didn't like us." He called Riley the brainchild of the violent response to Allen's death. "They call it 'the ride.' They go up to Malvern and look for anybody who looks like they're gangbanging or associated with gangbangers ... and if you looked a certain way, then basically you were a target."

Ellis also described how his relationship with Riley had fallen off the rails, giving the jury some indication of how he came to be in the witness box testifying against his childhood friends.

Watching it all was Charlton's mother, Valda Williams, dressed in a bright, sunshine yellow caftan and matching headwear, who had just toughed out another Mother's Day. "Roland isn't making it up," she told me. Throughout the trial, she would come into court, smiling and greeting everyone who crossed her path, including defence lawyers and the mothers of the young men accused of killing her son.

For the Crown, Ellis came across as credible and confident. "He's the politest, nicest crack dealer you'll ever know," Pasquino told me one day on her way into court. "It's a tragedy he's not working as a community leader."

But defence lawyers, obviously, had a different take. Midanik told me he believed Ellis was a "pathological liar" who had been "woodshedded"—carefully scripted by prosecutors. David Berg called Ellis "glib." Andy McKay, Atkins' lawyer at the preliminary hearing, sat in on the trial one afternoon. His assessment of Ellis? "A dope-smoking fiend liar, but a good witness."

Of course, defence lawyers, in their zeal to win, often overlook just how effective—and believable—a witness can be to the regular folks sitting in the jury box. It would be the defence's mission to discredit Ellis.

Initially, though, Midanik's line of questioning seemed to accomplish little.

"When did you do your first robbery?"

"I was 17."

"And you started by doing—stealing jackets and stuff like that with fake guns?"

"Yes."

"Do you remember the name of your first victim?"

"No, I do not."

"Do you remember the face of your first victim?"

"No, I do not."

"When you are perusing your Bible did you consider the effect, what you did, had on your victim?"

After Akhtar objected, Dambrot told Midanik he didn't understand the question. Was the lawyer asking: "When he looks at the Bible does he think about his victims? When he looks at his Bible when? Do you mean when he takes the oath? I don't understand what you mean."

"At any time when he reads his Bible, just generally, I want to know if he thinks about his victims—his victim," Midanik said.

Ellis then responded. "At the time I was committing the robberies I was not into the Bible. Later on I got into the Bible, sir."

Midanik continued to ask him questions about the "fifteen to twenty" robberies he had committed. "How many stores did you rob?"

"Two." The rest, Ellis said, were "mainly weed dealers, drug dealers."

Midanik did his best to undermine Ellis' credibility—mocking his new-found "morality" about drugs. "You're aware of the effects that crack cocaine has on people?" Midanik asked.

"Yes, I do. Now I do, yeah."

"Now you do?"

"Yes, I do."

"You didn't for the—you've been dealing crack cocaine since you were, what, 17?"

"Yes."

"And you're saying now you know the effects?"

Midanik continued, "Why did you sell crack cocaine?"

"To get money is the only way. That was how—that was how I grew up, sir. I was selling drugs from when I was a kid, when I was 17. I knew that was a way to make money. And it's just what I do. It's the last resort thing, sir."

Midanik moved on to Ellis' "love affair" with guns. The lawyer snidely asked if Ellis had complied with the government's registration program. He hadn't.

Midanik also tried to suggest Ellis had exaggerated his fear of Riley's death threats, that he needed a handgun and bullet-proof vest "to protect yourself from big, bad Mr. Riley." That was the kind of sarcasm that prompted a reprimand from the judge, who called it "editorial comments."

Midanik also peppered Ellis with questions about his life since leaving witness protection. What happened to get him kicked out of the program? Midanik asked.

"I breached security," Ellis answered. He had allowed someone from the Galloway neighbourhood to stay with him at his new secret location—in strict violation of the program's rules.

And why had he resumed drug dealing?

Ellis said it was either that or become a "homeless person." He had run out of money, and couldn't find a job. "I did what I had to do to survive, sir."

He had never used crack, the jury heard, though he liked to smoke pot. Ellis ended most of his answers with "sir." Midanik sometimes responded in kind.

Early on, the lawyer got nowhere with Ellis. But Midanik would eventually score some points. When Ellis gave his first statement to police he said he saw Riley in an SUV but later specified it was a Pathfinder. "I'm suggesting, sir, that you made that up," Midanik said.

"No, I did not."

Midanik also questioned Ellis' account of Riley's reaction to a TV newscast the night of the shooting of Charlton and Bell. Ellis had suggested Riley, in front of a group of friends, was upset he picked the wrong targets. "It's a blatant lie where you say that . . . Riley said these things watching the television on March 3, 2004," Midanik thundered. Ellis stood his ground.

Midanik asked Ellis about the level of organization of gangs in Galloway.

"It wasn't like a mafia, or anything like that," Ellis said.

"When people dealt drugs everybody basically made their own arrangements and kept their own money," the lawyer said. "Isn't that correct?"

"Yes, sir."

"And if people did a robbery or grime, the people who participated are the only people who would get anything out of it. Isn't that right?"

"Sometimes. Majority of the time, yes."

"So, like, did you ever watch *The Sopranos*?"

"No, sir."

A few questions later. "There's not a clubhouse like Buddabing," Midanik said, referring to the strip club in the acclaimed TV series.

"So there's no structure?"

"Not really," Ellis replied.

Midanik pushed the point, asking Ellis if there were joint bank accounts, letterhead, business cards, board of directors or blood oaths. "Did you take a knife and cut yourself and mingle blood and all that stuff?"

No, a straight-faced Ellis replied, but "there were tattoos for the gangs."

"So the only requirement really is that you grew up in the neighbourhood and knew some of the other guys?"

Ellis agreed.

"In fact," Midanik pressed, "these so-called gangs were really just a bunch of kids who grew up together who became criminals?"

"Yes, sir."

As he wound down his cross-examination, Midanik questioned Ellis about this "animosity towards Mr. Riley." Ellis repeated what he had said before, when he was asked about his refusal to accept blame for some charges laid against Riley. "Yeah, like he treats me like a piece of shit anyway, so why am I doing it when he has other people who are closer to him that could do it. So if you want to say there's animosity, you could say there's animosity. But I never had no animosity towards him personally."

Midanik ended by suggesting Ellis had made up seeing Riley in a Pathfinder on March 3, 2004.

"Sir, that is not correct," Ellis replied.

David Berg, the lawyer for Philip Atkins, zoomed in on a gun his client allegedly displayed on the night of the shooting of Charlton and Bell. Ellis had testified Atkins was trying to ditch a .357 Glock because the police were looking for him and the gun. But Berg reminded Ellis that he had never mentioned this in all previous statements.

"You did not ever mention that Mr. Atkins had said he didn't want to have that firearm anymore because he thought that the police were looking for him with that firearm, or any words resembling that idea. Would you agree with me that you did not so testify at the prelim?"

"I believe I did, sir."

After referring to transcripts of his preliminary hearing testimony, Ellis agreed they showed he did not mention police were looking for the firearm. But, he said, he had told police. After some back and forth—with Ellis insisting he told the cops—the former gangbanger and defence lawyer were at a stalemate.

"Mr. Ellis, this isn't a question like what colour of shoes were you wearing," Berg said. "This is the central point of the whole matter."

Ellis said he was certain he had mentioned it before, though he couldn't pinpoint when or to whom.

"I'm going to suggest to you, sir," Berg said, "you made that up today, you made up the words that my client said, [that] he did not want to have that firearm anymore because he thought that the police were looking for him with that firearm." Berg insisted Ellis bent the truth to help the Crown's case. But the witness did not break.

Maurice Mirosolin, Wisdom's lawyer, was next to try to pick apart Ellis' most damning evidence. Mirosolin focused on his client's alleged confession and Ellis' assertion that he saw the three defendants in a Pathfinder the night of the shootings.

Ellis had testified that on the night of March 3, 2004, he saw a dark, two-door Pathfinder at the bottom of an alleyway off Kingston Road, where gang members often hung out and sold drugs. Riley, Atkins and Wisdom were in the SUV, Ellis said.

"At no time during your statement to police on February 22, 2005, did you ever say that you saw my client in a Pathfinder [on March 3, 2004]. You remember that, yes?" Mirosolin asked.

"I told them that I seen him in the Jeep, yes."

"And I'm going to suggest to you that you never mentioned seeing my client in a Jeep on February 22, 2005."

"I believe I did, sir."

Mirosolin got Ellis to admit that the first time he spoke to police he didn't mention seeing anybody in a Jeep or Pathfinder on the night of the shooting. "I was withholding information at the time, sir," Ellis replied. "I wasn't fully—like I didn't fully explain everything to the officers at the time of the interview. Throughout the interview I was withholding information from the officers, sir."

Turning to Wisdom's purported confession at Smokey's, Mirosolin suggested Ellis had "taken a rumour" and portrayed it as a statement by his client. "Isn't that the case, Mr. Ellis?"

"No, it's not true."

"My client wasn't at Maxeen McPherson's on March 3, 2004. Isn't that correct, sir?"

"Yes, he was."

Mirosolin managed to trip up Ellis on who was in the room at the time, getting on the record that one of them, Damian Walton (a.k.a. Burns), was in Florida and an other man in jail. It was impossible to know what effect such inconsistencies would have on Ellis' credibility with the jury. The Crown would later call such discrepancies a "red herring" and say they were "peripheral" to the murder of Charlton and attempted murder of Bell.

Mirosolin suggested to Ellis he had a clear motive for testifying against his client: They had a conflict over the sale of drugs. Ellis denied that.

After several days of cross-examination, Ellis appeared exasperated, exhaling and shaking his head in disbelief. "I'm not here to lie or make up stories. I'm here to tell the truth to the best of my abilities," he said at one point.

The next Crown witness would not be in court to tell "the truth" or say much of anything, turning the next scene in the trial into a comic opera with a female prosecutor playing Marlon Wilson's part.

CHAPTER 22

Is the sky blue? Mum's the word

"I suspect Mr. Wilson will not be an easy witness for the Crown," the judge presciently predicted before the jury was brought in to hear his testimony.

Marlon Wilson, now 29, bounded into the courtroom, seemingly confident about what he was about to do. He looked nothing like the man in a T-shirt and baggy pants and closely cropped hair whom Burks and Linquist had interviewed in a Vancouver police station three years earlier. His black hair had grown in and he was sporting a moustache and beard. He was also wearing glasses and a pale blue button-down shirt.

He took the stand but quickly signalled he was not about to participate in the proceedings.

"Do you . . ." the clerk began before she was cut off.

"I'm not testifying. I'm not even putting my hand on the Bible."

"Pardon me?" Justice Dambrot said.

"I'm not testifying."

"You're required to testify, sir," Dambrot said.

"Well, I'm not gonna."

"You're refusing?"

"I'm not even gonna say my name. I'm not swearin' on no Bible. I'm not answering no questions." The judge quickly cleared the jury from the courtroom.

Crown attorney Maureen Pecknold stood mute while her recalcitrant witness stayed put.

The prosecution lawyers huddled. Dambrot flipped through the Criminal Code. But they were all flummoxed.

The judge asked Wilson: "Didn't you testify at the preliminary for seven days?"

"Yup."

So why not now?

"I'm in a federal penitentiary and I want to make it out of there and I have children on the street," Wilson replied. "I'm not throwing my life away for this."

Even for the seasoned courtroom participants this was a spectacle. Pecknold said to the judge, "I didn't quite see this coming."

But there had been signs that Wilson might clam up.

In spring 2007, while in the Walkerton jail, Wilson had sent two grovelling letters to Riley, written in neat, printed letters.

"Yo Ty," began the first. "I'm sorry I lied [to the police] and got them wound up. Everyday I, think 'bout, me, you, Brub [Atkins]. We all grew together, from when we were kidz, And I let some soft shit come between us.

"It's true, like you said, we had a fam. And I broke it apart. But I'm gonna make sure the truth comes out, and then everybody could live their lives again, ya dig. Even if I have to go to the pen, you niggahs been there 2 long for nothing. I'm sorry, nigga, I know it's probably 2 late to say that shit, but I got 2."

A month later, Wilson sent Riley a second letter, again trying to get back in his good graces. "Yo, Ty, what's good, nigga? I'm just shouting you, not to beg friends. 'cause I know what it is, but just to shout you," Wilson wrote. "I know all this madness got out of control, it's all gonna be nice soon. The truth has to come out."

Now, two years later, his refusal to testify forced an adjournment of the trial. A week later, on May 21, 2009, Wilson came back to court.

"Mr. Wilson, I understand you are now prepared to testify. Is that right?" asked Dambrot.

"No, Your Honour," he replied, "the reason I didn't testify last time is because I'm not gonna stand on the stand and lie on these guys. So . . ."

"Okay," Dambrot said. "Mr. Wilson, I just need to know you're going to take the oath and you're going to answer questions. Is that right or not?"

"I'm going to say that everything I said before was a lie—then okay."

This time he put his hand on the Bible and swore to tell the truth.

Once the jury was present, Pecknold asked if he was prepared to testify. When Wilson started to repeat "I'm here to say that everything . . ." Dambrot cut him off.

"Now, Mr. Wilson," the judge said, "I'm going to tell you this now and I want you to listen."

"Okay."

"You're here to answer questions like every other witness. You're not here to make speeches. You don't get to say whatever you feel like."

Wilson said "all right," before blurting out "every question that she asks me . . ."

Dambrot stopped him again. "Pay attention because you'll be out of the room so fast . . . that your head will spin."

Pecknold began by asking when and why Wilson had changed his mind about testifying. Wilson said he did so after contacting "a whole bunch of lawyers." Then, as she had done at the preliminary hearing, Pecknold read into the record Wilson's criminal history, which now included recent convictions and prison time for firearms possession—he was caught with a Mac-10 machine gun. A month before the trial, he was convicted of aggravated assault and received a sentence of two more years in prison. It took her eight minutes to go through the list.

But when she moved on to his testimony at the preliminary hearing, Wilson showed just how far he was prepared to go—or not go.

Acknowledging he knew a "gentleman" named Tyshan Riley, Wilson denied knowing him by any other name, though at the preliminary he identified him by the names Ty, Greeze and Nid.

"Do you see him today?" Pecknold asked.

"Yeah, I see him today."

"Can you point him out, please?"

"No, I'm not going to point him out. He is here."

Dambrot asked if Wilson could at least "describe where he is. You don't have to point."

"He's in the courtroom."

"Where in the courtroom, sir?" Dambrot said.

"Somewhere in the vicinity of the courtroom he's here," Wilson said.

"Why won't you tell us where he is?" the judge asked. "Everybody knows where he is."

"I'm not going to sit here and point at people in the courtroom," Wilson replied.

After some more fruitless back-and-forth, Dambrot instructed Pecknold to "move on." She did, and after a few glaring lies from Wilson the jury was excused.

Pecknold, after referring to Wilson's "feigned memory loss," received the judge's permission to ask tougher questions, to approach her wayward witness as if it was cross-examination. It hardly mattered. To most of the questions from the endlessly patient prosecutor, Wilson would respond, "I don't know," or "I don't remember" or "That is what I said but that wasn't the truth."

Pecknold read Wilson some of the statements he made against the defendants during the preliminary hearing. The Q&A went mainly like this:

"Do you remember being asked that question and giving that answer at the preliminary inquiry?" Pecknold asked.

"No."

"No. But if the transcript says you did, then you must have done, right?"

"You're gonna get the same answer that I gave a minute ago."

"Humour me, Mr. Wilson, what's your answer?"

"You keep asking me the same question over and my answer is not going to change. It's the same answer that I gave."

Throughout this farce, the defence lawyers tried to hide their grimaces. They did not want to support the impression that Wilson was either afraid of their clients or lying for his fellow gangbangers.

After more denials, Pecknold asked Wilson where he was on the night of the Charlton/Bell shooting.

"At home," he replied, contradicting his preliminary hearing testimony that he was with the rest of the gang at their usual hangout, Smokey's apartment. "I don't know who Smokey is."

After another break, Pecknold returned to the shooting on March 3, 2004.

"At the preliminary hearing, Mr. Wilson, my question to you was, reading from page sixty-two, line twenty-five: 'Do you know anything about a shooting that happened around Neilson and Finch in March or April of 2004?' And your answer was: 'Yes, I do.' My question was: 'And who did you get that information from about that shooting?' And your answer was: 'Philip and Tyshan.'"

Wilson said he lied.

"And you said you don't remember anything about somebody named Ross?"

"No."

"You don't know anybody by the name of Ross?"

"No, I don't."

Again she cited his preliminary hearing testimony. Had Wilson not told the court Riley phoned the night of March 3, 2004, and asked him to go to the liquor store because "they just caught that Ross guy," Pecknold said, reading from the transcript. "Did that happen or not?"

"No, it didn't," Wilson said.

"So when you told Justice Robertson that you and him [Ross] had problems, that was a lie?"

"Yeah."

"And when you told Justice Robertson that you wanted to find this guy Ross P, that was a lie?"

"I don't know Ross P. Why would I find him?"

"Well, I'm asking you the questions, Mr. Wilson," Pecknold said sternly.

On it went.

The judge sometimes looked amused by Wilson's performance but nonetheless tried to rein him in. "You're not here to pick and choose what questions you're going to answer," Dambrot told Wilson.

Pecknold kept her cool, trying to employ skilled lawyering to deal with Wilson. She continually referred to things he had testified to, which would draw his denial, and offered to refresh his memory by reading his previous statements aloud. So, the jury got two chances to hear Wilson's original evidence.

When Pecknold asked him to explain yet another discrepancy, Wilson blamed it on the authorities. "People were—kept telling me that these guys that were my friends were trying to plot against me to do things to me. So I just said that—whatever came to my head, what you guys wanted to hear."

Pecknold tried to get at Wilson's motivation for going mute on the stand. "You're changing your story now because you're afraid of what's going to happen to you. Isn't that right, Mr. Wilson?"

"Who am I afraid of?"

"Would you answer my question?"

"No."

How to frame Wilson's nonsensical testimony became a crucial matter for the court.

The defence was as shaken as the Crown. If Wilson thought he was doing his friends a favour, he was mistaken.

"If he wants to convict these men, he could not be doing a better job," Midanik told the judge in the absence of the jury. "Because the lies he's telling, some of them are so obvious . . . whether or not his purpose is to thwart the Crown or to send these men away forever is in my respectful submission some matter of debate." Midanik went on: "Can anybody be this stupid? I mean, really."

Dambrot said, "I don't disagree one bit from your description: Could anybody be this stupid? But, you know, he's lying and he's lying stupidly."

But while Midanik only saw damage to the defence, the judge saw both sides. "I appreciate this is not a helpful way for him to testify from the defence point of view. That's not lost on me, I can assure you," Dambrot said. "But, at the same time, I don't know that [Wilson] knows that. From his point of view, if he's not implicating the accused, then he's not helping the Crown."

Before the end of this interlude, Midanik mused: "I'm sitting here and I'm saying to myself: 'What in heaven's name am I supposed to do with this?'" And Midanik flashed a sense of humour. "My first question on cross is going to be: Do you or did you not at any time have a mother?"

With the jury back in the courtroom, when the defence took its turn, Wilson was no longer stupid or a liar. Midanik returned to his role as the serious advocate for his client.

He immediately zeroed in on one statement Wilson gave to police about the shooting of Charlton and Bell: "Basically they told you, before they started questioning you about the offence, that it's called Project Pathfinder and they told you the date and the location. Is that correct?"

"Yes."

Wilson also agreed he had read newspaper accounts of the crime and had watched a re-enactment on television, so he was aware police were looking for a dark Nissan Pathfinder.

"Now, you told us you were arrested [in Oshawa on] April 19, 2004, for something you didn't do. Right?"

"Right."

"And you were arrested with Riley and Atkins and they didn't do anything to cut you loose, did they?"

"No."

"They didn't do anything to help you or tell the authorities that you had nothing to do with it, right?"

"Right."

"And is that one of the reasons you're angry with them?"

"Yes."

"And you've now been in jail six months or so?"

"About that, yeah."

"Okay. For something you didn't do."

"Right."

Midanik then asked him about telling the cops Riley had said "they caught him at the legs in the purple Neon."

"Would it surprise you, sir, that no one, that neither Charlton nor Bell, were shot in the legs?"

"I don't . . . I don't know," said Wilson, apparently unsure as to what the right answer was.

"Well, sir, the reason you said Riley said that is because it was a total fabrication. Right?"

"Right."

Wilson agreed that he had placed Damian Walton with the rest of the gang at Smokey's apartment on the evening of March 3, 2004.

"Well, do you know that Burns wasn't even in the country on March 3, 2004?" Midanik asked.

"I didn't know that."

Midanik also used his cross-examination to paint a picture of Wilson as someone who had benefited from his cooperation with the Crown.

Midanik recounted details of a nasty beating Wilson had participated in on June 20, 2005, right before the preliminary hearing, and "somehow managed to get bail." (Wilson later pleaded guilty to assault causing bodily harm, and was given credit for six months' pre-sentence custody, received an additional two months, and was placed on probation for two years.)

Wilson agreed he was one of five or six people who had kicked a man when he was down. Midanik asked if he had a knife.

"I don't remember."

"You don't remember if you had a knife?"

"No, I don't think it was a knife. I think it was a beer bottle."

"And the complainant apparently lost the vision in his left eye," Midanik said. "When you pleaded guilty [he] had permanently lost sight of his eye?"

"I don't remember."

"You don't remember if the guy who you kicked when he was down lost the sight of his eye?"

"No I don't."

"Minor detail?"

"I don't remember."

"Anyway. You got bail on this," the lawyer said. "As far as you're concerned, when you got bail, did it have something to do with being a Crown witness?"

"I think so. But I don't know how I got bail. I was surprised." Wilson said he rarely was released from custody on a serious charge.

"So, most judges have the sense to keep you in jail where you belong, right?"

"Right."

Midanik reminded Wilson that he had gone to see Pecknold "to see if she could do something for you on those charges." Wilson said he figured she would help him out "'cause I was a witness in her case."

"And am I correct she wasn't prepared to play ball with you?" (Midanik knew this would be raised in Pecknold's re-examination of Wilson.)

"Right."

"But you still thought when you testified [at the preliminary hearing] that if you came across for the Crown, that they would do something for you, didn't you?"

"Yes."

Still, Wilson agreed with Midanik that the ultimate disposition of the assault case suggested somebody had "pulled some strings."

At times, both the questions and answers were laughable.

Wilson said he had expected better treatment for cooperating with authorities. "I thought it was like the movies. After, like, you end up a witness against people you get a big cheque, house, car, all of that. But nothin' ever went like that, ever."

"Did Ms. Pecknold offer you her house and her car?"

"No."

"What about the big cheque she gets from Her Majesty every week. Did she offer that to you?"

"No."

"Maybe you just didn't bargain well enough?"

"I don't know. All I got was a couple of hamburgers here and there. KFC. That was it."

When asking Wilson about his sojourn in Vancouver, Midanik demonstrated his scorn for the witness. "What were you doing there? Get a job logging or something?" Midanik also asked Wilson about the meetings he'd had at the Scarborough courthouse before the preliminary hearing. Wilson said he was able to watch movies and was given access to PlayStation 2.

Wilson agreed he testified at the preliminary hearing because he didn't want to be charged with perjury. (After this trial, Wilson *was* charged with perjury.)

"And now you don't care?"

"Nope."

"Why not?"

"I don't care no more. It's like this thing went too far."

Berg was up next. He knew he would be questioning a witness who had referred to his client, Philip Atkins, as "like a cousin."

Berg turned to Wilson's statement where he did not implicate Atkins in the Charlton/Bell shooting. "You were telling the truth at that point, is that fair?"

"Yes."

The first time he put Atkins at the shooting was during the pre-dawn interview with Burks, after they returned to Toronto from Vancouver.

"You didn't want to stay in jail. I'm going to suggest to you that you knew at that point that you had to give them something?"

"Right."

"And I'm going to suggest to you from an early age you had a fair bit of experience in saying whatever was required, doing whatever the situation called for to get out of trouble."

"Okay."

Berg continued for several minutes on that point, doing what lawyers do: asking questions not for the answers they might elicit but to create reasonable doubt.

Then there was the insinuation that Wilson's preliminary hearing testimony had sprung from a police threat to have him declared a dangerous offender, which meant life in prison without the chance of parole. "That must have been pretty scary," Berg said.

Wilson agreed.

Summing up, Berg suggested "anything that you have ever said about Mr. Atkins being involved in this murder is a complete and utter lie."

"You're right."

It was late in the day on May 25 when Mirosolin rose to ask just a few questions. Wilson had not implicated his client, Jason Wisdom, in any way, so the lawyer did not want to draw any association between the two.

"Sir, as I understand it your position today is simply that on the night of the Charlton and Bell shooting, you were not at Smokey's. Is that correct?"

"Right."

Wilson agreed that even in his preliminary hearing testimony, he never put Wisdom there that night.

Pecknold got one more chance to question Wilson, during what is known as "re-examination in chief." She went briskly through all of the inconsistencies. Again, there were moments that left courtroom observers trying to stifle laughter. One exchange had to do with the mother of Wilson's child, Shannon Anderson.

"Why are you asking me about her for?" Wilson said to Pecknold.

"Because there's a reference to her in the [Vancouver] interview, sir. Would you answer my question, please?"

"No, I'm not answering that question. I don't know—my baby mother doesn't have nothin' to do with this."

"I'm going to ask you again: There's reference to a Shannon at the beginning of that tape. Is that your baby mother, sir?"

"I don't know."

"You don't know?"

"No."

"So you don't know who Shannon is?"

"I know a lot of Shannons."

Dambrot stepped in: "The Shannon you were talking about in the tape?"

"There was two different Shannons out there."

"Tell us about the two Shannons you were talking about in the tape."

"When I was in Vancouver there was two different Shannons ..."

"No, no, no," the judge said. "I'm not concerned about how many Shannons there are in Vancouver. There are probably hundreds. I'm concerned about the Shannon you were talking about in the tape."

The Shannon issue remained unresolved.

Maintaining her composure throughout, no doubt suppressing considerable exasperation, Pecknold finally let the mask slip. "So are you determined to disagree with everything that I say, then?"

"Depends."

"If I say the sky is blue, you're going to disagree with that?"

"Today it's raining out, it's not blue."

A little while later, Wilson tried to shut it down.

"I'm not answering no more of these dumb questions. Now you're just trying to make me look stupid and I'm not dumb. I'm smart," he said. "So whatever questions you wanna keep askin' I'm not gonna answer them 'cause you're trying to make me look dumb. So I'm finished now."

But by the end of the afternoon, after Wilson made one last denial, Pecknold thanked and dismissed her ornery witness.

"Thank you, Ms. Pecknold," the judge said. "Mr. Wilson, your time with us is over."

"Am I allowed to use the phone now?" he asked in parting.

He then left the courtroom, not glancing at the prisoners' box where his "cousin" sat glowering.

The day after Midanik cross-examined Wilson, my cell phone rang. On the other end was the lawyer, irate because I had, admittedly, missed his cross-examination and my story in the *Toronto Star* quoted only Berg. (The testimony included here came from trial transcripts.) He scolded me for not giving proper due to his skilled cross-examination, suggesting I had given Berg undeserved credit.

That same morning, before the jury came in, Midanik said, in front of Dambrot, that he was being overlooked in media reports. The judge looked bewildered. By then, I was the only reporter showing up to cover the trial on a regular basis and hardly capturing front-page headlines.

While Wilson's two days on the stand may have appeared to be a fiasco for the Crown, they were also great theatre if you prefer comedy to tragedy. Many of his statements sparked chuckles and his sometimes bizarre behaviour drew puzzling looks from spectators and participants alike.

And what of his testimony against Atkins, their mothers still close at the time of the trial? What did the jurors think of the spectacle? How did they make sense of it all? Did they conclude Wilson was a liar? A wacko? Did his performance influence their verdict? We'll never know, because jurors in Canada are not allowed under law to publicly discuss their deliberations.

Jurors would also not be told whether the Crown *knew* its witness would recant everything he had said previously. If the answer was yes. So why did they still put him on the stand? Because they were determined to get his previous testimony on the record.

And that's exactly what they did in an equally strange piece of stage acting that saw a middle-aged white woman, with a British accent, playing the part of Marlon Wilson. For several hours, Pecknold reprised her role and that of defence lawyers from the preliminary hearing while Pasquino read Wilson's answers from court transcripts. Both Pasquino and Pecknold wore their hair in ponytails as they stood behind lecterns, flipping through binders marked with colour-coded tabs.

Midanik objected to Pasquino's "distinct and charming English accent" being substituted for Wilson's distinctively uncharming Toronto street-speak. The judge conceded Pasquino "sounds a great deal different" but added no one was going to mistake her for being as "surly and obnoxious as Wilson."

So the jury heard what Wilson had testified to at the preliminary hearing. They heard he had known Atkins all his life, and Riley since he was 12 years old. They heard about the existence of a gang in Scarborough, members' nicknames, and how Smokey's was a gang hangout. They heard that Wilson had seen Riley in a two-door dark-coloured Pathfinder and how on March 3, 2004, Wilson received a call from Riley telling him to go to a liquor store because "they had caught the Ross guy."

Crown attorneys Maureen Pecknold (left) and Lesley Pasquino (right) who had to read in prosecution witness Marlon Wilson's testimony when he refused to cooperate during the 2009 murder trial of his childhood friends.

Critically, they also heard Wilson admit he feared the repercussions for testifying—"I was in jail with all these guys"—as well as the contents of a wiretapped call between Riley and Wilson. In it, Riley told Wilson that his cooperation with police was "taking food out of people's mouths" by keeping him in jail.

After Wilson, the Crown really had few significant witnesses to help make its case. Two forensic firearms experts testified that bullets and bullet fragments recovered from the crime scene could have been fired from thousands of handguns in circulation at the time. After test firing the alleged murder weapon, a .357 pistol, bullets and fragments gathered up at the scene "could neither be identified nor eliminated as being fired from the seized gun," one of them testified. (The jury had already heard Atkins' and Wilson's DNA was on the gun.)

Also left to testify was a parking enforcement officer who knew Jamaican patois and had worked in the wire room. A few other police witnesses testified about non-contentious points, such as the Toronto police officer who had removed some items from Riley's cell.

The Crown was ready to wrap its case. That caught everyone off guard, including the judge. Remember, Dambrot had told the jurors they might still be there after Labour Day. But now it looked like things could be over by Canada Day.

So why did the Crown so quickly close its case in a first-degree murder trial involving three defendants? Its initial witness list was far from exhausted. Maybe the jurors never heard from them because they were part of the gang scene and likely to turn out as forthcoming as Marlon Wilson.

As prosecutors prepared to turn the trial over to the defence, key questions remained. Where was the evidence that Riley, Atkins and Wisdom were in the Pathfinder? Where was the vehicle itself? Where were all the guns—police said from two to six were used—fired at Charlton and Bell? Who could identify the defendants as the shooters? Where was the no-doubt confession, even on all those wiretaps?

Nonetheless, the Crown's case was completed on June 12, 2009. It was now up to the defence lawyers. Berg and Midanik didn't call any witnesses. Given their clients' baggage—and the fact neither Riley nor Atkins could offer a credible alibi—they had little choice. They were counting on the jury concluding the Crown failed to prove its case, or at least having reasonable doubt their clients killed Charlton and shot Bell. Confidence was higher than it had ever been.

The defence of Jason Wisdom was different.

"There is a strong possibility I will be calling evidence," Mirosolin told the judge. He would call witnesses including his client and Wisdom's mother.

On June 16, wearing a grey suit, pale blue shirt and striped tie, Wisdom took the stand.

"You guys hear me?" he said, tapping the microphone. Mirosolin told him yes, but asked him to keep his voice up when answering questions.

"I will."

Wisdom told the court he was born on September 3, 1985, in Toronto and raised by his mother in the Galloway area of Scarborough. He dropped out of high school to sell crack cocaine. Before his arrest in April 2005 for murder, he had a couple of driving offences and one drug-trafficking conviction on his record.

Under questioning by Mirosolin, Wisdom admitted he sold drugs in the Galloway area and confirmed he belonged to a gang whose members called it G-Way. He said Throwbacks was a rap group, not a "ride" squad. In any event, Wisdom said, he didn't have a Throwback tattoo anywhere on his body.

The prosecution couldn't have scripted better answers: Here was one of the accused admitting to the existence of G-Way, its leadership and its activities despite the fact the defence had previously refused to concede their clients belonged to a gang.

Moving to the night of March 3, 2004, Wisdom testified he was home watching television when his mother came in and switched the channels to show him a news report. There had been a drive-by shooting just down the street. Wisdom lived with his mother, Marcia Thomas, and siblings in Malvern, where the family had moved from Galloway.

"Were you responsible in any way?" Mirosolin asked.

"No, I was not," Wisdom said, shaking his head and looking directly at the jury.

"Were you ever in a Pathfinder with Tyshan Riley and Philip Atkins?"

"No."

"Roland Ellis says you told him you were involved," his lawyer said. "Is that true?"

"No."

Nor, he said, was he at Smokey's apartment that night. The first time he left his mother's house was around midnight to sell drugs, he said.

The cross-examination was by lead Crown attorney Suhail Akhtar. He would give Wisdom a lot rougher ride.

Akhtar challenged Wisdom to explain how he could have such a clear recollection of what he was doing on March 3, 2004, when he wasn't questioned about it until after he was arrested more than a year later. "[If] the shooting had nothing to do with you, why would you remember?" the prosecutor said with his arms crossed.

"My friend was charged for it," Wisdom said, referring to Riley.

Akhtar became more aggressive as his questioning grew more accusatory. "On March 3, 2004, you went into a Pathfinder with Riley and Atkins looking to shoot someone," the prosecutor said, raising his voice.

"I totally disagree with you."

The exchange continued with Akhtar making accusations and Wisdom, forcefully but politely, denying each one.

Of course, defence lawyers coach their clients to play down their rough side. Wisdom, while a physically imposing figure at more than six feet and 200 pounds, came across as genuinely mild-mannered, in part because of his dark, sad eyes and soft voice.

Before finishing his cross-examination the next day, Akhtar suggested Wisdom had "invented" his alibi.

"I'd never do that," Wisdom responded.

Midanik took notes as he listened and seethed.

When Wisdom was done and jurors were excused, Midanik asked the judge for a mistrial. He contended that Wisdom's evidence amounted to a "character attack" on Riley and had done "irreparable damage to my client's position." Midanik accused Mirosolin of turning into a "tag team" with the Crown. It would, for a while, be the end of Midanik's tennis matches with Mirosolin.

The judge refused Midanik's mistrial request.

Legal Wrangling

The adversarial antics in the court, from the beginning, had been at times heated and extreme—of course, mainly out of sight of the jury.

On some occasions, the judge must have thought Midanik and Akhtar were behaving like two boys in a sandbox in front of him. The rancour would hit its peak during pre-trial motions when Midanik alleged Crown misconduct, arguing he had been deliberately misled about wiretap evidence. Dambrot commented on the level of distrust and "ill-will" that existed between them in his ruling dismissing the misconduct application. He did, though, find Midanik was "entirely within his rights to raise the issues that he raised."

At that time, Midanik sent an email to Akhtar that captured the tone. "I am not aware of all the witnesses you are calling. You have refused to be more specific," said the email signed by Midanik, though his secretary would have sent it. (He had little use for computers.) "I understand neither your refusal to focus the prosecution nor what seems to be an attempt on your part to lengthen proceedings and waste valuable court time." That was exactly what Akhtar thought Midanik was doing.

A recurring theme became Midanik's suggestion that Dambrot was on the side of the Crown. In many instances this provoked an angry reaction from Akhtar, growing increasingly frustrated that Midanik was trying to hijack the proceedings. One time, during the trial, with the jury absent, Midanik accused Dambrot of "assisting the Crown," by offering to clarify some minor points in the evidence.

"Can you give me an example?" Dambrot asked.

It wasn't the substance, Midanik responded, "it's the number of interjections."

Akhtar leapt to his feet. "Don't be intimidated," he told the judge. As Midanik began to demand Akhtar apologize, Dambrot cut him off.

"I don't feel intimidated," the judge said. "I have no interest in advancing anyone's case and I hope nothing I do will be seen to do that."

Another exchange occurred during Midanik's cross-examination of Ellis. "Mr. Midanik has made sarcastic comments," Akhtar told the judge.

"[He's] mocked the witness on occasion and he's now making comments—editorial comments which are unnecessary. And now when I make an objection that I'm entitled to make sure, he's now mocking the Crown in front of the jury."

Midanik didn't deny making "little sarcastic comments" but said it was "fair comment." Dambrot asked him to refrain from using sarcasm.

"I'll try to frame the questions so there won't be any further objections," Midanik said.

But Midanik and Akhtar would, on a rare occasion, make light of their differences.

When a witness was late for court one day, Akhtar apologized to the court. The judge told him it related to transportation and an apology wasn't necessary.

"Even I don't blame Mr. Akhtar," Midanik said with a smirk.

"This month has been a month of firsts, Your Honour," said Akhtar, also grinning.

A Mother Takes the Stand

Jason Wisdom's mother, Marcia Thomas, followed her son to the stand. A friendly woman in her mid-forties who worked at two long-term care facilities helping the elderly, she had brought her uniform inside her purse in case she had to go straight from court to work. Thomas had raised Jason and his older brother, Dwight, on her own. As their run-ins with the law grew more serious, she lost weight and developed diabetes.

Thomas testified that after making dinner on March 3, 2004, she sat down to watch television. Thomas said she heard a TV announcer say: "Breaking news, breaking news, drive-by shooting" at Finch and Neilson. "I rushed to Jason's room and turned the TV [channel] and said, 'Holy shit it happened just up the street,'" Thomas testified.

After backing her son's story, Thomas was now through with questions from Mirosolin. He turned her over to Akhtar—who launched a vigorous attack. While Thomas could recall a lot of details about the events of March 3, she could not answer a barrage of Akhtar's questions concerning other dates. What was the date of the preliminary hearing? What was the date of your son's bail hearing? What was the date that she first came forward with an alibi? Mostly her responses were "I don't remember." But one question from the prosecutor elicited an emotional and sympathetic response.

"You're doing this to help Jason out," Akhtar said harshly.

"I've lived here for thirty-two years, I've never broken the law," she said, becoming increasingly upset. "A lady lost her son, I would never lie."

Pressing further, Akhtar read a statement Thomas had once given to police about her eldest son, Dwight, reminding her she had said "no mom wants to see their kids in jail."

"That's how you feel, but you're not going to lie to get them out of jail," she responded tearfully, as her younger son sat in the prisoners' box with his head buried in his hands.

Mirosolin got another chance to question his witness. Had she given Dwight an alibi when he was charged with murder?

"No," she said emphatically.

After Thomas left the stand and the jury was excused, Midanik was on his feet again, asking Dambrot again for a mistrial. Sitting in her usual spot in the front row of the gallery, Valda Williams groaned at this latest act of lawyering. But Midanik wasn't talking about her dead son when he said "suddenly there's another murder before this court." He said the reference to Dwight Wisdom's murder charge had brought "great prejudice" to the accused.

"So?" Dambrot said. "They are separate people. Jason is not his brother's keeper and is not responsible for whatever Dwight has done." (The murder charge against Dwight was earlier dropped.) Again, there would be no mistrial.

It was soon time to move on and prepare for the closing addresses. Dambrot adjourned court for a week to give the lawyers time to prepare.

CHAPTER 23

The verdict: agony and ecstasy

"All right, Mr. Midanik, are you ready?" Dambrot asked on the morning of June 29, about three months ahead of schedule.

"Not really, Your Honour."

He proceeded to the lectern anyway. "I will be rather lengthy," he said, leaning over to face the jurors. "The Crown hasn't proven its case," he began. Nor was there "a scrap of physical evidence linking my client to this crime."

"Mr. Riley is a very soft target. He's a bad man," the lawyer conceded. "I'm not asking you to like him, or take him home with you, or hire him," Midanik said, smiling. He called the two main witnesses, Ellis and Wilson, "liars, criminals, disreputable people." Ellis was "slicker" than Wilson, Midanik said, "but perhaps he was more dangerous."

Where was the independent corroboration of the Crown's evidence? he asked.

"Everybody had a grudge against Mr. Riley," he said. "Did these persons have a motive to lie?" Wilson, he said, didn't like Riley because he had tried to have sex with his girlfriend—the mysterious Shannon. As for Ellis, he believed Riley wanted to kill him. "Now, is that a strong motivation to falsely accuse someone?" he asked. These friends, Midanik said, had turned into enemies. "He didn't share the wealth," Midanik said. "He doesn't treat people very well."

Midanik suggested that Ellis and Wilson had concocted their stories from jailhouse gossip and information released publicly at Toronto police news conferences. "It's called stimulation," he said. "The information is put out there in order to further their investigation but the problem is the information you're getting back is the same information you're putting out." Garbage in, garbage out, went the argument.

Midanik's approach in a courtroom can be exhaustive and exhausting, apparently even to him. After speaking for nearly four hours, he asked Dambrot to adjourn for the day. "I've given myself a headache," Midanik said.

The next morning, he focused on some of the wiretap evidence and invited jurors to follow along with the transcripts provided. Some did, others didn't.

Summing up after a couple more hours, Midanik urged the jury not to convict Riley "for who he is." . . . "Maybe he deserves to be in jail for a long time—but he doesn't deserve to be in jail for something he didn't do." He apologized for taking so long. "I hope you come up with the right result."

Taking it all in was Dana Lee Williams, who had again brought her two daughters to court. "It's a new variation of bring-your-kids-to-work day," Crown attorney Patrick Clement, who came to the case late, was overheard saying.

Next up for the defence was David Berg. He walked to the lectern with a stack of transcripts. "It's worse than it looks," he told the jury with a smile.

"I represent Mr. Atkins," he said, pointing to his client in the box between Riley and Wisdom.

Berg divided the evidence against his client into three categories: the .357, the testimony of Wilson and Ellis, and a "handful of intercepted calls."

Yes, Atkins' DNA was on the gun. "But it's impossible to say if it was before or after the murder," he said. "All we know is that Mr. Atkins touched the gun—not when—and there's no evidence he had it on March 3."

As for Wilson, Berg said: "How can one believe anything this man has said?" Turning to Ellis, Berg reminded jurors that the witness mentioned Atkins' attempt to ditch the alleged murder weapon for the first time when he testified at the trial. Berg suggested Ellis would have told police or the Crown earlier if this were true. "Ladies and gentlemen, you saw him make it up." And none of the wiretap evidence presented by the Crown amounted to much of anything, Berg said. "Philip Atkins liked to smoke marijuana and have people throw it at the jail. That does not make Philip Atkins a murderer."

The summation marathon—though Berg had been relatively concise—was at the halfway mark as Mirosolin approached the lectern with a prepared address. There would be no extemporaneous delivery.

"The spectacle of this trial cannot be lost on anyone," he said, glancing around the courtroom. "Jason Wisdom sits in the prisoners' box surrounded by guards. At any given time, there are as many as seven guards in the courtroom. Although you have heard from His Honour that Jason Wisdom is presumed innocent, the imagery suggests otherwise."

Mirosolin expressed an understanding of the jury's task. "Your desire to see justice done for all those affected by the shooting of Mr. Charlton and Mr. Bell creates a powerful cocktail of emotions, emotions which could lead to a potential miscarriage of justice." All the jurors appeared to be paying close attention.

Ellis, again, came in for a withering attack. "He is a gun-toting criminal and a proven liar," Mirosolin said, adding, "there was no love lost between Jason Wisdom and Roland Ellis."

Mirosolin played up his client's decision to take the stand. He noted that Wisdom was under no obligation to do so, without noting Riley and Atkins didn't testify. "He did not portray himself as an angel." He called Wisdom's mother, Marcia Thomas, "among the most credible of the witnesses who testified at this trial."

In conclusion, he said: "When you deconstruct the Crown's case, the only verdict that you can deliver in relation to Jason Wisdom is one of not guilty on all counts."

Under the rules governing criminal trials, when the defence calls evidence, as in this case, the Crown gets the last word.

On July 3, Akhtar rose to speak. "The Crown has met the high standard of proving beyond a reasonable doubt that Mr. Riley, Mr. Atkins and Mr. Wisdom murdered Brenton Charlton and attempted to murder Leonard Bell," the prosecutor began in a loud and confident voice. "This murder was planned and deliberate and committed for the benefit of a criminal organization, in this case the street gang that all three accused belonged to."

Standing in front of the jurors, with his arms crossed, Akhtar asked them to look at the "big picture." The crux of his argument was that the jury should believe Roland Ellis and the statements Marlon Wilson made before recanting at the trial. He pointed out that Ellis and Wilson did not know each other. Yet they had both incriminated their childhood friends with evidence that "may not be identical, but it's certainly very consistent," Akhtar said.

He chided the defence for attacking Ellis as an "evil, insidious liar trying to frame three innocent men." What benefit did Ellis receive for talking to the police? None. Still, he had to come into court again and again over three years, only to face a barrage of questions from defence lawyers who branded him a liar. Meanwhile, in his community, he was labelled a rat and a snitch. "He can never go back to the area that he lived and was raised in. Ever. For the most obvious of reasons he can never go home."

And, if Ellis wanted to frame his friends for first-degree murder, why "concoct such a strange, convoluted story?" If he was lying, why didn't he simply say all three had confessed?

Akhtar said he would have preferred to call witnesses with unblemished records—"a doctor, charity worker, a good-Samaritan-Mother-Teresa type." But, he said, none of them would have been knowledgeable about the violence that transpired on the streets of

Scarborough. "None of them would be able to tell you about 'ride' missions, G-checks, street names or the beef with Malvern," he said.

Akhtar turned to Wilson, whom he described as a "thoroughly reprehensible individual who was concerned with only one thing: his own well-being." Akhtar asked the jury to consider the motivation for Wilson's performance. "His testimony in this courtroom is simply worthless and that includes his assertion that he lied at the preliminary inquiry," Akhtar said. "He was telling the truth then, but has changed his story now because he is trying to help the accused."

Over the course of two days, the Crown attorney picked apart defence arguments while advancing his line of attack, punctuated by arm waving, finger snapping and knuckle rapping. Akhtar's remarks covered 103 written pages. But, after five years, he knew the case well and often left his script on the lectern to pace in front of the jury box. It was a persuasive and forceful show rarely seen in Canadian courtrooms.

He also harkened back to his opening address when he told the jury the evidence would be pieces of a "jigsaw puzzle." Now, he put a couple of pieces together for the first time.

He reminded jurors that Wilson, at the preliminary hearing, testified that he was told by Riley and Atkins that they followed a Neon to Mornelle Court. "This account is confirmed by Leonard Bell, who told this court that prior to making their way to Neilson and Finch, both he and Brenton Charlton stopped at Bell's apartment at Mornelle Court."

"There's no way Mr. Wilson could know that," Akhtar continued, if Riley and Atkins had not confessed to tailing the Neon. "That information was never released by police." Akhtar was trying to connect the dots, suggesting the accused had mistakenly followed Charlton's Neon instead of a similar car driven by their intended target, Alton Reid.

Akhtar highlighted another piece of evidence—when linked to the surveillance photos—which was Wilson putting the silver Impala at the scene of the crime. Wilson had testified at the preliminary hearing that Riley and Atkins had also told him that the Neon had been pursued not only by the Pathfinder but also by a silver Impala. "This Impala was a car that Wilson had rented and loaned out to one of the gang members. It was returned to him a day after the shooting by Philip Atkins."

Akhtar stopped momentarily so jurors could look at the large screen where images of the Pathfinder, Neon and Impala were being beamed. "See how the big picture is working here—how the evidence is drawing together?" Akhtar said.

The Crown, he concluded, had met the high standard of proof. Riley, Atkins and Wisdom murdered Charlton and attempted to murder Leonard Bell. The murder was planned and deliberate and committed for the benefit of a criminal organization, in this case G-Way, a street gang the three defendants belonged to.

(Alton Reid, also known as Ross P, allegedly the intended target who too drove a Neon, was killed in a shooting at a birthday party in Scarborough in late 2009.)

On July 6, the lawyers met with the judge to discuss what instructions he would give to jurors before sending them off to deliberate. Dambrot asked both sides to send him summaries of their arguments and laid out his game plan. This was designed to ensure there would be smooth sailing right up to the verdict. It was anything but.

Dambrot spent a week preparing his charge to the jury. On July 10, before the jurors were brought in, the judge asked all those assembled, "Anything anyone needs to say before we get started?" Midanik again had a problem. The lights over the prisoners' boxes were off. He objected to the "psychological impact" of jurors seeing the "accused sitting in the dark."

As was the case during closing arguments, Dambrot insisted no one be permitted to enter or leave the courtroom during his charge. The mood inside the courtroom was tense and sombre as jurors filed in.

At Midanik's request, the judge told the jury "there's no significance" to the dimmed lighting. With that out of the way, Dambrot did what all good judges do. He made the twelve jurors feel they were the most important people in the room. He even apologized for a bit of a sore throat. "If I start to lose my voice, you'll know why."

For nearly eight hours over two days, Dambrot spoke to the jury. He told them the verdicts for Riley, Atkins and Wisdom did not have to be the same. He explained the difference between second- and first-degree murder before instructing them on how the law should be applied. He also posed a question: "The Crown's position is that all three accused committed the killing together. How, you might ask, can anyone other than the shooter who shot the deadly bullet have participated in the killing?"

The judge provided an answer: "Where a killing is committed by two or more persons, each may play a different part. So long as they are acting together as part of a joint plan or agreement to commit the killing, each may be found guilty of it."

Dambrot then ran through the evidence against each of the defendants. It was a painstaking process and was undoubtedly a challenge for the twelve jurors to focus on all his words.

"Don't concern yourself with consequences, including punishment," Dambrot told jurors, winding down. "Decide based on what you've seen and heard." It was just after 1:00 p.m. on Monday, July 13, when Dambrot excused the jurors to begin deliberations.

No sooner had the jurors left to begin their deliberations than Midanik was on his feet, objecting to the judge's charge and demanding corrections on numerous points. "You went through the reasons to convict," Midanik said. "They needed the flip side." The lawyer also objected to the judge repeating the evidence against each of the three. "You could have done it once." He added the judge had "put the Crown's case before the jury better than the Crown did."

The judge attempted to appease the lawyer by calling the jurors back to amend his charge. That night, the now-sequestered jurors retired to a nearby hotel. When they returned the next day to the jury room, they were out of earshot when Midanik and Akhtar engaged in a final dramatic clash.

Akhtar said it was "truly offensive" that Midanik claimed Dambrot had presented the Crown's case better than the Crown. "He's saying, 'redo my arguments.' He wants you to repeat that. You can't do it at this stage," Akhtar told the judge.

Shortly after asking Akhtar to lower his voice, Dambrot adjourned court for a few minutes so tempers could cool. At one point, the judge, obviously exasperated, warned the lawyers: "This is not an endless exercise."

But soon the jury had a question: What is reasonable doubt? A buzz went through the courtroom. Atkins smiled and adjusted his tie.

He and the other defendants appeared encouraged. But the lawyers knew better, that this was one of the most common questions for a jury to ask. One veteran prosecutor not connected to the case said the question was usually a sign a jury was close to a verdict.

He was right. The following morning, Wednesday, July 15, was warm and sunny, rare in that rainy month of 2009.

Alice Atkins was doing her best to stay calm as she sipped a coffee and smoked a cigarette outside the courthouse. Valda Williams passed by, wearing her bright lemon-yellow caftan. She stopped, smiled, and said good morning before continuing on her way inside. Similar scenes had played out throughout the years this case was in court. The mother of the victim would cross paths with the mothers of the accused. Valda Williams would always utter a cordial greeting and even a smile. Some, like Marie Riley, would sneer in return. But on this day, Alice Atkins could only shake her head. She had often wanted to offer condolences to Williams but was never able to muster the words.

At 10:45 a.m., my cell phone rang. There was a "motion" of some kind, so court was reconvening. But just as everyone was settling into their usual seats, the court had news. The jury had reached a verdict. Dambrot told everyone to return in an hour. Riley, Atkins and Wisdom were taken back down to the cells.

The Verdict

As is typical in big trials, word spread quickly that a verdict was coming down. Before long, the spectators' benches were filled. Valda Williams and her sister Uleth Harvey, the aunt who had brought Brenton Charlton to Canada, took their place. Leonard Bell was on a renovation job out of town and not able to get to the courthouse. The families and friends of the defendants, including Riley's mother, father, a younger brother and girlfriend, gathered in groups to support the three young men in the box.

Detective Wayne Banks, who had been on the case at the beginning, was there, as was his new boss, Kathryn Martin, who had investigated Eric Mutiisa's murder and was now head of the Toronto police homicide squad. About a dozen lawyers, some of whom had participated in the early stages of the case and others just curious to witness the final act, crowded in to see the show. So did a flock of reporters, most of whom hadn't been there since Day One. The extraordinary security force that had been in place from the start was now ever present in the courtroom. Armed police officers stood at the back, in addition to the regular court security officers.

Five years had passed since Riley and Atkins had been arrested on April 19, 2004, when Barack Obama was a little-known U.S. senator from Illinois, before Facebook was a popular social network and only birds twittered. It had been four years since the preliminary hearing began. There had been fourteen months of pre-trial motions, and a surprisingly short eight-week trial.

"I assume you all know that we have a verdict," the judge said at 11:40 a.m. "I know this is an emotional time, but whatever your views, out of respect, please restrain yourself and not make this any more difficult for anyone." His words would not be heeded.

The three gangbangers from the streets of Scarborough appeared stricken. Still in their twenties, they faced the possibility of a twenty-five-year sentence, not emerging from prison until they were in their fifties or older. Riley, now 25, wore a suit vest over a pale blue shirt. He took tiny sips of water from a plastic cup. Atkins, who had turned 26 during the trial, wore a sleeveless sweater over a button-down shirt. He glanced at his mother and sat with his back pressed up against the Plexiglas. Wisdom, wearing a grey button-down shirt and dark suit, rocked back and forth, occasionally looking up at his mother and aunt.

Prosecutor Maureen Pecknold was "nearly hyperventilating," she told me later.

The jurors took their seats. The foreman, an analyst for a bank, rose to deliver the verdicts.

"Mr. Riley, please rise," the clerk said. Riley pulled up his baggy pants as he stood up. Within seconds he got the news.

"Guilty, of first-degree murder," the fair-haired foreman said, looking directly at Riley. He went on to say "guilty" to attempted murder and "guilty" of committing murder for the benefit of a criminal organization. Riley sat down, shut his eyes and rubbed his head.

Apparently realizing what was coming, Atkins ignored the court clerk's request to stand. He remained sitting in the prisoners' box with his head in his hands. It may not have been an act of defiance. He seemed to lack the strength and will to get up. He didn't move as the foreman said "guilty" three times.

Wisdom was shaking his head. Tears streaked down his face as he stood. Again: three times guilty.

As a wave of sobbing in the courtroom grew louder, Dambrot quickly asked staff to escort the jurors out of the courtroom. They were gone when the accused and their supporters erupted.

Riley started yelling: "How am I guilty of murder? How is this?" He stood up, shaking his head back and forth.

"It's okay, baby," shouted his girlfriend, Dana Lee Williams, tears streaming down her face. "It's the system. They want to show they did something for society."

Atkins had finally found his legs and was standing. "I love you, Mom. You raised a good kid, you know that," Atkins called out to his mother, Alice, who stood bawling and blowing him kisses. "What am I going to tell my daughter?" Atkins moaned. For the past five years, since she was two, Atkins' daughter had been told her father was in jail for shoplifting.

Wisdom lost it. "I told the truth," he screamed, pounding the Plexiglas divider separating him from Atkins. "I told the truth."

"I know you were home," his mother shouted.

Dambrot abruptly ordered a recess so everyone could "cool down." Court security rushed to usher out the spectators and get the convicts in handcuffs and out of the courtroom. Passing by Dambrot, Riley and Atkins yelled "you're biased," parroting what Midanik had been saying for the previous two days. Seconds later, the sound of glass smashing resonated through the courtroom. It was Atkins punching the casing for a fire extinguisher in a back hallway.

The hysteria spilled onto the sidewalk outside. Wisdom's aunt collapsed and writhed on the ground, surrounded by TV cameras and photographers. Marcia Thomas helped her up. She was defiant as she faced reporters to defend her son. "I know Jason wasn't there," she said. "Regardless of what he's done in the past . . . I will sit on my

Marcia Thomas, mother of Jason Wisdom, comforting her sister outside the courthouse.

grandmother's grave and I'll swear to death I am not a liar. I did not lie when I testified."

Her son's lawyer would call it "the worst day of my life." Maurice Mirosolin said later that he believed his client was innocent. "It was devastating. I just wanted to find a hole and disappear."

Other family and friends of the three men did not hang around to answer questions, though a TV cameraman followed Alice Atkins and recorded her in tears, sitting by herself.

Outside the revolving doors of the courthouse, relieved members of the prosecution team and police officers came out to address reporters. Akhtar did the talking to the cameras. The verdict, he said, sent a message that "these types of offences cannot be tolerated in Canadian society." The jury's finding that members of a street gang had committed first-degree murder for the benefit of a criminal organization was a first in this country, he said. He also gave credit to a "hero," Roland Ellis. "This was a unique case in many ways, not least of all because the Crown relied upon a former gang member to lay bare many of the secrets of the gang that was operating in Galloway."

Valda Williams came outside with a huge smile and hugged Detective Wayne Banks. She smiled as she stood in front of reporters

Toronto Police officers Wayne Banks (left) and Dean Burks (right) and Valda Williams (centre) in July 2009 after a jury convicted three Galloway gang members in the first-degree murder of her son, Brenton "Junior" Charlton.

and cameras. "I just felt sorry for them and I forgive them 100 per cent, I really do," she said of the men convicted of killing her only son. Williams said she felt the spirit of Junior beside her when the verdict was read out. "I was hugging him. I was holding him. I was talking to him."

That afternoon, Riley, Atkins and Wisdom were back in court to get a date for sentencing, though they knew there would be no suspense on the term for a conviction for first-degree murder. Dambrot had ordered they be brought into court one at a time. Only court staff, members of the legal team, reporters and police would be allowed inside Courtroom 2-7—everyone else could watch via a video link.

Riley was first, and he stood in the court in handcuffs. First, Dambrot put on the record there had been an "uproar" in the court after the verdict. The judge set July 29 for sentencing. Riley had something else to say. "You're biased and I did not commit this crime.

Leonard Bell, shot multiple times on March 3, 2004,
was not in court for the verdicts but appeared here after
sentencing of three Galloway gang members convicted
of attempted murder.

You're biased, that is all I have to say," Riley told Dambrot before the
judge ordered him removed. "It is what it is, you're biased," Atkins
said when it was his turn. He too left. Wisdom just kept shaking his
head before being led out of court.

That night, police began guarding the judge's house.

Bell, who wasn't in court for the verdicts and chaotic aftermath,
sent me a text message: "Brenton died. I am suffering and three young
black men have now lost their lives to their own stupidity. I hope
others on the same path of destruction will see that crime is hopeless
and change their ways."

CHAPTER 24

Cool poses and baby mamas

The Galloway Boys came of age during a time of heightened tensions between members of Toronto's black community and the police. The early 1990s was also a time when Toronto media reports were filled with stories about people of Jamaican heritage involved in violent crime.

"Murderous [Jamaican] posses gain Metro foothold," read a headline in the *Star* in February 1990. Two years later, the *Globe and Mail* ran a series called "Crime Story: The Jamaica Connection." In it, an unnamed homicide investigator said that of 1991's record eighty-nine homicides, up to twenty of the twenty-four black victims were Jamaican.

Reaction was mixed to the *Globe* stories, written by veteran reporter Timothy Appleby.

"A lot of people told me I had written about something that should have been written about before. There was a lot of positive reaction from the Jamaican community but there was also a lot of negative feedback too. I was accused of being a racist, the *Globe and Mail* was picketed, we got a visit from the Jamaican consul. It was pretty unpleasant, which bothered me," he told me many years later.

"I'd spent a lot of my earlier life working against racism. I spent the night in jail [in Manchester, England] for Nelson Mandela, my sister is married to a non-white person and I just grew up with that culture, feeling comfortable around people of different races. It certainly hurt me to be called a racist, which I wasn't."

In his article, Appleby included a prescient comment by Trinidad-born Arnold Auguste, then publisher of the black community newspaper *Share*: "A lot of white people don't like to hear this, but the root of the whole thing [the violence] is racism and I think the situation is fairly serious because of the number of kids out there with no hope. The problem is a Canadian problem. Somehow, we missed the boat, we let this situation develop. If we ignore it, it's not going to go away; it's going to grow."

Later in 1992, waves of young people, many of them black, invaded downtown and rioted on Yonge Street, smashing windows, looting stores and fighting with police. Why? Because a jury in California—3,500 kilometres away, in another country—had acquitted four white cops in the videotaped beating of black motorist Rodney King? Because some teenagers in Toronto had seen the live images of the riot in Los Angeles that followed the verdict and wanted to be on TV too?

The demonstration started at the U.S. consulate—to protest the verdict—before moving throughout the downtown core. Protesters chanted: "No justice, no peace." A homemade sign read: "We denounce racist murder." The next morning, Ben Chin, a young reporter with Citytv, decided: "Last night's looting was not about skin colour, it was mostly about teenagers, of many races . . . Although there have been a lot of gratuitous comparisons to L.A., this was nothing like L.A. and this city can get over this."

But others were not so sure. Some said the riot was in part a reaction to the killing of 22-year-old Raymond Lawrence, shot dead by police two days earlier, the fourth black person killed by Toronto police in four years.

The first, in 1988, was 44-year-old Lester Donaldson, fatally shot in the bedroom of his rooming house in the city's west end. Toronto police constable David Deviney was charged with manslaughter. At his trial, the officer testified he shot Donaldson in the chest after the man thrust a small knife at the throat of Deviney's partner. The constable said it wouldn't have mattered if the assailant was "blue or green or another colour," he would fire his weapon again to save a life. When Deviney was acquitted, dozens of officers in the packed courtroom cheered. A few raised their fists to salute the verdict.

Activists cited the Donaldson shooting, and others of blacks by white police, as evidence of widespread racism in the Toronto police department.

So, was the Yonge Street riot primarily a response to the shooting death of Raymond Lawrence, the father of two shot by Constable Robert Rice? Toronto police said Lawrence, brandishing a knife, approached the officer in the Bloor Street-Lansdowne Road area, and ignored an initial warning shot. (The province's Special Investigations Unit, which investigated all police shootings, cleared Rice of wrongdoing. A coroner's inquest, convened at the request of the Lawrence family, concluded his race was not a factor. However, the five-person jury recommended police receive training in race relations and that members of visible-minority groups provide some of that training.)

So, was the rampage on Yonge Street a manifestation of the latest shooting and all the rage that had been building for years? Many thought so.

"What happened … was the frustration and anger coming out. We have waited for the justice system to deal justly with our community, and they have failed," Dudley Laws, the beret-wearing leader of the Black Action Defence Council, said the day after the mayhem. "You cannot control people who are being brutalized and seeing their people being murdered from time to time by a so-called police force."

In the aftermath of the Yonge Street riot, Ontario NDP premier Bob Rae appointed Stephen Lewis, a former New Democratic Party leader and United Nations envoy, as his special advisor on race relations. The report he produced was not the first or last on the subject of racism in Toronto. Lewis recommended setting up a public inquiry into the entire criminal justice system. He also urged the Ontario government to quickly introduce employment equity legislation and set up a cabinet committee on race relations. "If ever I've felt two solitudes in life, it's the apparent chasm between the Metropolitan Toronto Police and many representatives of the black community," he wrote.

In response, the Rae government launched an inquiry into racial bias in the justice system. Judge David Cole and community legal worker Margaret Gittens spent three years interviewing hundreds of people and issued a 445-page report in 1996. She was black; Cole, white.

The conclusion: Racial bias permeated the entire justice system, from arrests and detention through to the bail process and the penal system. Among its many revelations was that, on drug charges, white suspects were twice as likely as blacks to be released on bail. The report also found that blacks in Toronto between the ages of 18 and 24 were randomly stopped by police twice as often as white youths. It wasn't that they were committing more crimes—they were under greater scrutiny.

An unambiguous example of this played out in the media in 1993, while Cole and Gittens were involved in their inquiry. Dwight Drummond, who would become a popular crime reporter and anchor at Citytv, was the station's chief assignment editor on the late news show that October. He was driving home with a companion along Dundas Street in downtown Toronto when a police cruiser with flashing lights pulled up behind him. A voice on a loudhailer ordered him and his passenger to get out of the car and put their hands on the roof. They did so, and soon found themselves face-down on the street, spread-eagled and handcuffed. Police searched Drummond's Volkswagen Passat, found nothing and said he and his friend were free to go. The incident sparked an uproar.

The officers told Drummond the reason for their high-risk takedown was that a prostitute had reported she thought she had heard gunfire and that "you looked at us as you drove by." Drummond, who came from Jamaica as a youngster and grew up in the Jane-Finch area, said he had been stopped on at least five previous occasions. He described it as a "rite of passage" for young black men.

This time, however, he lodged an official complaint, saying the only reason he was stopped was because of the colour of his skin. A board of inquiry found the two white police constables were justified in pulling over Drummond. Angry, Drummond, then in his late 20s, declared "it's open season on young black men in this city." Years later, in addition to covering crime for Citytv, he would host a phone-in show with Toronto police chiefs.

Judge Cole's report also examined sixteen shootings of black people—ten of them fatal—by police in Ontario since 1978. In nine cases, criminal charges were brought against the officers. None were convicted. "The shootings are perceived," said the report, "not as isolated incidents, but as tragedies that affect the entire black community—and as a reflection of the destructive force of systemic racism."

Another report, more than a decade later, in 2008, would suggest that little had changed. "Inequality, disadvantage and racism are tightly interwoven into many of the roots of violence involving youth," wrote Roy McMurtry, a former Ontario attorney general and chief judge, and Alvin Curling, a prominent black politician and one-time provincial cabinet minister. "We were taken aback by the extent to which racism is alive and well and wreaking its deeply harmful effects on Ontarians and on the very fabric of this province."

But the McMurtry-Curling report came at a time when youth violence and the black-white divide was nearly accepted as normal in Toronto. Whereas Cole's report, more than a decade earlier, in 1994, the situation was much different. At that time, the white community was gripped by anxiety after two sensational murders in Toronto, in which young black men killed white people.

On April 5, 1994, Georgina (Vivi) Leimonis, who was 23, was shot to death while chatting with a friend in a restaurant called Just Desserts in the Annex neighbourhood of Toronto. (Three black men would go on trial. One was convicted of first-degree murder, the other of manslaughter and a third acquitted—before being deported and himself murdered in Jamaica. Midanik's client, of course, went free.)

Then, on June 16, 1994, 26-year-old Clinton Gayle shot and killed Constable Todd Baylis and wounded Constable Mike Leone behind a northwest Toronto housing complex.

Gayle had come to Canada from Jamaica in 1977 to join his mother, who worked as a domestic in Toronto, when he was eight years old. His father, who was a policeman, remained in Jamaica. Gayle had convictions for assault, weapons and theft by the time he was in his teens. He had been facing a deportation order, and packing a handgun, when he had his run-in with Baylis and Leone. Gayle admitted he shot Baylis and Leone but said he was acting in self-defence after the officers assaulted him. He was convicted of first-degree murder and attempted murder and sentenced to life in prison.

The furor surrounding the case came right before the creation of a nationwide gun registry and federal legislation making it easier to deport immigrants with serious criminal records by denying them appeal rights.

The murders of Vivi Leimonis and Constable Baylis helped to fuel the perception that "the entire city had become lawless—black youths with ski masks running rampant throughout the city, and anyone, especially whites, could be slaughtered," Cecil Foster, a black journalist, author and educator wrote in his 1996 book, *A Place Called Heaven: The Meaning of Being Black in Canada.* "The killing had spilled over into a middle-class and largely white area [the Annex], the mainstream was sitting up and taking notice."

Journalist Margaret Cannon, "who grew up in the profoundly racist society of the American south," before emigrating to Canada, wrote that Leimonis' murder was what many regarded as a "racial watershed in Toronto's multicultural history: the day the town got mean," she wrote in her 1995 book, *The Invisible Empire: Racism in Canada.* "The Other had killed our innocence, destroyed our faith and we wanted revenge. As one person put it '. . . Toronto the Good or Toronto the 'Hood? It's up to us.'"

Both Cannon and Foster identified other casualties of the violence: the law-abiding young members of Toronto's black community. "The harshest effects were felt on the streets of Toronto, especially in neighbourhoods with a strong black presence. In one fell swoop, blacks were painted as gangsters, irresponsible louts who had little respect for life," Foster wrote.

In the Just Desserts case, police released grainy black-and-white photos of the suspects taken by the café's security camera. Repeatedly aired on every television newscast and published in newspapers, the images "looked like any young black man in town," Cannon wrote. "There were very real fears that the vague photographs of the suspects could lead to an open season for attacks on black men," she wrote. "Black parents, watching their sons head for work or school, asked children to call in upon arrival and to telephone again before they left for home."

While these fears were genuine in the black community, the reality was, in some ways, more troubling. Decades of poverty and alienation had left most black Torontonians vulnerable in their own neighbourhoods. "It is possible that the city has become more dangerous for some people and less dangerous for others," University of Toronto criminologists Rosemary Gartner and Sara Thompson wrote in a paper called "Trends in Homicide" in Toronto, published in 2004. Using estimates of Toronto's black population for the years 1991 through 2001, they concluded the homicide rate in the black population was five times that of the average overall rate of 2.4 homicides per 100,000. "Black Torontonians have faced much higher risks of homicide victimization than non-blacks at least since the early 1990s," they wrote.

Similar research in Canada and elsewhere consistently showed that most racial and ethnic groups killed their own kind. "Young black men are killing each other," Pastor Orim Meikle, who delivered that damning eulogy at Omar Hortley's funeral, told yet another congregation of mourners years later. "It's not the Chinese that are doing it. It's not the Italians. It's our own." All of this underscored the commonly used phrase "black-on-black crime." Gangsters, thieves and drug dealers were preying on their neighbours.

"I can guarantee you that no matter what court I'm in, there will be a huge overrepresentation of black people," Judge Cole told me in 2009 as he waited to learn whether he would be in youth or adult court that day. "In addition to being black, they will be young, they will be poor, they will be male—because that's what we instruct our police to do—and poor people tend to commit their offences in public spaces. And so the police go out and arrest them, we process them through the system and there's an overrepresentation, but that's not simply because they're black. It's a lot more complex than that."

Where Did It All Begin?

Some traced racial inequities—and the eventual growth of youth violence—to this country's immigration policies, enlisting its poor cousins in the Commonwealth to fill the jobs no self-respecting Canadian wanted to do, such as work as domestics.

"From the 1950s on, [Canada] saw the Caribbean as a pool of cheap labour, primarily for women who could become babysitters, childcare givers, and who could look after the sick and elderly," Cecil Foster wrote in *A Place Called Heaven*. "Many young women across the Caribbean took this opportunity to escape," wrote Foster, who moved to Canada from his native Barbados in 1979. "Canada did not intend that these visitors should stay."

So, only young women were recruited, "ideally unattached romantically and without children. If they were, the spouses and children were left behind. The reasoning was obvious: if these workers had no family ties in Canada, they would not want to stay in the country." That wasn't the case. Many wanted to remain to raise their own families "and whether or not the Canadian government wanted the men and children to follow, they would come anyway, many of them illegally," Foster wrote. Some of those children had difficulty adjusting—not only to Canada but also to living with mothers they barely knew after being cared for in their home countries by aunts and grandmothers.

By the late 1970s and into the '80s, the children who had reunited with their mothers in Canada were having children of their own. They included the parents of both Tyshan Riley and Jason Wisdom. (Philip Atkins' mother was born in Toronto. His father, who had little to do with his son after he and Alice Atkins split up, had been born in Jamaica before coming to Canada.)

The immigrant parents retained strong ties to their homeland, where they would often return to visit. Many Jamaicans who settled in Toronto lived alongside each other, conversed in patois, ate West Indian food and socialized in clubs playing reggae music. This left their Canadian-born children feeling "displaced and dysfunctional—don't understand who they are," said Michael Crawford, a Jamaican-born court stenographer in Toronto with a ringside seat to the daily parade of black suspects. "They're black kids born here but they feel like they don't belong because the parents are always talking about what life was like back home."

This clash of cultures seemed to be especially difficult for black males who were born in Canada and coming of age at the end of the 20th century. They did seem to understand one thing—that they were descendents of slaves, who were chattel and existed to sire children.

This may, in part, explain what Crawford called the "sperm donor syndrome"—men of no means who impregnate numerous women, free of commitment and financial responsibility. "It also shows 'I'm virile, I'm the don, I'm cool, I'm the mandingo.' Sex is seen as conquest," he said. The term "baby mama"—used to describe women who are not married to a child's father—originated in Jamaica's matriarchal society but by the late 20th century was in widespread use to describe young women—black and white—living in Toronto public housing complexes.

To Crawford, it wasn't so much that absentee fathers were the problem. What was missing was "good parenting." That was American comedian Bill Cosby's message in his controversial May 2004 speech at an event to commemorate the fiftieth anniversary of the landmark U.S. Supreme Court ruling in the case of Brown v. Board of Education of Topeka, Kansas, which sought to end segregation in schools, declaring "separate educational facilities are inherently unequal."

Cosby, the beloved comedian then in his mid-sixties, used the occasion to scold members of his race. "Women having children by five, six different men. Under what excuse? 'I want somebody to love me,'" Cosby told the gathering. "And as soon as you have it, you forget to parent. Grandmother, mother, and great-grandmother in the same room, raising children, and the child knows nothing about love or respect from any one of the three of them.

"All this child knows is 'gimme, gimme, gimme.' These people want to buy the friendship of a child, and the child couldn't care less. Those of us sitting out here who have gone on to some college or whatever we've done, we still fear our parents. And these people are not parenting. They're buying things for the kid—$500 sneakers—for what? They won't buy or spend $250 on *Hooked on Phonics*." Cosby was saying out loud what only a black man of his stature could say. And he wasn't the only one saying it.

Before Cosby was making headlines in the United States, Pastor Meikle, in Toronto, at Omar Hortley's 2004 funeral, said black men needed to stop "breeding children as if they're racehorses—we are not racehorses." The *Toronto Star*'s Royson James, who is black, in a 2005 column also addressed the issue of stopping sex-crazed men from being absentee fathers.

"Great. But how?" James asked. "Yes, the 'baby mother syndrome' and fatherless homes are the single most debilitating and self-inflicted cause of social dysfunction for black families. Everybody knows that. But nobody knows how to exorcise that demon seed, bred into huge segments of a race that's been emasculated by slavery and socialized by colonialism."

This was published a day after police rounded up one notorious Toronto gang. "Yes we may have smashed the Ardwick Blood Crew," James wrote. "But we didn't get the conditions that breed such deviants. In our hearts we know that. In our hearts we must find the courage and empathy to ease the conditions that incubate such evil."

The following year, south of the border, a renowned black author and professor of sociology at Harvard University was stirring the pot in an op-ed piece in the *New York Times*. Orlando Patterson, born in Jamaica, called for a new "multi-disciplinary approach toward understanding what makes young black men behave so self-destructively."

In the piece, he related an anecdote: One of his students had returned to her high school to find out why nearly all the black girls graduated and went to college, whereas most of the black boys dropped out or did not continue their education.

So why were they flunking out? Their candid answer was that what sociologists call the 'cool-pose culture' of young black men was simply too gratifying to give up. For these young men, it was almost like a drug, hanging out on the street after school, shopping and dressing sharply, sexual conquests, party drugs, hip-hop music and culture, the fact that almost all the superstar athletes and a great many of the nation's best entertainers were black.

Not only was living this subculture immensely fulfilling, the boys said, it also brought them a great deal of respect from white youths. This also explains the otherwise puzzling finding by social psychologists that young black men and women tend to have the highest levels of self-esteem of all ethnic groups, and that their self-image is independent of how badly they were doing in school.

I call this the Dionysian trap for young black men. The important thing to note about the subculture that ensnares them is that it is not disconnected from the mainstream culture. To the contrary, it has powerful support from some of America's largest corporations. Hip-hop, professional basketball and homeboy fashions are as American as cherry pie. Young white Americans are very much into these things, but selectively; they know when it is time to turn off Fifty Cent and get out the SAT prep book.

Canada's Other "Two Solitudes"

In the United States, such discourses on race, racism and race relations were integral to the national dialogue for much of the 20th century. Yet in Canada, during the same time, the discussion had always been about French and English, not black and white. For many, this was a white country. Then suddenly, almost without warning, the complexion changed. Great waves of Asians arrived. And those children of immigrants from the Caribbean grew up. For years, in the 1990s and beyond, the whites who still ran things rarely acknowledged any conflicts that arose based on colour. But, in Toronto, tension and suspicion, especially between its black citizenry and the police, became a way of life.

In 2002, the *Toronto Star* published a series on race and crime. The investigative project, led by reporter Jim Rankin, analyzed the Toronto Police Service arrest database. The statistical evidence suggested blacks were subjected to more stringent policing than whites. It also concluded "blacks arrested by Toronto police are treated more harshly than whites" and police engaged in racial profiling, defined by the newspaper "as the practice of stopping people for little reason other than their skin colour."

Chief Julian Fantino angrily denied his officers were singling out blacks. Mayor Mel Lastman said in a statement: "I don't believe the Toronto police engage in racial profiling in any way, shape or form. Quite the opposite, they're very sensitive to our different communities." (This was the same Lastman who famously said in 2001 that he wouldn't be going to Africa to support Toronto's ultimately failed bid for the 2008 Olympics. "I just see myself in a pot of boiling water with all these natives dancing around me.")

The police service's civilian oversight body commissioned an independent review of the *Star*'s analysis by a criminal lawyer and a University of Toronto sociology professor. Their review called the *Star* analysis "junk science." The newspaper countered with its own university expert in statistics, who concluded the methodology and findings were accurate. Whatever the interpretation of the facts or the stats, the story was out there and the word was on the streets. And police headquarters was doing little to change the perception.

Fantino would say later, to the *Toronto Star* in 2004, that he did not deny the existence of racial profiling on the force, but that it wasn't official policy. "We didn't resist that there's racism or bigots or some officers behave inappropriately, including with racist conduct. I resisted then, and still resist today that we, as an institution, go out there and systemically do any of this stuff."

By 2005, Toronto had a new police chief who not only openly acknowledged racial profiling existed but said he would do something about it. In his first remarks as chief of police, Bill Blair signalled a different tone. Making Toronto safe could not be done if "substantial segments of our society perceive that police are not trustworthy, that they are the victims of police bias, or that the criminal justice system is unjust for them," Blair told the audience at his swearing-in ceremony.

He acknowledged that losing the trust of any segment of society would make it "more likely to withhold their participation in community problem-solving and may demonstrate their disaffection by refusing to cooperate with us." Blair devoted a substantial part of his inaugural remarks to the city's diversity and didn't duck the R-word. "There is no greater challenge to our relationship with diverse communities than the corrosive issues of racism and racial bias," he said. "It will not be tolerated in the Toronto Police Service and must not be tolerated anywhere in our society," he said, to applause. Blair, at 51 the youngest chief the city had ever had, promised to work at creating a "culture within our service that truly values diversity ... We need to be vigilant against the influence that bias can have on our decision-making."

During his tenure, Fantino had seized every opportunity to advocate tougher sentencing while slamming Canada's too-lax laws and "revolving-door justice system." Blair, in his first five years on the job, rarely preached from that law-and-order soapbox, which some believed made a positive difference in police–minority relations. "We frankly have a police leadership that's a lot more sensible," Judge Cole told me. "One can disagree with Bill Blair but he and the senior leaders are way out ahead of the previous regimes."

True to Blair's word, the force was becoming more diverse. By mid-June, 2009, 19.6 per cent of all 5,500 uniformed officers were visible minorities. A decade earlier, the figure was 10 per cent.

That year, there also seemed to be some quieting of the gunfire. Blair and other senior police officers would credit TAVIS (Toronto Anti-Violence Intervention Strategy)—teams of Toronto police officers who would "flood" an area after an outbreak of violence. As a *Star* crime reporter, I spent five nights on patrol with TAVIS officers, all of whom seemed committed and determined to make a difference.

Part of the TAVIS approach was for officers to stop and speak to as many people in a community as possible, handing out business cards but also collecting information about the people who agreed to these informal chats. While there was no question many residents seemed pleased police were so visible, I wondered about the effect on young black men who were being stopped and asked for their names and backgrounds simply because they happened to be walking through an apartment lobby or parking lot. I've lived in Toronto all my life and have never once had an officer ask me who I was or where I was going.

University of Windsor professor David Tanovich also questioned such practices by police. He wrote that focusing on people in designated neighbourhoods would, in the long run, make the problem worse. "It is an inefficient and unreliable use of resources to be conducting countless numbers of stops when the overwhelming majority of those stopped will not be in possession of a gun or be a member of a gang," he wrote in a 2005 article published in the *Star*—a year before the release of his book, *The Colour of Justice: Policing Race in Canada*. "It is an alienating, humiliating and frightening experience to be confronted by the police when you have done nothing wrong. It confirms that race still matters and that no matter what you do or who you become, you will always be perceived as the usual suspect." He continued: "This is, in part, why racial profiling engenders a sense of anger, injustice and a lack of respect for law enforcement and the law."

An aggravating factor was the perception that all those hyped war on drugs were inherently biased because most offenders caught for possession and trafficking were black, despite evidence "that drug use and trafficking is overwhelmingly a white activity," Tanovich wrote.

In their 2008 report, McMurtry and Curling still noted "deteriorating police relations" with Toronto's black community. By late 2009, unfavourable perceptions of police and the criminal justice system persisted in the city, with the most negative views held by Canadian-born racial minorities, said University of Toronto criminology professor Scot Wortley and doctoral student Akwasi Owusu-Bempah in a study published in the *Journal of International Migration and Integration*.

Among Torontonians, the study showed the perception that the police and courts were biased appeared to have increased between 1994 and 2007 for all racial groups—including whites, who thought others were discriminated against. Aggressive street policing strategies, the authors wrote, "may help reduce gun and gang crime in targeted communities, and perhaps save lives, [but] they might also draw innocent people into the web of suspicion and directly contribute to the perception among some civilians that the police are biased or unfair."

Is It Getting Better—Or Worse?

In November 2009, I sat down with Justice David Cole in his office in the Ontario Court of Justice building in the northwestern edge of the city. I wanted to talk to him about the changes he has seen in the thirteen years since he wrote his report on racism in the justice system. Before being appointed to the bench in 1991, Cole was a defence lawyer for sixteen years, specializing in penal and parole litigation. "Cole for Parole" was reportedly scribbled on one of the walls of the Don Jail.

He acknowledged the justice system still traps too many black kids but there is little, as a judge, that he could do about it. "There's kind of a snowball rolling down the hill effect: the police officer perceives a black young male selling a twenty-piece [of crack] around the corner, so he goes and arrests him. He then gets put into the justice system. He then gets bail. Because of our delays in the justice system, he screws up his bail. He then winds up before a judge and gets sentenced to time. There aren't the programs that are necessary, there isn't the environment that is necessary to do something about it when he comes out of jail. So he goes back to the same environment. That has not changed."

What had changed, in Cole's view, was an increased "sensitivity" to some issues. "In terms of criminal justice personnel, I don't think there's any doubt of that," said Cole, married to prominent child psychologist Esther Cole. The couple's two grown children are both lawyers.

He gave himself as an example to this new sensitivity. In his 1996 report, there were documented instances of inappropriate language in the courtroom, particularly in distinguishing between people who were born here and those who immigrated. "The tendency for judges, justices of peace and lawyers to refer to individuals' foreign origins or ethnic background is a significant cause of perceptions of racial injustice in courts," the report said. It cited non-whites in courtrooms being questioned about being Canadian. Why would a Crown attorney need to ask a person of Asian origin if he was born in this country? Why would a defence lawyer need to do the same with a black person?

"In both examples, the lawyers' words create doubt, however momentarily, about the Canadian identity of the accused person ... send subtle and unpleasant messages to black and other racialized Canadians. They suggest that the speaker, who represents the justice system to them, believes persons who are not white are outsiders whose rights to belong to the Canadian community must be established." Cole, who turned 61 in 2009, said: "Certainly, I've learned to temper my language."

"So, for example, I largely think that whether or not someone is a citizen is simply an irrelevant factor, for bail purposes, for sentencing purposes, reliability. If counsel mentions the defendant is a Canadian citizen, I now regularly say to counsel, 'Why are you telling me that?' I wouldn't have done that before my experience on the commission."

Cole identified other changes that had happened in the years since his report, including more sensitivity training for police and corrections staff, and better education on race bias for judges. But while a lot more could still be done, there needs to be political will. Governments, Cole noted, "have different priorities—and scarce dollars."

By the time Cole and Gittens released their report in 1996, the Progressive Conservatives under Mike Harris were in power in Ontario after campaigning on a law-and-order agenda that promised to slash welfare rates and establish boot camps for young offenders, though the latter never happened. "The government to which we reported in 1996 didn't have much interest in these issues," Cole told me.

Globe and Mail justice reporter Kirk Makin had a less diplomatic and funnier assessment. "Wiping systemic racism from the justice system ranked somewhere between funding creative dance and preserving the common loon," he wrote in 2003 of the Tories' Common Sense Revolution.

But in fairness, no government, of any political stripe, has made equity within the justice system a top priority. Cole recalled a conversation in the 1980s with then Liberal attorney general Ian Scott. At the time, Cole was still practising law and looking for funding increases for legal aid. He recalled Scott telling him: "Around the cabinet table, justice does not have a particularly high priority—it's not an income producer."

To further make the point, Scott added that throwing money at lawyers is a hard sell when "it's costing farmers $4 a bushel to grow stuff and they're only able to sell it at $2 a bushel." The message was: Don't ask for vast amounts of taxpayer funds to defend criminals. "Putting this money into programs for those rapists? No."

Or for gangbangers in 2009 for that matter. By then, defence lawyers in southern Ontario were refusing to take on clients in gangs and guns cases. The reason, they said, was because they were being paid an average of $87 an hour for handling complicated cases involving great numbers of gang members being swept up. Defence lawyers said the scales were already tipped in favour of the small army of Crowns and police working—on government salaries—on the various anti-gang projects. Even David Midanik, the white knight eager to defend poor young black men, had joined the legal aid boycott that ended with a settlement in January 2010.

This was not really a concern to the lawyers willing to take only cases that billed handsomely, up to $800 an hour for the biggest hired guns. So, without lawyers stepping up to represent them, more black youths and other minorities would remain in jail until they got proper legal representation. "When they build in the budgets for these gang sweeps, they don't build in an extra line for the legal aid budget. It's all very easy to do the big press conference and announcement but the follow-through is the issue," Cole said.

The justice system would repeatedly wrestle with the perception of racism. For example, after a 1993 Ontario Court of Appeal ruling, it became routine practice that prospective jurors in Toronto and the surrounding area would be asked whether their ability to judge a case impartially could be affected by the race of the accused, as was done in the murder trial of Riley, Atkins and Wisdom.

More difficult was how to change the culture of the judicial system reflected in a 2005 Supreme Court of Canada decision that found: "The courts have acknowledged that racial prejudice against visible minorities is . . . notorious and indisputable . . . [It is] a social fact not capable of reasonable dispute."

Yet Cole remained optimistic the system would one day become fairer to all. "You have to keep in mind what a very wise English historian, Harold Laski [1893-1950], said of his study of British royal commissions: It takes about thirty years for recommendations of royal commissions to come into effect. We have to realize change is a slow process."

CHAPTER 25

Forgiveness and thanksgiving

Riley, Atkins and Wisdom returned to court on July 29, 2009, to hear the judge pronounce sentence. It was pouring rain, a grey day to fit the mood of their grim-faced family members.

The now-convicted killers were back in their street clothes, swapping ties and suits for hoodies and T-shirts. This time the guards didn't remove their handcuffs for court. Everyone knew it was an automatic life sentence in a maximum-security prison with no eligibility for parole for twenty-five years.

Akhtar, seeing Leonard Bell sitting in court, went over to shake his hand. Once Justice Dambrot was on the bench, Pasquino told the court that Bell, Williams and her sister, Uleth Harvey, would read victim-impact statements.

Atkins wanted no part of what was to come. "I'm taking my sentence. I'd like to be brought downstairs," he said in his deep voice. Berg exchanged a few words with his defiant client before asking Dambrot if Atkins could be excused. The judge refused.

"I don't want to be here to hear these people talk," Atkins insisted. "I didn't do nothing to their families." Nonetheless, Atkins stayed put.

Harvey, a nursing student, went first. Standing with her arms behind her back, she spoke about life after the death of her nephew, Junior, with whom she came to Canada in 1989. "One's life should not be defined by tragedy. In my family's situation, our life is defined by the untimely death of Brenton Charlton," she said. "We often speak of life before Junior's death and life after Junior's death. March 3, 2004, is seen as a hallmark in the loss of innocence in our family."

Harvey had been the one to identify her nephew's body at the coroner's office. She had had to tell her older sister her only son was gone. "Upon telling Valda that Junior was dead, the pain and anguish that emanated from her is etched in my memory for the rest of my life." She said that her nephew, only 31 when he was killed, had been like his mother, "always well composed and gentle."

His death, she said, caused his father, Brenton Charlton Sr., to lapse into depression and stop caring for himself. "The last time I visited him in Hamilton, Ontario, he had no food in his refrigerator, his home was dirty and he was unkempt." He gave up the will to live and died at age 60 before the case even came to trial. "He was very angry, up to the time of his death, about his son's murder."

Jason Wisdom kept his head bowed. Atkins sat with his arms crossed. Riley kept exchanging glances with his girlfriend, Dana Lee Williams.

Valda Williams followed her sister to the podium in the middle of the courtroom. Wearing her hair braided and in a bun, she held a paper with prepared remarks but began off the page. "To forgive is healing and bitterness a barrier," she said, looking at the three young men. "Losing a child, at any age, is going against nature. It is harder for me to face as he was my only child." She sobbed softly as she said her dream of seeing her son getting married and having children was "shattered as the glass of his Neon on March 3, 2004."

"I can't imagine his last moments, the fear, terror and shock he was experiencing. I wonder if a friendly face was there when he took his last breath."

The courtroom was silent when Bell approached the podium. He said he was still haunted by "recurring sounds of gunshots," the tension he still felt "when I am driving and get to an intersection or traffic light." He mentioned the "trauma and stigmatization" of being a black man who had taken nine slugs. This, he said, made him distrustful of other people of colour "unless they were previous acquaintances of mine." Bell ended by saying he took comfort that God had spared his life. And he extended his faith to the three young men in the prisoners' box. "From my heart, I forgive them."

The prosecutors entered into evidence the criminal records of the three. Riley had twelve convictions at the time of his arrest in Oshawa in 2004, including weapons and drug offences. Atkins had seven convictions. Wisdom, who had three convictions, "is not the worst of these three," the Crown said.

Before passing sentence, Dambrot asked the three convicted killers if they had anything to say.

Riley got up. "I never did this crime," he began. "I'm sorry for the loss of your son but I never did this to your son," he said, addressing Williams. "Mr. Bell, I'm sorry for your pain." He added, to no one in particular: "Do what you want to do."

Atkins declined to say anything and remained sitting with his arms crossed.

Wisdom stood up and turned to face Bell and Williams, who were sitting together. "I took the stand, Mr. Bell and Ms. Williams. I am not responsible, I thought that was clear," he said plaintively, appearing troubled. "The citizens of Toronto are sick of guns and gang violence but I did not do this," he said. "I'm a young black man. I was selling drugs. That's why I got convicted."

Annoyed that convicted killers may have caused pain to Bell and Williams, Dambrot apologized. And then he passed sentence on the three who had "filled a car with bullets," killing and wounding "honourable, decent men." Calling it an "ugly and mindless" crime, Dambrot said there wasn't much for him to do at this point. "I impose the sentence and it's up to correctional authorities to determine how the sentences are to be administered."

He sentenced each to an automatic life term for first-degree murder, with no parole eligibility for twenty-five years. Their sentences for attempted murder and gangsterism would run concurrently. They would be credited for pre-trial time served, dating back to their arrest, making them eligible to apply for parole in roughly twenty years. (The average time someone convicted of first-degree murder spends locked up is 28.4 years, according to the John Howard Society. However, in late 2009, the federal Conservative government introduced legislation designed to keep "multiple murderers" behind bars for even longer terms.)

Then the three men were taken from the courtroom in cuffs.

"I'll be all right, Mom," Wisdom said as he was being led out. "I'll keep the faith. Don't worry."

Wisdom's mother, Marcia Thomas—who had taken the stand in her son's defence—remained a fervent believer in his innocence, establishing a Facebook group called Freedom for Jason Wisdom. It said: "My name is Marcia Thomas, the mother of Jason Wisdom, and I am 100 per cent sure that he did not murder or attempt to murder any of these people!!!"

There was a photo of Roland Ellis and another alongside showing a mound of cash, suggesting that was the money he was paid to rat out her son, Atkins and Riley. "His freedom was sold to Roland Ellis for $11,000," Thomas wrote of the money spent to relocate Ellis. "Life should never be up for a police bribe. Police should be able to solve crimes without making deals with other criminals because in most cases like this one, the innocent goes to prison."

Was it possible that Wisdom had been wrongly convicted? That he had falsely boasted about his involvement in Riley's ride squads? As for his alleged confession to Ellis, Wisdom, the youngest of the three, 18 at the time of his arrest, was known to "big himself up."

Galloway's Legacy

So, how did this case, these verdicts, change life on the streets of Toronto? And did the convictions validate the millions of dollars spent to prosecute the Galloway Boys as a criminal organization?

The federal government introduced criminal organization legislation in 1997, largely in response to violence by outlaw motorcycle gangs in Quebec. But by 2004, police in Toronto and later in Montreal and Vancouver were using it to combat street gangs. Prosecutors in the United States had for years used federal racketeering statutes to target street gangs.

The law in Canada allows for stiffer penalties for anyone found guilty of committing crimes for the benefit of a criminal organization—which can be as few as three people. (In this country, the maximum sentence anyone can receive is life without parole eligibility for twenty-five years, with no additional time for being found guilty of committing murder for a criminal organization, even if someone is found guilty of multiple counts of first-degree murder. On lesser offences, such as drug trafficking, a criminal organization conviction can mean more jail or prison time.)

More practically, it gives police grounds to request a judge's permission to intercept multiple phone calls based on the contention a group is engaged in an ongoing criminal enterprise. If the wiretap evidence collected is the equivalent of a smoking gun, it can be a persuasive tool to extract guilty pleas, as it did eventually in the case of all those arrested in the initial Galloway gang sweep.

In any case, it sets the stage for endless legal haggling as both sides of the bar try to prove or disprove that a group is or isn't a criminal organization. One of the main criticisms of the legislation is that it must be applied on a case-by-case basis. In other words, the Crown must prove a group is in fact working in concert to commit crimes to benefit the group. For example, one judge may find the Hells Angels to be a criminal organization, but the case must be made each and every time.

The province of Ontario and Toronto police were quick to say Project Pathfinder demonstrated the success of prosecuting street gangs as criminal organizations. Critics—many of them defence lawyers—suggest such claims are self-serving and designed to ensure resources continue to flow to what they call public-relations exercises. As one said to me, "Authorities can say, 'Look, we're winning the war against crime.'"

Yet if the measure of success is a decline in gun violence in a particular area, then Project Impact in Malvern and Project Pathfinder in Galloway seemed unqualified victories. While recurring gunfire got 2004 off to a bloody start in Malvern, by year's end residents were once again venturing outdoors to shopping malls and parks. "Whether it was true or not, innocent people were afraid of being mowed down," then Toronto police superintendent Tony Warr told me in late 2004 as we sat in a food court at Malvern Town Centre. "We still have crime here, but not what was going on before, when bullets were going through people's houses."

Around the same time, city councillor Michael Thompson, representing Scarborough Centre, vice-chair of the mayor's panel on community safety, said the two gang projects let the community reclaim its neighbourhood. "It has dramatically altered the perception that these people could do whatever they wanted with impunity."

Tyshan Riley certainly acted like he was above the law, armed, dangerous and apparently convinced that nobody within his circle of influence would dare rat him out to the cops. He also counted on the community's distrust of police to maintain a wall of silence. That's one of the problems with widespread gang crackdowns (which is what the investigation against Riley turned into): they don't change the way people live in these communities and may even widen the divide between residents and police.

"Gang interventions have a suppression emphasis . . . that inhibits effective relationships between the police and the community, serves to further isolate the police from the community and threatens already fragile relationships," prominent U.S. gang researcher Scott Decker wrote in a 2007 article called "Expand the Use of Police Gang Units" published in the *Criminology and Public Policy* journal.

What ought to be required reading for all Canadian policymakers interested in curbing the growth of gangs is a 2007 study from the United States called *Gang Wars: The Failure of Enforcement Tactics and the Need for Effective Public Safety Strategies.* It pointed to Los Angeles and Chicago as examples of "the tragic failure of the most popular suppression approaches to gangs. Despite decades of aggressive gang enforcement—including mass arrests and surveillance, huge gang databases, and increased prison sentences for gang crimes—gang violence continues at unacceptable rates."

New York, by contrast, did not embrace such aggressive tactics and experienced far less gang violence. "When gang violence became a serious problem, the city established a system of well-trained street workers and gang intervention programs, grounded in effective social work practices and independent of law enforcement," the study noted. Gang crackdowns were a reactive response to clean up a problem until the next turf war. They were also expensive and placed a tremendous load on an already burdened court system. Invariably, they involved electronic surveillance—dramatically illustrated in the critically acclaimed HBO series *The Wire*—which legal experts said was one of the reasons criminal trials were getting longer and costlier.

The alternative, some say, is to invest in jobs, schools and social programs to try to create healthy communities where young people could imagine a future that has nothing to do with selling crack and carrying a gun. But long-term initiatives lack the political payoff of hiring more police and prosecutors, which, admittedly, can have a more immediate impact on a community experiencing gang violence.

The primarily white power-brokers in places like Toronto don't have to care about what's happening on the fringes of their city, the kind of people who don't generally get out to vote. "Let's face it, most people will say: 'As long as they're killing each other, who gives a shit,'" Detective Dean Burks told me after the trial ended. "The problem is, they're not going to be just killing themselves."

But only when gangsters come into white neighbourhoods—shooting Vivi Leimonis or Jane Creba—do the murders get national headlines or lead newscasts. If street gangs continue to proliferate in Toronto and across the country, more innocents—white and black, like Charlton and Bell—will be caught in the crossfire.

One Galloway gang member predicted it was inevitable. "It is never going to stop. The next generation is coming up," Ernesto Gayle told Riley.

A Way Forward

On a sweltering hot Sunday, August 16, 2009, a few weeks after the verdict, Leonard Bell and Valda Williams held a "thanksgiving" service at their makeshift church in an industrial area of northwestern Toronto.

They wanted to pay tribute to the Crown attorneys and police officers who had brought the case to a successful resolution.

Some of the prosecutors, including Akhtar and Pecknold, were on vacation and couldn't be there. Crown Patrick Clement represented them. Wayne Banks and Dean Burks were there. So was Al Comeau, by this time retired from the force. The cops were all wearing suits, a sign of respect for the victims and the occasion. Burks brought his wife and two teenaged children. Bell—Leo, as I came to call him—invited me. We had kept in touch throughout the case, and he knew I was writing a book.

He had initially been suspicious of me and my newspaper, since the *Star* had published his photo the day after he was shot. I'm still unclear how we got the picture. But he feared the people who shot him might come back to finish the job. Over time, I won his trust. We talked often. Those sweet and sad text messages he sent me—on the anniversary of the shooting and after the verdict—solidified the bond.

I drove south from Ontario's sparkling cottage country, where I had been visiting friends, to the dull world of an industrial complex filled with rusted-out cars parked in somewhat haphazard fashion. An older woman, wearing a crisp, white dress and matching wide-brimmed hat from a long-gone era, directed me inside where the familiar faces from the courthouse were standing in a circle.

Leo, a deacon at the church, soon showed up with his wife, Winnifred, both dressed up. Valda Williams and her always friendly husband, Dennis—the man her son had been talking about welcoming into the family the day he died—soon followed. We all took our seats in the several rows of chairs inside the windowless space.

There were prayer readings and hymns. We were given books and tambourines. Bible passages were read before Valda, and then Leo, addressed the group. Leo sang—he has a lovely voice—and thanked the "special guests." He recalled lying in the hospital after he was shot and Comeau and Banks coming to see him. He remembered their assurances the shooters would be brought to justice. He publicly, and very graciously, thanked me for my very small part—keeping in touch over the years.

In some ways it was an odd occasion. I was not there as a reporter. I wasn't taking notes or turning on a tape recorder. I was an invited guest, not there to document the event.

As the small group of celebrants exhorted "praise the Lord" I felt very much an outsider—except these were people I had grown close to in some way, and cared about. No one talked about gangs or guns. In their own miraculous way, they were moving on.

INDEX